CW814125989

Dianarama

Dianarama

The Betrayal of Princess Diana

ANDY WEBB

MICHAEL JOSEPH

PENGUIN MICHAEL JOSEPH

UK | USA | Canada | Ireland | Australia
India | New Zealand | South Africa

Penguin Michael Joseph is part of the Penguin Random House group of companies
whose addresses can be found at global.penguinrandomhouse.com

Penguin Random House UK
One Embassy Gardens, 8 Viaduct Gardens, London sw11 7bw

penguin.co.uk

Penguin
Random House
UK

First published 2025
002

Set in 13.5/16pt Garamond MT Std
Typeset by Six Red Marbles UK, Thetford, Norfolk
Printed and bound in Great Britain by Clays Ltd, Elcograf S.p.A.

The authorized representative in the EEA is Penguin Random House Ireland,
Morrison Chambers, 32 Nassau Street, Dublin D02 YH68

A CIP catalogue record for this book is available from the British Library

HARDBACK ISBN: 978-0-241-78464-8
TRADE PAPERBACK ISBN: 978-1-405-98259-7

Penguin Random House is committed to a sustainable future
for our business, our readers and our planet. This book is made from
Forest Stewardship Council® certified paper

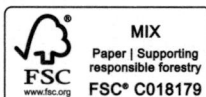

MIX
Paper | Supporting
responsible forestry
FSC
www.fsc.org   FSC® C018179

To my dear family, patient listeners.

Contents

CONTENTS

CONTENTS

PART SEVEN

Open Questions

'. . . we want to open up our journalistic
processes so people can see how we work;
radical transparency driving increased trust.'

– Tim Davie, BBC director-general,
speaking on 14 May 2025

'. . . trust is the most vital quality necessary
in our journalism . . .'

– Lord Hall, former BBC director-general, speaking
during the cover-up of the Bashir scandal, 25 April 1996

Prologue: What Saddens Me Most

On an overcast spring day four years ago Prince William looked straight into the TV camera, at all of us, and said, 'It brings indescribable sadness to know that the BBC's failures contributed significantly to her fear, paranoia and isolation that I remember from those final years with her.' He was speaking, of course, of his mother, Diana, and reflecting on the report which had been published that day, 20 May 2021, dealing with the biggest scandal in BBC history. It had been promised that this document, the Dyson report, would reveal after an inquiry lasting six months how the BBC had hoaxed Princess Diana into appearing on the *Panorama* programme on 20 November 1995. The interview which Diana gave reporter Martin Bashir was damning of the royal family and especially William's father – in fact, so damaging that in less than a year Diana had been stripped of her royal status and, newly untethered, was dead once another year had passed.

What William said next was startling: 'But what saddens me most is that if the BBC had properly investigated the complaints and concerns first raised in 1995, my mother would have known that she had been deceived. She was failed not just by a rogue reporter but by leaders at the BBC who looked the other way rather than asking the tough questions.' It is those words which tell us that what happened to Princess Diana thirty years ago is still a matter of burning intensity for her son. Because here William goes considerably beyond the verdict of the inquiry report, which looks at the conduct of those leaders at the BBC and decides that they were not guilty. They were, in William's judgement, not hapless and blameless stooges plagued by ill fortune. Instead they 'looked the other way'.

When the *Panorama* programme threatened in 1995 to erupt into an enormous scandal, key people at the BBC had to make a crucial ethical choice: *Do we cover things up, or do we come clean?* The person who has taken the rap for the scandal, pretty much all of it, is the hoaxer, Martin Bashir. If this were a cowboy movie, he would be wearing a black hat, the blackest hat of all, to signify his villainy. Bashir's boss, the man who was running the BBC at the time, Lord Birt, has said, 'Unless you understand that this was a serial liar on an industrial scale you simply cannot understand the story . . . in 100 years of BBC journalism can we think of anybody else who behaved in that kind of way?' But though Bashir is a villain, he is not an interesting villain. His motivation is plain. The people who might have explained to Diana that she had been the victim of a hoax, who might have stopped the runaway train that Bashir had set in motion, were what William calls the 'leaders at the BBC'. And so the concern of this book is to consider their likely motivation. Were they all truly taken in, like Diana, by the man in the black hat?

Lord Dyson's report, though compiled at a cost of more than £1 million, does not tell us how Bashir hoaxed Diana. It says simply that in the autumn of 1995 Diana was bursting to have her say on TV and that Bashir, a charming rogue, was lucky to catch her at the right time. Dyson says that when, the following year, BBC bosses looked into what Bashir had done, they bumbled and they faffed and they failed to get an answer yet nobody can be blamed for their failure. Lord Dyson does not tell us how the BBC then covered up the scandal for twenty-five years, nor who was in charge of the cover-up. And the malign effect of Dyson's report is more serious than even these omissions about what happened long ago. It is in 2025 being used by the BBC as both a deterrent to further inquiry and as a shield by those people who, as William put it, looked the other way.

This book will present evidence to answer the questions which the inquiry ought to have settled, but did not, and it will also explain William's most poignant words: 'what saddens me most'. Consider the sadness of this man whose life has been shaped by what the BBC did to his mother. How William, as a thirteen-year-old schoolboy, had to watch Diana talk of sex with a lover, then trash his father, on television – *on television on the BBC*. The news that Diana and Charles would divorce followed exactly one month after the *Panorama* interview. For a youngster desperately hoping, as kids do, that Mum and Dad will fall back in love, that will have been heartbreaking. The effect of learning that this wrecking ball set swinging by the BBC might have been grabbed, should have been grabbed, before Diana died is beyond imagining.

The story of Diana's life between autumn 1995 and her death two years later will also be of enduring historical interest, and so this book may serve, I hope, as at least a first draft of history. I sometimes think that even thirty years on we are still too close to those surreal-sounding events to properly see how bizarre the circumstances remain. Can it really be true that the woman who was supposed to now be our queen, our Queen Diana, had been assured by the BBC that her husband was a potential killer? Did she, because of that assurance, really set off on the crazy strategy described later in this book, merely to keep herself alive?

The answer to both questions is yes – and it is a story

more lurid, more fantastical, than anything that happened at the Tudor court of Henry VIII, which so fascinates historians today. Indeed Diana's last two years sound rather like a twisting Shakespeare plot, written as soap opera. A beautiful princess is betrayed by a heartless husband, pining for his own lost love. A character sidles up, whispering sinister warnings of murder and betrayal, but our heroine cannot see that she is being duped by a worm-tongued villain. Cast out, her own destiny now linked with a feckless ne'er-do-well, only a tragic death awaits them both. It is Shakespearean but it is horribly true, a story which will be picked over by historians and retold for centuries.

For that reason alone it is a story which deserves to be told in a way that is more complete than the Dyson report, a document studded with omissions and marked by its apparent failure, in at least one case, to grasp the importance of critical evidence. I believe that inasmuch as the report has established a temporary orthodoxy it will be rapidly dismantled by historical researchers. But consider right away that the *Panorama* interview, the most controversial broadcast ever made by the BBC, is not at all what you think it is. It is in reality not an *interview* but a *performance*. A double act, devised, rehearsed and delivered with a specific object in mind. There was a quite separate interview, carried out seven days earlier, but which has passed under the radar. *That* is the important encounter, the one which reveals the truth about these extraordinary times.

Many journalists have looked at the Bashir scandal over the last thirty years. I can say without being too swell-headed that something I did five years ago, described later in this book, finally brought it to light. I have studied these matters for something close to twenty years and have confidence in my judgement because it is made, I believe, from a unique position. As you will see I have been able to obtain formerly secret documents, despite enormous opposition from the BBC, and at the same time I have had close inside access to those who knew Diana best at this critical moment in her life, especially her brother Charles Spencer. He has shared with me his archive showing how he tried, and failed, to get the BBC to admit what they had done to his sister.

As you will also see, as the story unfolds, the revelations I was able to make have had a profoundly personal effect on many people who were shabbily treated by the BBC. Some were handed hundreds of thousands of pounds in reparations; for others the knowledge of the BBC's duplicity has at least provided some comfort in explaining why Diana behaved as recklessly as she did, harming not just herself but those she loved. Prince William's speech of May 2021 can be regarded as a victim impact statement which, it seems to me, might have caused Lord Dyson to think a little deeper had it been delivered, as usually happens, *before* sentence was delivered, rather than after.

William concludes with a sentence which is itself remarkable when the implications are fully considered. The BBC, perhaps the world's most respected journalistic enterprise, one that should be shouting loud for truth and honesty, instead worked furtively to prevent people like me uncovering the BBC's misdeeds. As William put it: 'These failings, identified by investigative journalists, not only let my mother down and my family down; they let the public down too.'

Introduction: The Million-Pound Question

In June 2024 I did something I had not done for thirty years. I drove to a nearby shopping mall, went into what used to be called a gentlemen's outfitter and bought a dark suit, a white shirt and the most sober tie I could see. It felt like choosing kit for a sports event, or, more exactly, determining my look for a gladiatorial bout. Swords and shields here, nets and tridents across the aisle. At the very least it would prove that I was serious about my upcoming two days in court and I needed to grasp every small advantage I could.

My summons to court came three years after I had used the Freedom of Information Act to put to the BBC a very simple question, but a question which it turned out people there were determined not to answer. And I mean *really* determined. The issue would come to occupy not only the most highly paid lawyers inside New Broadcasting House but also the most expensive lawyers from London's elite legal chambers. People who charge upward of £5,000 per day. As my request was repeatedly denied for those three years, I had been forced to run a solo guerrilla campaign from my kitchen table. I had to become my own lawyer, trying to match the constantly shifting legal manoeuvres of the pros being paid, to my intense annoyance, by me, from my BBC licence fee. And the BBC would clearly spend whatever it took to make sure I did not win this case when it finally came to court. The BBC's bill just for *external* legal fees would come to a staggering £646,694.95. In all, considering likely internal costs as well, something well over £1 million.

So what was this million-pound question, one which required such extraordinary legal might to prevent it being answered? The question was simple, the circumstances which prompted it a little more complicated. Looking back from our viewpoint today, thirty years on, it is clear that the BBC managed to cover up the worst elements of the scandal concerning their infamous *Panorama* interview with Princess Diana in November 1995. It is now clear beyond doubt that Martin Bashir used forged documents to get his foot in the door, to gain his first introduction to Diana, six weeks before the interview took place.

But these facts did not emerge until 2020. As described in more detail later, it was only when I was able to get hold of a formerly secret document from the BBC, after a thirteen-year struggle, that the scandal burst into the open and Bashir's duplicity was revealed for the first time. Fully twenty-five years had elapsed from the moment the BBC cover-up was first devised, in 1995, to the point where it collapsed in ruins, in 2020. It seemed to me that during that time certain BBC managers must have actively sought to keep matters secret for as long as they possibly could. And so to test my theory I had used the Freedom of Information Act to demand sight of emails which passed between the likeliest suspects at a critical period in 2020. If they had been trying to keep things under wraps, to sustain the cover-up, perhaps an incautious email would betray them? My question to the BBC, posed on 4 June 2021, said, 'I would like to request all documents that exist relating to email or other correspondence between BBC managers and the BBC Information Office, between September 2020 and November 2020, which has any bearing on the November 1995 *Panorama* programme with the Princess of Wales.'

It sounds simple enough. But what would happen over the next three years would involve the most astonishing twists and turns, the mysterious disappearance of certain documents and the miraculous appearance of thousands more. The case would become, at least in the BBC's own estimation, the biggest Freedom of Information case there has *ever* been. And the weirdest, altogether hardest-to-believe moment came roughly halfway through, eighteen months after I had made my initial request. The BBC had declared, in a statement signed by one of its lawyers, that the total number of emails relevant to my request was eighty. *Eight zero.* A short time later a different BBC lawyer said, in effect, 'Scratch that. The correct number is 3,288.' *Three thousand, two hundred and eighty-eight.* They had lost 3,208 emails, this lawyer said, through a computer error. Now, instead of a fistful of documents, it turned out that there were 10,336 pages, enough to fill twenty bulky lever arch folders. A page count equal to *War and Peace* ten times over. And that, as you will see, provided just one of the tricky questions to be decided. How do more than ten thousand pages of documents go missing, from one day to the next? Especially ones which might implicate senior BBC managers in a cover-up?

It was at 10 a.m. on Tuesday, 18 June 2024 that the court was scheduled to convene, in a workaday modern building in London's Bloomsbury. The BBC had a legal team of seven, including a thoroughly terrifying KC, the topmost grade of lawyer, described, on her own website, as 'the silent assassin of cross-examination'. But I did have my new suit.

PART ONE
Mindset

'I was so fed up with being seen as someone who was a basket case. Because I am a very strong person. And I know that causes complications in the system that I live in.'

– Princess Diana, *Panorama*, 20 November 1995

1. Take Two

My court case was a question of peeling back three layers of history. Could we, in June 2024, discover something that a particular set of BBC bosses had done in the autumn of 2020 to hide what another set of bosses had done way back in 1995? Had the *first* cover-up, thirty years ago, perhaps inspired a second one? Complicated, yes, but I knew that somewhere underneath these layers the truth must lie. As a journalist it is that feeling that the answer has to be right there, maybe in the very next document you flip open, that is thrilling. Friends often asked me, considering the years of work involved in this court case, 'Why do you care so much?' But the answer always seemed to me perfectly obvious. Here was a story with real historical resonance, something which will be debated when juicy scandals about newsreaders, handsy ministers and disgraced DJs, the things which reporters so often become obsessed by, are long forgotten. Indeed, when I am long forgotten.

The BBC would like all of us to believe that this is old news, done and dusted. I suspect if it were, the people running the BBC today would not have scrambled quite so quickly to throw those lawyers a million pounds, your money and mine. But there is also a personal factor. Through the pure coincidence of a family connection I was granted, more than thirty years ago, a unique insight into the fractious sparring between Prince Charles and Princess Diana, what was called in the late 1980s and early 90s the 'War of the Waleses'.

That phrase, evoking a 'war', was used in a thousand and one tabloid headlines to describe the way that the royal marriage was pulled apart, before being finally sundered by the BBC. And there was one remarkable day, in June 1994, which constituted a huge set-piece battle in this war, a day that is familiar from TV clips played endlessly ever since. Looked back on now it seems to be one of those sliding-doors moments when had one of the characters acted even the tiniest bit differently then all that followed would have been vastly altered. Because this was the day on which Prince Charles went on television to admit that he had not been sexually faithful to Diana.

To understand how this event set so many other things in motion, consider where he and Diana were, where the royal marriage was, in June 1994. What had begun in 1981 as a fairy tale, the sun-speckled wedding of the twenty-year-old bride and her thirty-two-year-old prince had seemed blessed at first, with baby William arriving in 1982, Harry in 1984. But then year by year the happiness slipped away. By the end of the 1980s the prince and princess did indeed seem to be engaged in a war, greedily chronicled by the tabloids and the broadsheets, in books and on TV. Queen Elizabeth chose the famous phrase *'annus horribilis'* to describe 1992, her especially horrible year, the one in which Charles and Diana's formal separation was finally announced.

Charles's confession, two years later, seemed to put an end to something which had been slowly dying, privately at first, then for everyone to see. But what is remarkable is that, in reality, Prince Charles had not been prepared to make that critical admission of adultery until the very last minute. It is not widely known that at first he simply refused, but then he buckled, setting history on an entirely new course. And, as so often in the Diana story, this single extraordinary day, 29 June 1994, yields drama so unlikely that it might have been conceived as a soap opera season finale. An air crash, an agonizing twist in the sex saga, and all in the space of just a few hours.

Shortly after 11 a.m. on that June morning, in the sky over Islay, a rugged scrap of island off Scotland's west coast, a BAe 146 airliner in the red and white colours of the Queen's Flight swung into view. Islay's distilleries produce a rich, peat-stained malt whisky, and Prince Charles, also titled Lord of the Isles, was scheduled to visit one of them. Another title Charles carried was that of RAF Group Captain, and he was indeed a trained pilot, qualified to bring the jet and its eleven occupants safely to earth. Charles had agreed with the aircraft captain, Squadron Leader Graham Laurie, that he would take control once the aircraft began its descent to the miniature airport at Glenegedale.

The weather that day was typical for the Hebrides in June: cloudy, the wind thirty miles an hour. As Islay grew larger below, Charles asked which of the two landing strips, designated RW13 and RW31, he should aim for. Laurie advised RW13, aware that this would mean landing with a troublesome tailwind, though that should present no danger if all went according to plan. But as the plane began its approach, a little under four miles out, people on the ground could see something was wrong. The plane was approaching too fast, at too steep an angle. In pilot's jargon, she was coming in hot. Voice recordings from the cockpit have not been made public but we can imagine the barely restrained terror of the next few seconds as twenty-five tons of aircraft thudded down on the twin nosewheels.

The main wheels locked and smoke billowed as the tyres melted with the friction. Five hundred metres from touchdown a tyre in the right main undercarriage exploded, sparks flying as the metal rim screeched across the tarmac. Then a tyre on the left undercarriage burst, the plane still careering forward with just 150 metres of runway remaining. As the airport fire truck raced towards the scene, Laurie, wrestling the controls from Charles, tried to veer the aircraft on to a taxiway to his left. Instead the aeroplane slid from the runway, the undercarriage biting deep into the soft ground before collapsing. The aircraft slewed to a halt, its jet turbines still whining as the fire truck arrived.

As Charles, deeply shaken by the ordeal, was hurried to the small terminal, he may have looked back to assess the damage. The tangled wreckage beneath the aircraft, the smashed undercarriage, crumpled nose cone and radar array, would cost more than £1 million to repair. Charles was never called to explain his role in what accident investigators would coyly term a 'mishandled approach'. But had the prince been required to enter a plea in mitigation he might fairly have offered: 'Well – I did have rather a lot on my mind that day.'

In London, 600 miles away, Princess Diana steeled herself for an ordeal of a different kind. Not the sudden prospect of extinction in an air crash but a challenge that had been threatening for nearly two years. Because she knew that tonight the eyes of the world, and in particular the lenses of scores of photographers, would be trained on her even more closely than usual. She knew that almost every TV viewer in Britain would be anxious for a particular programme to begin, a documentary film which had been hyped for days in the press, its contents guessed at, debated, disputed. At 8 p.m. ITV would finally unveil the contents of a two-and-a-half-hour film, *Charles: The Private Man, the Public Role,* a programme without which it is doubtful that Diana would have agreed to talk with Martin Bashir at all, far less agree to discuss her own history of adultery in public.

The big question dangled by the tabloids before the programme aired was, essentially, would Charles cough? Would he admit that he had been playing away, and with his former girlfriend, Camilla Parker Bowles? Because what could there be to say over the space of two and a half hours, longer than most Hollywood epics, if not that? In many ways the question was already redundant. By June 1994 anyone with an interest in these matters could have read what sounded suspiciously like the truth in their favourite newspaper; if the two were not an item, it damned well looked like it. And so the thrill that night for the 13 million people who tuned in was rather: How will Charles play this? Will he confess, and take his whacks? Will he lie? Or will he sidestep the issue altogether?

Diana understood her part in the drama perfectly. Instead of watching the show, curled privately on a sofa in Kensington Palace, she would put on a public display of insouciance, her stage a glittering *Vanity Fair* gala at the Serpentine Gallery in Hyde Park. But what to wear on this night of nights? The answer Diana came up with is clear from the astonishing photographic record of that night, the most memorable of all Diana's fashion gambles. This was the night of the so-called 'revenge dress', the cleavage- and shoulder-baring cocoon of black silk by Christina Stambolian, perfectly projecting allure and defiance, body language raised to a holler. Events unfolded perfectly for the TV crews and photographers. Backlit in the soft evening sunlight, Diana bounded from a black Jaguar, smile radiant as she double-kissed her host, Lord Palumbo, startled and beguiled, half a head shorter but standing proxy for every red-blooded man watching that night. The *Sun* captured it the next morning: **'THE THRILLA HE LEFT TO WOO CAMILLA'**.

The headline writers judged Charles's big moment on TV much more harshly. Yes, he made a halting admission of adultery, with an unspecified partner, but when two and a half hours of unwrapping revealed such a trifling gift, the prince won far less sympathy than he may have felt was his due. What emerged was less mea culpa than woe is me, bemoaning the utter beastliness of a foundered marriage, leaving one forced, obliged almost, to take up with an old flame. Would not anyone? Charles had squirmed and contorted, straining for the mot juste in a way which seemed intended to make what he said appear especially profound, that extraordinarily he had been singled out to face an ordeal which few had experienced and few could possibly comprehend. I talked about this with Sir Max Hastings, the distinguished writer, former newspaper editor and an acquaintance of Prince Charles at that time. He said, 'With the Prince of Wales, you can always see this poor man asking himself, "How do I feel about this? How do I see this?"'

'He spent maybe an hour and a half at the dinner table, with just me and Nicholas Soames, banging on and on, quite soon after the separation from Diana, about how ghastly everything was. How nobody understood it. After literally an hour and a half of uninterrupted monologue I said, "Look, sir. All three of us around this table have broken marriages. But there comes a moment when we have to recognize that we're all, even you, sir, deeply privileged people. And we've just got to shut up and get on with it."

'He didn't like this at all. Banged his fists on the table so that all the china rattled. He did not like anybody contradicting him. And he said, "Nobody but me can possibly understand how utterly bloody it is to be Prince of Wales!"

'Nicholas Soames behaved wonderfully on that occasion. Nicholas was always accused of being a courtier who sucked up to him, but on that occasion Nicholas said, "No, sir, no, sir. Max is absolutely right, sir! We must box on, sir, box on!"

'And he didn't like that either!'

The truth is that Prince Charles was far more conflicted during that interview than even his tortured delivery conveys. I was given special insight into the making of the ITV documentary because it was my father-in-law, Christopher Martin, who spent two years at the prince's side, filming roughly 180 hours' worth of material, whittled down to the film's 150 minutes. The unseen footage, surrendered to the prince's people at the end of the process, is today held in a vault at Windsor Castle and would provide fascinating material for any future historian lucky enough to study it. For what we see on-screen is only half the truth. Take *two*. When first challenged to confirm or deny his adultery Prince Charles refused.

So what changed his mind? To answer that we need to look at the genesis of the television film, in those years when the 'War of the Waleses' was at its height. Remarkably, the wrecking ball which was ultimately to strike Diana was set swinging by her husband's profound concern for architecture. Charles's belief in TV as a potent weapon stemmed from a rare moment when he'd discovered that a deeply held personal belief could actually win him admirers rather than mockery. Constantly derided for what most of the papers portrayed as hippy nonsense, homeopathy, talking to the

Highgrove shrubbery, Charles discovered that when he talked about architecture people seemed happy to listen. More than that, his pronouncements had a dramatic effect – plans for buildings he considered inappropriate were magically swept away. Here, if only in one aspect of life, was what it *should* be like to be king.

Charles's partner and enabler in this field was Christopher Martin, a long-time producer and director in the BBC department of Music and Arts. In the early 1980s Christopher picked up on Charles's sparring with architecture's avant-garde, whom he saw as wanton destroyers of a precious heritage. This was the time of Charles's famous denunciation of the proposed extension to London's National Gallery, a 'monstrous carbuncle on the face of a much-loved and elegant friend'. Amid a huge media fuss the public sided mainly with the prince. Christopher spoke with Charles, offering prime airtime if the prince cared to put his case on BBC1. The resulting film, *HRH The Prince of Wales: A Vision of Britain*, aired in October 1988 and was an enormous success. The prince spoke wisely, informedly, and the papers loved him for it. Buoyed with this success Christopher proposed broadening the scope, to show Charles's concern for the environment. In 1990 the BBC broadcast *HRH The Prince of Wales: The Earth in Balance*, warning of an unfolding ecological horror story. Again, a hit with the public, a second proud feather in Charles's cap.

And so negotiations began for a far more ambitious project, difficult now not to imagine under what would have been a much simpler title: *Charles: The Movie*. It would go much further than the previous films, offering Charles the opportunity to do more than simply bat for elegant buildings and nature. This time he would be batting for himself, demonstrating his desire to make the country he would one day rule a somewhat better place than he'd found it. And this new film would be an independent production, with Christopher quitting the BBC after more than twenty years' service, offering the prince to the corporation's main rival instead. Three decades ago royals on TV were a much rarer sight than they have become, and ITV jumped at what they judged would be a ratings triumph in the UK and sell briskly abroad. Christopher assembled a team to trail the prince right around the world, from Mexico to the Middle East, Scotland to Australia, with the celebrated journalist Jonathan Dimbleby, then compiling his authorized biography of the prince, called in at key moments to conduct the interviews. The entire budget for such an undertaking? At today's prices, perhaps £2 million.

The aim was to portray the prince as a serious man, doing serious things, a broadsheet blast against tabloid sniping. But as the team gathered material on a vast range of lofty subjects, events from the tackier side of life began to intrude. On 16 June 1992 a book appeared which was very different from the usual stream of lightweight gossip. Andrew Morton's book *Diana: Her True Story* was published amid a colossal media storm and clearly offered something in a wholly different category from simple tabloid rumours of a rift between the royal couple. Here was a book, rumoured to be endorsed by Diana herself, describing a life so wretched that she had tried to kill herself. And there was another character now in the cast. Charles's lover, Camilla.

At first the documentary makers were as horrified, as unbelieving, as the rest of the population. Talking soon after with Richard Aylard, private secretary to the prince, Christopher expressed his astonishment that something so outrageously false could be published at all. 'Yes,' came the reply. 'The problem is, it's all true.' In December 1992, at the end of that *annus horribilis*, Charles and Diana announced their formal separation. And by now the commissioners at ITV had begun to twitchily enquire whether the time spent with Charles, two years at the battlefront, would yield something more than monologues about racial harmony, youth clubs and organic fertilizer. What about the shagging?

It was these hard-faced commissioners, £2 million in the hole, who ultimately tipped the balance and brought about the public confession which, certainly in its secondary effect, changed history. In late 1993 Jonathan Dimbleby had been called to conduct a major set-piece interview with Prince Charles, in St George's Chapel close to Windsor Castle. Here is where Charles revealed his view that the historic title of the British monarch as 'Defender of the Faith', current since the days of Henry VIII, was outdated. Rather than '*the* Faith', implying a staunch defence of the Established Church, Charles said that he would prefer 'Defender of *Faith*', a kumbaya-ish embracing of all things spiritual from Anglicanism to Zen. And then, with one good story in the bag, Dimbleby shifted tack, with words to this effect: 'There has been speculation about your marriage, about your difficult relations with the Princess of Wales. How much of that is justified?' I have only a summary of the encounter, never having viewed the actual footage. But at this point Charles paused, for rather a long time. The pause endured. And then he replied, to the effect of: 'These are personal matters. The speculation you have talked about is not a helpful thing.'

He knew where Dimbleby wanted to take him, but he would not follow. Adultery was off the table. Dimbleby, Christopher and the crew packed up their cameras and lights.

Reporting back to their ITV commissioners, their paymasters, they had good news and bad. The good? A humongous kerfuffle over governance of the Anglican Church. Probably screaming headlines in the *Church Times*. Back of the net.

And Camilla?

Dimbleby and Christopher knew they were powerless on how far Prince Charles could be pushed. Royals do not do contracts, guarantees of revelation. But when the filmmakers were told by ITV's executives to go back to Charles's people, to lean on the flunkeys one more time, they knew there was at least a glimmer of hope. Did Charles seriously believe he could be allowed more than two hours in the nation's ear without telling it the single thing it was yearning to hear? This made for a powerful argument, but there was an additional strand, one which appeared sensible at the time but proved fatally mistaken. If the tabloid machine ran on the fuel of speculation, then why not cut off that fuel, in order that the machine would stop?

Christopher and Dimbleby returned for talks with Aylard and put forth just such a case for confession. Only say yes, adultery happened, with Camilla Parker Bowles, and from that point on there will be nothing for the horrid journalists to speculate about. Aylard reported this fresh approach. But Charles was receiving conflicting advice, some of it from one of the wisest journalists in the land. Max Hastings told me, 'I wrote to the Prince of Wales at some length about the whole Dimbleby project. And I said, "You are potty if you think that telling all could possibly do you personally, or the monarchy, any good. The only sensible way to behave in these situations is to say nothing, say nothing, and let the other side make mistakes."

'Throughout this whole ghastly drama all the parties

involved kidded themselves that telling their side of it to newspapers or television companies was somehow going to make things better. All it did was, at every turn, give the story new legs. And, of course, it was great for newspaper sales and television audiences. I think it was pretty awful for the monarchy.'

The prince pondered, knowing that the way he was perceived for evermore would now hinge on this single decision. He reflected further. And then the fatal deal was done. As Aylard told Christopher, surprised but hugely relieved, regarding the tabloid newshounds on Camilla's scent: 'We've decided to shoot their fox!'

The setting decided upon for this final critical encounter was the place where Charles would feel most comfortable, literally at home, Highgrove, the prince's eighteenth-century estate in Gloucestershire. In the film we see Dimbleby and Charles stroll amiably through the garden, nonchalant, talking flowers but clearly headed to conduct important business of some kind. Once indoors, the mood of the interview is set from the beginning.

DIMBLEBY: The most damaging charge that is made, in relation to your marriage, is that you were, because of your relationship with Camilla Parker Bowles, from the beginning, persistently unfaithful to your wife and thus caused the breakdown. What is your response to that persistent criticism?

CHARLES: Oh, that's the persistent criticism, is it?

The prince's retort comes across as petulant, a final squeak of defiance. It establishes the tone which runs throughout the interview, building to its unsatisfactory climax, the clip which fuelled headlines then and has been replayed countlessly over thirty years.

DIMBLEBY: Did you try to be faithful and honourable to your wife when you took on the vow of marriage?

CHARLES: Yes. Absolutely.

DIMBLEBY: And you were?

CHARLES: Yes. Until it became irretrievably broken down. Us both having tried.

Dimbleby adopts the tone of a legal inquisitor, his questions precise and unrelenting. But this is the gentle probing of the defending silk, the friend who has got your back, not the prosecutor drawing the net slowly tighter around his prey. Patrick Jephson, Diana's private secretary at this time, told me, 'What is significant is the prince uses this term "irretrievably broken down". That's a piece of legalese. It's not a natural thing to say. What was glossed over was the question of whether the marriage was broken by the adultery, or did the adultery happen because of the breakage? And I would say, having observed these people over a long period at close range, the adultery came first.'

The who, what, why, where and when remained unexplored, leaving Dimbleby's client unchallenged, allowed to fill the void with a facial pantomime evoking by turns pain, wisdom, sorrow and regret, but for what we are never entirely clear. The impression is of a man who is certainly sorry for himself, regretful of where life has led him, but faintly shifty, faintly weird. In Max Hastings' words: 'This was the absolute reverse of Diana. When you went to see Diana she was brilliant at pretending to be a normal human being. Every time I came out of a conversation with her, I'd always think she's brilliant at simulating frankness. She appears to be really telling it like it is, which is quite a gift. None of the rest of them know how to pretend to be normal human beings.'

The film finally wound to a halt at 10.30 p.m. On a day which saw Charles come close to death on a remote Hebridean landing strip, a story which would normally have claimed top spot on the front pages was beaten by his own television appearance. But the *Daily Mail* forged a link between the two, carrying a photograph of the crippled airliner and asking: **'ANOTHER ERROR OF JUDGEMENT?'** Charles has never since piloted an aircraft.

Tabloid editors appear to have presumed that their readers would condemn Charles's boldness. The *Daily Mirror* next day carried the banner headline **'NOT FIT TO REIGN'**, while the *Sun* declared readers had jammed its switchboard because 'they did not want an adulterer on the throne'. But by the weekend it was all change, an indication perhaps that those editors had misread the tea leaves. Opinion appeared to have swung through 180 degrees, the *Mirror* revealing an opinion poll which showed 61 per cent support for the prince, the *Sun* reporting that 'thousands of *Sun* readers flooded our hotline with calls of support'. Charles appeared to have pulled off a victory – if not the six–nil virtuoso triumph he had expected then at least a hard-won one–nil, after extra time. But as history has shown, the response of millions of newspaper readers was inconsequential, set aside the reaction of a single individual.

The most important of the 13 million viewers was the

one who had not watched the programme at all that night. Viewed on tape, Charles's halting half-confession – the public embracing of Camilla as a 'great friend' yet with no explicit admission that she was his lover – put Diana into an icy rage, oddly tinged with a sense of exultant relief. Suddenly, after two years of Palace disdain for having briefed Andrew Morton, Diana felt herself to be back on the moral high ground. Patrick Jephson told me, 'She was vindicated. She said to me, "Patrick, now people can see what we've been dealing with." And, of course, for Diana's divorce lawyers, it was an absolute gift because at that stage the lawyers were engaged in a protracted legal dance to gain advantage in the litigation. This was a spectacular own goal.' In a way that is intriguing considering what came later: Diana had learned just how damaging a television interview could be. Jephson said, 'I think it was a huge mistake and rebounded badly against the prince. But her main concern was for William and Harry. This was something that had not been previously discussed with them and it was a terrible thing to discover in that way.'

Charles's decision to ignore his instinct for discretion, to allow take two and admit adultery, would reap a bitter harvest. Diana's revenge would come, on 20 November 1995, certainly not determined by Charles's interview, though perhaps somehow *permitted* by it. And what a difference there would be in the delivery. Where Charles had struggled with each agonized sentence, Diana would sparkle and dance through almost an hour of candid-sounding eloquence. But she would leave out, as we will see, almost all that she believed to be *truly* important, *truly* scary. The secrets which she had been told by Martin Bashir.

2. How Much Is True?

The long road leading to Martin Bashir's *Panorama* interview, in turn to the horror of Paris's Pont de l'Alma tunnel in 1997, can be traced back to a far more prosaic setting, a junction on the A1199 at Snaresbrook, in the eastern suburbs of London, on a rain-drenched night eight years earlier. There, where Hermitage Walk joins the Woodford Road, a little after 10.15 p.m. on 14 May 1987, blue ambulance lights played over a small scene of tragedy.

A red Ford Fiesta, dented and slewed sideways in the road; an overturned Suzuki GS400 motorbike with the body of its helmeted passenger lying close by. 'The man appeared to be dead when I reached him. There was no movement,' said a GP who had been driving past and stopped to help. The mundane horror of just another dreadful road accident was in this case far more. The man lying dead on the wet tarmac had been, in Princess Diana's words, 'the greatest love I've ever had'. And because of that, she said, he had been murdered.

The dead man was thirty-nine-year-old Barry Mannakee, who only nine months earlier had been Diana's police bodyguard. He was a plain-clothes sergeant, married, good-looking in a TV detective kind of way, appointed in April 1985 to guard William and Harry as well as their mother, a job which involved shadowing the princess both in the UK and on tours to Italy, Australia and America. At that point in time the royal marriage was less than five years old. The evidence on the exact nature of Diana's relationship with her bodyguard is mixed and it would be unfair to dwell on whether he offered merely emotional support or something more. Either way, in July 1986 Sgt Mannakee was abruptly switched to other duties after rumours of what was called 'over-familiar behaviour' began to spread from palace circles to Scotland Yard.

It is Diana's response to Barry Mannakee's death which matters. Andrew Morton, the journalist she briefed, secretly over a long period, for his revelatory book published in June 1992, told me, 'When I was first involved with Diana back in 1991, the first question she asked me was, "Was Barry Mannakee murdered by the security forces?" You could say it was him that got me the gig. And she asked me that question because she'd had an affectionate relationship with him, and she'd always had suspicions. It showed you what was brewing inside her mind on a daily basis.'

When in 2005 police came to investigate claims that the bodyguard had been done away with, perhaps by British secret services, to prevent a scandal emerging, they recorded that Diana many times had expressed her belief that this was murder. Detectives noted how Diana had reported her suspicions to Inspector Ken Wharfe, Sgt Mannakee's successor as bodyguard; to Paul Burrell, her butler; to two subsequent boyfriends, James Hewitt and Hasnat Khan. But most remarkably we can hear Diana's own words; we can see her describing the relationship and outlining her belief that her former minder had been taken out.

In late 1992 Diana had set out to improve her public-speaking style, to do away with the slightly daffy voice of the Sloane Ranger. Diana decided that in future all public pronouncements would be delivered in a way that commanded respect and inspired belief. And so she hired an expert, a former *Coronation Street* actor turned voice coach called Peter Settelen, part of whose method involved shooting clips of his pupils on the clunky video recorders available thirty years ago, to watch and analyse later. He recommended that Diana choose subjects which were deeply personal, drawing out emotion and honesty. Recorded in the sitting room at Kensington Palace, Diana had no idea that what she put on tape would ever go beyond those walls. The material was indeed kept under lock and key within the palace, only reaching the public domain seven years after Diana's death. It is remarkable to study the grainy footage, Diana relaxed, laughing occasionally, sharing what it is impossible to believe is anything other than the truth, at least as she saw it.

'I'll tell you one of the biggest crushes of my life, which I don't find easy to discuss. When I was twenty-four or twenty-five I fell deeply in love with someone who worked in this environment. And he was the greatest friend I ever had. I was always wandering around trying to see him. I just, you know, wore my heart on my sleeve and was only happy when he was around. I was like a little girl in front of him the whole time.

'It got so difficult. People got so jealous and bitchy in this house and eventually he had to go. It was all found out and he was chucked out and then he was killed. Charles said to me, "He was killed in a motorbike accident." And that was the biggest blow of my life I must say. I think he was bumped off.

'I used to have really disturbing dreams about him. And he was very unhappy wherever he's gone to, and so I went and found out where he was buried and I went to put some flowers on his grave. And the day I did that the dreams stopped. It's strange, isn't it?

'I should never have played with fire and I did. I got very burned.'

Diana did in fact question the terrifying prospect that Barry Mannakee, the father of two young daughters, had been murdered, all because of her, and it is uncomfortable to imagine Diana's fear, curdled with guilt. In 1991 she asked Andrew Morton to discover what he could about the incident and a short time later the reporter relayed his findings: the motorbike had collided with a car being driven by trainee beauty therapist Nicola Chopp, a seventeen-year-old who had passed her driving test only six weeks earlier and caused the motorbike to swerve by performing a dangerous right turn. Admitting dangerous driving, she was fined £85 and surely sounded the least likely agent to be involved in a secret service-inspired assassination. Nonetheless, Morton said, 'I told Diana that. And whilst the logic of it was there, and whilst the evidence was there, she never really believed that. She always felt that some unseen forces had engineered that death.'

Barry Mannakee's death remains just one of the extraordinary events in Diana's story which provide rich material for conspiracy theorists. In a parallel to the notorious 'blinding white light' said to have disoriented chauffeur Henri Paul on the night of Diana's deadly crash, police investigators themselves suggested that the bright lights of a mystery vehicle could have been a factor in the collision in east London. Miss Chopp, at the wheel of the Ford Fiesta, would say in 2003, 'I do believe that accidents can be arranged and that something suspicious happened that night.' Barry Mannakee's brother-in-law, Richard Emmins, spoke in 2017 about his continuing doubts: 'First, my brother-in-law has this accident, then Diana dies in a Paris car crash. But trying to get to the truth will probably be impossible.' There, that lingering doubt, even from people who attended Sgt Mannakee's inquest, who will have studied the police reports line by line.

So what did Diana truly believe? Someone whose judgement counts is Patrick Jephson, Diana's private secretary between 1988 and 1996, who spent virtually every working day with the princess during those turbulent years. I have discussed these things many times with him. In his view it is only possible to understand how Diana and Martin Bashir came together, in fatal combination, by looking at the extraordinary build-up to autumn 1995. Patrick said to me, 'Who could have predicted half the things that had happened in the preceding five, ten years? It was hard work to decide what was real, what was unreal, what was believable, what was malicious. So it may seem naive of her, but in the context, it's not so far-fetched. It may seem strange that she would believe these things, but let me tell you, from my own experience, you didn't know what was coming from day to day.'

I have talked about these things too with Diana's brother, Charles Spencer. He told me, 'Diana didn't start off her adult life in an unhappy place, or one verging on paranoia. But I think repeated extraordinary revelations in public had left her very vulnerable and very suspicious. She was not academic, but she had a very clever mind, she had a very high emotional intelligence. And I think it really played on that clever, alert mind. There was a feeling among all of us who cared for, and loved, Diana that she was very beleaguered and was up against a big opponent and we felt beholden to help.'

Another person Diana confided in at this time was the then thirty-eight-year-old *Daily Mail* journalist Richard Kay, who told me, 'I knew her socially as a friend, as well as being a journalist. This idea that she was some sort of empty-headed young woman who couldn't string two words together was simply not the princess I knew. She was someone who was witty, quite well read. Certainly she was very up with current affairs.' He says Diana's belief, that she was a surveillance target, whether true or not, was entirely genuine: 'Diana felt that she was being spied on, watched, recorded, observed by shadowy people. She didn't trust "the enemy", as she called them, the courtiers who served Prince Charles, because she felt that they were taking notes on who she saw, what she did. She felt at times quite alone. That she was one woman against the system, which in many ways she was.'

It is hard to imagine that a shiver did not run down Diana's spine when she first heard the news of Mannakee's death in May 1987. She told Peter Settelen that it was Prince Charles himself who passed on the news as they were preparing to board a royal flight to the south of France, their destination the Cannes Film Festival: 'Charles just dumped it on me like that and I wasn't able to do anything. I just sat there all day going through this huge high-profile visit to Cannes, just devastated.' Twenty miles along the coast from Cannes is Monaco, which Diana had visited five years earlier in an equally troubled frame of mind. The funeral of Princess Grace of Monaco took place on 18 September 1982, she having died from head injuries after losing control of the Rover she was driving, plunging from a winding mountain road.

Diana's attendance at the funeral was evidence of a long fascination with the former Hollywood star Grace Kelly, a figure whom she regarded as something of a kindred spirit. Diana recounted to Andrew Morton how Grace had taken her discreetly aside at a London palace reception, shortly before the 1981 royal wedding, to offer private words of solace to the nervous young princess-to-be. Diana told Morton, 'I learned a lesson that night. I remember meeting Princess Grace and how wonderful and serene she was. But there was troubled water under her, I saw that.'

By the time of that shared confidence with Morton, in 1992, the marriage of Grace and her husband Prince Rainier of Monaco had been picked over by biographers, revealing infidelity and intrigue remarkably similar to Diana's own experience. And so the car crash? Do princesses who step out of line need to look out for not just the safety of discarded lovers but indeed their own? So much of Diana's story sounds improbable that it is no great leap at all from reality to fantasy. The boundary between the two is gossamer-thin. So what was it like for the person living inside this chamber of smoke and mirrors, when, for them, deciding between fact and fancy might literally mean life or death? Even if the deaths of Barry Mannakee and Princess Grace spelled only *imagined* menace, there was plenty of the real thing headed Diana's way.

In August 1992, shortly before her public-speaking lessons with Peter Settelen, with the aftershock of Andrew Morton's book still rippling through the country six weeks after publication, Diana arrived at Balmoral, Queen Victoria's turreted Highland retreat, for what must have been the least jolly getaway it is possible to imagine. Balmoral was the venue for an annual invasion by the entire royal family, a private place, in the pre-internet era a remarkably insulated place, creating conditions eerily similar to a modern-day reality TV compound where imported hatreds are carefully nurtured into bloom.

Thirty years ago, with no newspapers available on mobiles

or iPads, the mood for the day ahead at Balmoral, certainly the atmosphere over breakfast, was determined by the arrival of the London newspapers, flown first to Aberdeen and then driven the fifty miles along forest roads. On Monday, 24 August 1992, in thick letters three inches high, the *Sun* headline read simply: **'MY LIFE IS TORTURE'**, Diana's words, but much more worryingly Diana's words as captured in a hacked phone conversation between the princess and a boyfriend, James Gilbey, which had actually taken place long before, on New Year's Eve 1989.

This was what has gone down in history as 'Squidgygate', so called because Gilbey uses his pet name for the princess, Squidgy, fourteen times during the call. The evidence shows that the call took place around 7 p.m. on 31 December, Diana speaking on a landline, miserable and alone in her bedroom at Sandringham, Gilbey on a mobile inside his parked car in a lay-by in north Oxfordshire some 150 miles away. The language is occasionally salty, sometimes fruity, as the chat meanders for twenty-three minutes across subjects ranging from their next dinner date to how Jimmy Savile, then a royal favourite, has been called on to offer tips on handling the media. For just a flavour of hinted-at hanky-panky, of how ghastly it is to be married to Prince Charles:

DIANA: He makes my life real torture, I've decided. Bloody hell, the things I have done for this fucking family.

GILBEY: I haven't played with myself, for a full forty-eight hours. Not for a full forty-eight hours.

DIANA: I don't want to get pregnant.

GILBEY: Darling, that's not going to happen. All right?

DIANA: Yeah.

GILBEY: Don't think like that. It's not going to happen. Darling, you won't get pregnant.

Anybody who has known the routine fraughtness of being a guest of the in-laws can imagine how the leaking of this conversation played over breakfast at Balmoral on this and succeeding days. The *Sun* revelled in its exclusive as every other paper, red-top and posh alike, picked over the scraps. For Diana it was beyond cringe-making, she being reduced to relying on Patrick Jephson, on holiday 700 miles away in Devon, to buy an armful of newspapers the moment they arrived at his local newsagent's at 6 a.m., to brief Diana before her descent to breakfast: 'I stood in a call box outside the newsagent's, reading to the princess as calmly as I could the printed transcript of her intimate conversation with James Gilbey and the damning chorus of comment that accompanied it.' Diana would shortly be able to relieve her private secretary of that task. The *Sun* made audio of the entire call available to readers who dialled a premium-rate number at 36p a minute. Roughly 120,000 people did, within hours.

Patrick told me, 'It was intended to diminish her in the public's eyes, to embarrass her. But curiously, it had the opposite effect. She came across as vulnerable, trying her best in a loveless marriage, finding some consolation somewhere. It actually, in a curious way, made her look more human, approachable, lovable, forgivable. She was quite pragmatic about it. You could dial a number and listen to it. So I did dial the number, just to satisfy myself that it really was her. And I told her about it later and she said, "Well, I hope you used the office phone. I wouldn't want you to have to pay the charge." '

Extraordinary as it may sound, the eruption of Squidgygate may have been, for Diana, a relief. The *Sun* had received a taped copy of the phone call in January 1990, within ten days of its having been made, and hours later confronted Gilbey outside his home in London's Lennox Gardens. The newspapermen announced their discovery before Gilbey fled, to share the terrible news with Diana herself. But then nothing appeared in print for a torturously long time. To finally see her words in the newspapers, then hear her own voice in radio and television reports, was a horror Diana had anticipated for more than two years. The *Sun* had held back so long from going to print not because they doubted the veracity of the tape but because even the rhino-hided bosses of what was then the country's top-selling paper knew how damaging publication would prove, for the princess, for the monarchy as a whole. With the appearance of Andrew Morton's book, revealing the emotional knife-fighting that had been going on for years, the bar for acceptable outrage had been dropped by several notches. Squidgy could debut.

There is no certainty even today whether Squidgygate was part of a plot pulled together by spooks, or a crazy bit of happenstance unkindly targeting a very unlucky princess. When technical experts listened to the tape they immediately pointed to electronic pulses which seemed to say it could not have been recorded live, as the conversation occurred, rather that it must first have been captured from Diana's landline and then *rebroadcast*. Why? In the hope that some member of the public, equipped with the correct scanning device, would tune in to the couple's chat and take it to the papers? But surely that sounded fantastical, a carefully engineered plot which still depended entirely on luck to be carried through. And who could be behind it? To first tap one of Sandringham's phones and then cleverly reintroduce the audio into the broadcast sphere suggested skills and resources only available to MI5, or more likely the UK intelligence-gathering wizards at GCHQ.

The informant who brought the tape to the *Sun* seemed a model of rectitude. Seventy-year-old retired TSB bank manager Cyril Reenan freely volunteered that his hobby was to listen in to random phone calls, on a £900 receiving device in his home in Abingdon, close to where Gilbey had been at the time of the conversation. Mr Reenan told his local newspaper the *Oxford Mail* that, no, he didn't just snoop out of nosiness. He listened to phone calls hoping that he would pick up insider gossip from people in the horse-racing world, which he could then use as tips for betting. To add to the confusion, Mr Reenan said he had not happened upon the call at the time it was made, on New Year's Eve 1989, but on 4 January 1990. Surely that was evidence for the rebroadcast theory, and an indication of something very sophisticated, very murky, going on? But how he was able to seize on the sotto voce back-and-forth between Diana and Gilbey, amid the thousands of calls floating through the airwaves, remains a puzzle to this day. Mr Reenan died, aged eighty-two, in 2004.

The story which brought such toe-curling mortification for Diana also troubled the government. Once the official spy agencies began to fall under suspicion, the then Home Secretary, Kenneth Clarke, was forced to publicly deny any suggestion that MI5 or GCHQ had been involved. But if this official denial was to be believed, then it surely left only possibilities which were even more chilling than surveillance by the state: surveillance by agents with all the expertise and resources of the state, but with their own rogue agenda. And so for Diana here was the worst of all possible worlds. Not only were her private conversations being bugged, by persons unknown, but they would be released to the world in a way and at a time to cause her maximum damage. And, just as in the case of Barry Mannakee, Diana had not got a clue where the truth lay. She was sure of only one thing. As she would go on to tell Martin Bashir, in November 1995, in her *Panorama* interview:

> BASHIR: Have you any idea how that conversation came to be published in the national press?
>
> DIANA: No, but it was done to harm me in a serious manner. And that was the first time I'd experienced what it was like to be outside the net, so to speak. To not be in the family.

In Diana's analysis, August 1992 marked the first instance where the dark forces ranged against her decided to demonstrate their awesome power. While she had run a homespun operation, with a friend literally ferrying the tapes of her anguish, by bicycle, to Andrew Morton, here was evidence of magisterial technical competence as well as terrifying audacity. In deciding to trash Diana so publicly, whoever was calling the shots was even prepared to risk collateral damage to the Windsor brand, so long as this late recruit was squashed like a bug. But at least the enemy seemed to have declared himself. Imagine how even that degree of certainty was shaken when, a little over four months later, Diana's attempt to build a cogent narrative was crushed, instantly.

3. Tapped and Bugged and Hacked?

On 17 January 1993 the Sunday newspaper the *People* ran the simple headline: **'CHARLES AND CAMILLA – THE TAPE'**. Inside was a transcript of a tape they had possessed for months, the record of a playful late-night phone conversation between Charles and Camilla in which the prince joked about a life so dreadful that he likened his ill fortune to a flush-resistant tampon. The analogy was grimly poetic, the whole effect desperately tawdry. Never had a senior member of the royal family suffered such scarifying humiliation, the worse because it came not from the pen of a cruel satirist but from the subject himself.

Desperately embarrassing then, decades later this conversation between our king and queen is so deeply embedded in the national psyche that it kindles mainly amused affection. Tina Brown, a close observer of the royal pageant, describes it well: 'The script, delivered in the prince's familiar mannered tones and Camilla's breathless basso, plays like a two-hander for Jeremy Irons and Emma Thompson at the National Theatre, so illuminating is it of adultery as performed at the top end of the class spectrum.' But in 1993 the nation's reaction was astonishment, perhaps disgust, certainly a profound sense of having been lied to. The problem was not merely Charles's cack-handed drollery concerning tampons but this clear demonstration that he and Camilla were a cavorting couple when any suggestions to that effect had always been dismissed.

But how did it surface? Analysis of the tape reveals that the 'Camillagate' conversation actually took place thirteen days before Diana's Squidgygate chat with James Gilbey. It had taken even longer to come to light. On 18 December 1989 Prince Charles had been a guest of the Dowager Duchess of Westminster at Eaton Hall in Cheshire, with Camilla 200 miles away at her home, Middlewick House in Wiltshire. Once again there is an impenetrable lack of clarity about the journey of the audio from speech to publication. The narrative offered by *People* newspaper editor Richard Stott is that an amateur radio geek trawling through the airwaves close to where Charles was based simply stumbled upon the call by accident. Stott recalled: 'The tape was made by a Scouser who had had a few pints of lager and a curry and decided he would test out his latest gadget, an electronic homing device that picks up cellnet signals. As the time was around 2 a.m. there weren't too many about, so he homed straight into Charles and Camilla.' The story goes that the owner of the tape recognized Charles's voice and decided to record what followed. He then sat on his discovery for more than two years, until in the riot of publicity following Squidgygate he realized there could be money to be made, and a £30,000 deal with the newspaper followed.

There is a counter-narrative. Former Conservative MP Gyles Brandreth, an author with close connections to King Charles, reports how he and other members of Parliament tried to investigate the security breach at the time. Despite assurances from Prime Minister John Major that no government agency had been involved, Brandreth reports that the sceptics were not convinced, believing instead: 'The only people with equipment of sufficient sophistication to make the recordings were members of an intelligence service, either our own or that of another country.' Voicing the most popular theory from this quarter he said, 'The Camillagate tape that was published was unofficially leaked by a mischief-maker at GCHQ, anxious to expose the private behaviour of the heir to the throne.'

Murky waters indeed. As Patrick Jephson told me, 'When something strange happens, like a tape appearing out of nowhere, of course speculation is pretty much impossible to control. And given the kind of theatrical nature of royal life, you know, "We Are Royal People, We Don't Do Ordinary Things." It couldn't just be a radio ham, having a bit of fun. It has to be something more. Some rogue actor from one of the intelligence services? Yeah, that's an attractive theory. Everybody loves spy stories. Why not?'

Either way, for Diana here was a swooping curveball. Just when she had begun to face up to the challenge of dealing with the tappers and hackers, it now appeared that some of the spooks might actually be on *her* side. Was there a faction at GCHQ cheering for the princess, as keen to embarrass Charles as their colleagues had been to humiliate her? The story unfolded under a cloud of unknowing. Were the spooks good, or bad? Were they following Diana's activities at all? And if not, with someone so potentially vulnerable, why not?

The *Daily Mail*'s Richard Kay, the best-informed Diana-whisperer of that period, said to me, 'Diana had this enormous capacity to cause trouble, wittingly or unwittingly, for the royal family. And I think there was a view that if they had an idea of what she was up to, they could head it off, or deal with it before it became a major issue.' Certainly, Diana's cooperation with author Andrew Morton would cause the royal family plenty of trouble, as Diana herself seemed to recognize. Morton told me, 'She was worried about being overheard on the telephone, so we had to buy these scrambler telephones, which were utterly useless, quite frankly. Cost us three grand. And we paid for her rooms at Kensington Palace to be looked at, for bugs and other devices. She was always looking for that kind of suspicious behaviour.'

As we get closer to that fateful day when Diana and Martin Bashir first met in 1995, there are clear signs that Diana was not only convinced that she was the subject of malign surveillance but increasingly determined to evade it. The evidence I have chosen to look at seems to me the most credible kind, Diana's own words, and in this case her words reported in a document which was never expected to become public. On 18 October 1994 Met Police Deputy Assistant Commissioner David Meynell, head of the Royalty and Diplomatic Protection Department, compiled a three-page memorandum marked 'SECRET' with, at the bottom of the first page, the handwritten note: 'Home Secretary briefed.' What Meynell was recording was a meeting earlier that day with Diana, referred to simply as HRH.

HRH did not display any of the confrontational attitude which was evident during our last meeting. She was 'friendly and bright' on the surface.

His optimistic opening quickly turns much darker.

During the course of the conversation HRH bluntly asked me if her car had been bugged . . . She then said to me, 'Even when no one knows where I am going in my car there are people waiting for me at the other end.' She then told me that she knew her telephones were being tapped and that she was certain the same applied to her vehicle. She stated that she had proof that her phones were being tapped because she had 'set traps on four occasions and she had got the necessary evidence'.

[She stated that] . . . whilst she had a lot of enemies she had a lot of friends, some in places of knowledge. She could not name them because they could lose their jobs but she had been told that without any doubt five people from an organisation had been assigned full time to 'oversee' her activities, including listening to her private phone conversations . . . She stated that whilst she was certain of her ground she could not assist further without jeopardising the identities of her friends and this she was not prepared to do.

In navigating a life where disturbing events happened almost daily, Diana had done her damnedest to seek out a rational explanation. She had gone to the very top, the head of royal security, and said, 'Are you watching me, following me?' They'd said, 'Of course not.' But in the early 1990s, at the height of the terror campaign then being waged by the IRA in London, it seems much easier to believe that Diana *was* being secretly surveilled than that she was not. It seems likely that at the very least the authorities would have been desperate to keep eyes on young William, next king but one, and therefore felt it their duty to keep tabs on his mum. As Richard Kay put it, 'I think it would be naive, frankly, to assume that there weren't some sort of eyes being kept on Diana to see what she was up to. I wouldn't be at all surprised if people were being asked to keep an eye on who she saw and where she went.'

Meynell's memo would remain secret for thirteen years, until the inquest into Diana's death opened in October 2007. Those proceedings offer a priceless glimpse into Diana's solo tussle with the authorities. A witness called to give evidence on 7 January 2008 was Grahame Harding, a former military policeman who had started a company providing electronic security services, including checking for phone taps and sweeping for bugs. Four times, in 1994, Diana asked Harding to conduct a sweep of her apartment. Three times he drew a blank, but then, as Harding said, 'My equipment detected an electronic signal which indicated that a possible bugging device may have been present behind a wall in her bedroom. Princess Diana was present when I found this signal. I did not know what was on the other side of this wall and was not able to investigate further as I did not have access.'

When he returned the following day, Harding said, 'It was gone, there was nothing. I went to exactly the same place, with exactly the same equipment, with exactly the same things and there was no evidence at all of any transmission.' A false reading, a technical glitch? Diana felt she needed to do something and so Grahame Harding became a key player in Diana's homegrown security set-up. He would describe to the inquest how, to protect her privacy, he would take out mobile phone contracts with Vodafone in *his* name, yet give the Nokia handset to Diana to use, changing the number every three or four weeks. When the phone bill arrived at his address he would pay it, Diana settling up later.

Even with these precautions Diana felt unsafe. I have spoken with her brother Charles Spencer many times on these issues and he believes his sister was an early victim of the technique which became notorious more than a decade later. He said, 'Reading things in the paper that she'd only said to really close friends made her extremely unsettled. It's my theory that, before anyone even knew the term, she was probably being phone hacked. It looks like paranoia, but I think she was finding very, very private things she had only said to close friends or confidants were getting in the papers. I have talked to various members of my family; we believe she was phone hacked, even though she didn't know such a phenomenon existed.'

Diana's dread would be proven in stark terms in August 1995, not long before her first, fateful encounter with Martin Bashir. One of Diana's senior confidants at this time was Sir Max Hastings, one of the country's most distinguished journalists, someone whom Diana knew it was safe to use as a sounding board. He told me, 'I was rung up by our neighbour in the country, Peter Palumbo, and he said, "Diana wants to see you." So I went and I spent a couple of hours with Diana and she asked me what I knew about a conspiracy, allegedly funded by a mining tycoon called Peter Munk, to get David Wynne-Morgan, the public relations man, to arrange to have her "put down".' Peter Munk, who died in 2018, was at the time the sixty-eight-year-old billionaire boss of the world's biggest gold-mining company and counted Prince Charles among his friends. David Wynne-Morgan was a sixty-four-year-old former journalist with a roster of blue-chip clients. No shred of evidence exists for either man's involvement in a plot to murder Diana.

Max Hastings recalled, 'I said, well, I know absolutely nothing about this. I knew both Peter Munk and David Morgan and it sounded absolutely crazy to me. But she did believe this sort of stuff. I don't know who was feeding her this sort of thing. But I do think she was ready to believe it.'

Diana's fears were often clearly off target. In 1993, six months after fire had torn through Windsor Castle, destroying

115 rooms, causing damage of more than £30 million, she announced an astonishing find to Patrick Jephson. He told me, 'She took me upstairs to the nursery floor. Finger to her lips. Pulled back the carpet. And there were these little holes bored in the floorboard. "Look," she said. "These are for bugs for microphones!" And I said, "No, they're not. Ever since the Windsor fire, we've been putting in new motion detectors, things like that." That wasn't the answer that she wanted.'

By the summer of 1995 Princess Diana was in a strange place. But then she was always in a strange place. How could it be otherwise for the most famous, certainly the most scrutinized, person in the world? Many people find the business of dragging themselves out of bed, doing a job, handling the routine fallout of a failed marriage, the kids one weekend but not the next, more than enough to cope with. Diana's job meant touring an AIDS ward, or the Taj Mahal, touring Croydon, or Japan. But it was still a job and one which had to be done every day in front of a million cameras, waiting for her to be slightly fatter, or thinner, or wear the same dress twice over. So Diana had all that, and strong evidence too that she was being bugged and tapped and hacked. So, in her place, do you shrug and hope for the best? Or decide it is safer to fear the worst?

4. The Crook, the Earl and the Whistleblower

Customers lunching at a trendy Clapham music and wine bar, Numero Uno, one Sunday in the spring of 2000 will have nudged one another, whispered and pointed. Tapping a set of bongo drums, really quite well, was a thirty-seven-year-old leather-jacketed figure everyone recognized, at that point in history probably the most famous television reporter in the world. Martin Bashir had come up to join the house band Surf'n'Turf as they launched into the old Dionne Warwick hit 'Walk on By'. Their bassist, Jonathan Maitland, was, like the rest of the line-up, a media guy who just liked to play a bit for fun, free drinks, taxi money. Bashir was a hit, according to Maitland: 'He was fucking excellent. He's serious about music.'

And he *was* serious. In due course, when more famous still, Bashir would write songs with strange-sounding titles like 'Evevry Likkle Boy' and 'Jah Help I From Bout Ya', singing harmony and playing bass on a reggae album he recorded in New York called *Bass Lion*. Promoting the album, he told an interviewer, 'I grew up on a very large housing project in London. There were a large number of Jamaican families who came on HMS *Windrush* in the 1950s, they all lived on this housing project. That was the first time I heard reggae and from there I grew to love it.' Did he sing for Princess Diana in the autumn of 1995? If it would have assisted, he surely would have. People who know him well say that when he set out to charm he was inventive, and irresistible.

THE CROOK, THE EARL AND THE WHISTLEBLOWER

Maitland, a close colleague and sort-of friend for six years, offered, 'With Diana he would've found out whatever it was that made her tick. She would've been pretty gullible and vulnerable at the moment of maximum stress.'

Before the famous *Panorama* broadcast Bashir was more or less a nobody, but a striver. Born on a Wandsworth council estate, one of five children of parents who were immigrants from Pakistan, he went to the local comprehensive before studying English at King Alfred's College, Winchester. He did very well to win a researcher job at the BBC, aged twenty-three, in 1986, going front of camera for the first time on the BBC2 current affairs programme *Public Eye*, a worthy but low-wattage strand looking at UK domestic issues with a furrowed brow. Bashir's episodes had titles like 'The Doctor's Dilemma: Cash or Care?' and 'Youth Crime: Targeting the Tearaways'. It was solid BBC fare, though the first indication that Bashir might not always play by the rules came during his time on this show.

In 1991 he persuaded Michelle Hadaway, the mother of nine-year-old Karen Hadaway, murdered five years previously, to help an investigation he was undertaking for the programme. Bashir pleaded that if he could only take away the clothes Karen had worn on the night she was murdered, by then returned to the family by police, he would have them DNA tested. Perhaps it would lead them to Karen's killer? I am told by someone who witnessed this encounter that Bashir gave the appearance of being horror-stricken by Karen's death. That he sobbed, openly. He won permission to take away Karen's vest, knickers, T-shirt and sweatshirt. But there was no DNA testing. The investigation was dropped and there was no programme – which might happen for any number of reasons – but it was Bashir's failure to return the items to Karen's poor mum, indeed to acknowledge that he had taken them at all, which hurt, and seems to indicate heartlessness. Mrs Hadaway raised it with the BBC, tentatively at first, forcefully later, and as recently as 2023 finally received an apology and compensation.

Bashir, even that early in his career, would have found Mrs Hadaway a pushover. As he demonstrated later he had wiles enough to bewitch even the most skittish, the most media-wary subjects, to have them trust him before destroying themselves. It is a remarkable record to have interviewed arguably the two most famous people in the world – Princess Diana and Michael Jackson – to have beaten off a thousand other reporters to get the scoop, and in both cases to be accused of hastening their demise. But the charm was not something which oozed naturally, like the 100-watt charisma of a Hollywood star. In my brief dealings with Bashir at the BBC he didn't seem to sparkle at all. When he engaged the chosen gear, that's when the magic happened. In Maitland's experience: 'He was fantastic at looking in your eyes and telling you, "You're brilliant!" It's like a snake charmer, you know. You're in the intense glare of his spotlight, and you don't know any better. He was brilliant at doing sincerity.'

Without having yet done much that was brilliant as a journalist, Bashir was promoted from *Public Eye* to *Panorama* in 1992. But this was an era when the BBC's formerly magisterial public affairs strand was in trouble. The grande dame of BBC journalism, born in 1953, almost as old as *The Archers*, was at that time the victim of scatterbrain policies originating with Director-General John Birt and roundly shunned by viewers. The new regime had fired many of the experienced reporters and were forced to fill the void with recruits, like

Bashir, only too happy to whistle a new tune even though it meant whistling largely in the dark.

When Bashir joined *Panorama* one of the few remaining old-school reporters was Tom Mangold, then approaching sixty years of age, with thirty years' BBC experience behind him and a swashbuckling Fleet Street career before that. Mangold told me, 'Bashir was brought on to the programme by the deputy editor, who'd worked with him on *Public Eye*. He was ambitious, had sharp elbows.' After decades of reporting villainy of all kinds, with 120 *Panorama* films under his belt, Mangold prides himself on sniffing out a charlatan better than most. And so he still gives Bashir amused respect today: 'We were all drinking at Albertine's, at the bottom of Wood Lane. One day Martin came up to me, took me to one side and said, "Mr Mangold, I'm sorry to trouble you, but I just wanted to tell you that my brother recently died, and on his deathbed he said to me, 'Martin, when you get to *Panorama*, imitate Tom Mangold. Write like Tom Mangold. Operate like him, and you will become as successful as he is.'"

'And I was really touched. I thought, "How nice, nobody flatters anybody else in this business." What I didn't know, until later, was that he told exactly the same story to Mike Nicholson at ITV. To John Humphrys. So this was Martin's introduction to famous reporters. To make sure that they were on his side. Neat technique. I kind of admire him for it.'

Bashir had indeed experienced family heartbreak. His father suffered recurrent bouts of mental suffering, which made him frequently suicidal. His twenty-nine-year-old brother Tommy died, in 1991, after a lifelong struggle with muscular dystrophy. Tommy's death came up during Bashir's appearance on ITV's *Celebrity X Factor* in 2019. Bashir recalled then how his brother's fortitude remained an inspiration, telling the audience and judges, with a catch in his throat, 'Every time I have faced a challenge I have heard him whispering, saying, "What excuse do you have?" That is my motivation.' Jonathan Maitland, working closely alongside Bashir on the ITV programme *Tonight* shortly after he achieved worldwide fame with the Diana interview, remembers a steelier kind of motivation: 'He used techniques back then that were considered acceptable. Aggressive, ruthless shit-bagging.'

Bashir's techniques will be described later, but as a guide to how well they might work on someone particularly susceptible, we have Diana's own words. She sent him a note, written as she sat surrounded by the newspapers, one story everywhere, the morning after the infamous *Panorama* interview went out in November 1995. This is more than a polite thank you. This is from a co-conspirator, but one still chugging the Kool-Aid, unaware that they have been totally shit-bagged.

November 21st 1995

Dearest Martin,

Apart from the fact that you're able to produce a mean pasta in my kitchen, you have other extraordinary qualities of which I have seen and 'worked with' during the last months . . .

Since you choose to be deaf to my verbal recognition and admiration you leave me no choice, but to revert to the pen! There are no words adequate to express how I now feel having had my wings returned to me and with that so many other doors opening. I never dreamt that such a response was possible and I am immensely humbled by the reaction. You have made [no argument please!] enormous sacrifices to release me and have had to pay a high price for such dedication . . .

Thank you, Martin, for listening to me, for supporting me and for understanding this particular lady, no-one has <u>ever</u> shown such belief and acted upon it . . .

Lots of love from
Diana

Only three months before that note was written Martin Bashir had made his first tentative approach to Diana's family. On 24 August 1995 he telephoned the Spencer family home in Northamptonshire, Althorp, asking for her brother Charles. He wasn't there but his secretary, Carol Sprigg, took a note: 'Not seeking interview or info. 15 mins of time to talk . . . No filming or interview . . . just talk.' Bashir followed up with a letter addressed to her that same day: 'Thanks for your helpfulness during our telephone conversation earlier today. It was much appreciated. As I said it is not my intention to record or publish any discussion with Earl Spencer but simply to share some information which, I believe, may be of interest.' The letter, on *Panorama*'s branded notepaper, seemed like something one could trust. Bashir offered to back it up with a note from management, what he called 'a letter of comfort', guaranteeing confidentiality: 'I do hope that this will allay any natural anxieties that may arise.'

Charles Spencer did not reply. Ironically, although a journalist himself, he hated journalists. Ever since Diana had been named as Prince Charles's fiancée, more than fifteen years earlier, he had been a target for the tabloids, simply by being Di's younger brother. But there was meat there too. Besides being the brother of the world's most famous woman, uncle of a king-to-be, some events in Spencer's own life seemed almost too rambunctious for the most rollicking Jilly Cooper novel.

Spencer's best man at his wedding in 1989 was the handsomely exotic half-Iranian ex-Bullingdon Club roisterer Darius Guppy, a friend since Eton and Oxford, and a gold smuggler. Guppy was happily, and illegally, shipping large amounts of bullion to India but then devised a much bigger scheme, to defraud the Lloyd's insurance giant of £1.8 million by staging a jewel robbery, hiring a stooge to fire a handgun to heighten the stakes. When the scheme unravelled, in 1993, Guppy was sentenced to five years in jail, but the fallout seemed to threaten Spencer too. The *Daily Express* published a piece claiming that Spencer had helped launder the proceeds of the insurance scam. Precisely at the time when Bashir made his approach, Spencer was deep in discussions with lawyers about taking the *Express* to court. He did, winning damages for a story which would prove to be grossly untrue.

Spencer also had another beef with the media just then. In 1991 he had struck up an acquaintance with Alan Waller, an ex-Para he had met on a news assignment to the war-torn Balkans. From that meeting came the offer of a job. Would Waller like to be security chief at Althorp, cottage provided? He would, though by the end of 1993 the relationship had broken down. Spencer suspected Waller of selling gossip to the tabloids and, in March 1994, had secured an injunction preventing him 'disclosing, publishing or revealing to any party whomsoever information concerning the private lives, personal affairs or private conduct of the Earl, his wife, children or members of the Royal family'. Crucially, it was this feud, between Spencer and Waller, which Bashir would pick up on before making his move.

So who was Charles Spencer, the then thirty-one-year-old media-averse journalist being targeted by the thirty-two-year-old *Panorama* reporter? The Spencers are one of those very few families in England who, thanks to their own extraordinarily long lineage, are able to glance ever so slightly askance at the royals. It was a John Spencer who first moved into Althorp in 1486, when the Tudors were still very new. And so Spencer descendants might consider the tumble of monarchs calling themselves Stuart, then Hanover, then Saxe-Coburg, then Windsor, and, though I guess they never do, whisper, 'New money?' The Spencer money derived from canny investment in vast flocks of sheep, reared on pastures throughout Northamptonshire, Warwickshire and Leicestershire. So much wool, and so lucrative, that in 1756 the first Earl Spencer was able to build what remains one of the grandest houses in London, Spencer House in St James's, leased now to the Rothschild family but valued at something around £50 million.

A writer, still, by profession, Spencer has been remarkably open in describing a family history which, shorn of the gilding of great wealth and fame, sounds remarkably human, too often sad. As a small boy he sensed the tension between the two men he adored most, his father and grandfather. He would write: 'It was sad, particularly in the years following my parents' divorce, that these two lonely men, who both had so much to give, could not break through the distance they had established between one another, to enjoy each other as men, even if not as father and son.'

So grand were the Spencer connections that the queen stood as Charles's godmother for his christening in West-minster Abbey. The first eleven years of his boyhood were spent at Park House, on the Sandringham Estate. But for a boy still too little to know that he had been dealt a magnificent hand, the cards must have seemed desperately cruel.

Spencer was just three when his parents' marriage collapsed. He has described in detail how, at eight years old, he was packed off to a boarding school where he suffered not just intense loneliness but beatings and sexual abuse.

Even when apart his parents carried on fighting, in an acrimonious court battle for custody of Charles and Diana. The court sided with Spencer's father, who then poisoned the emotional brew still further by marrying the seeming stepmother from hell, Raine – dubbed Acid Raine by the children – whom Spencer castigates for selling off family heirlooms and revamping stately Althorp in shades of pink and electric green, what he describes as 'the wedding cake vulgarity of a five-star hotel in Monaco'. It was only when his father died, in March 1992, that Spencer was able to assume control, turf Raine out and, as ninth Earl Spencer, make his own rules.

By then he was already a well-known face, certainly for viewers of the American television network NBC. In 1986 twenty-two-year-old Spencer had taken on a correspondent role for the company. The skills that would make him a successful writer were evident even then, and he was a good reporter, though his bosses were not blind to the glamour of the English milord, probably more famous than anyone he would be called upon to interview. Because, of course, all that had gone on in the Spencer family since 1981 had played out in the harsh reflected gleam of Diana's fame. Tabloids which would have discounted upper-class shenanigans elsewhere were avid for any gossip concerning 'Di's dad', 'Di's stepmum' and 'Di's brother'.

In 1995 his friendship with the gold smuggler Darius Guppy had brought some media attention. Yet more intrusive still were the reporters trying to get inside the Spencer marriage, then six years old and clearly in trouble, almost a proxy for the collapsing union of Diana and that other Charles. So furious had Spencer become that by that summer he was planning to uproot the family, wife Victoria and already four children – Kitty, aged four; twins Eliza and Amelia, aged two; and the one-year-old Spencer heir, Louis. Their bolthole was to be in South Africa, a mansion inside the gated Silverhurst Estate in the Constantia wine country, just south of Cape Town. It was while these plans were being finalized that Bashir first cornered Spencer. And, in some-thing of a coincidence, Bashir's plan would depend entirely on a clever piece of work carried out by a young man from the Constantia Valley.

Matt Wiessler is the third character it is vital to know in understanding what happened to Princess Diana. How Matt sees his role in the scandal is complicated, even to this day, but certainly there is a large measure of guilt, plus a willing-ness to own up, which I have found entirely absent when it comes to most other BBC characters who had a hand in events. On 6 September 1997, the day of Diana's funeral, Matt didn't know anything like the full story of what had gone on. But he did have a sense that something very bad had happened, and that he had been partly responsible. Alone among the million people who gathered along the funeral route that bright morning, to watch the flag-draped coffin trundle by, young William and Harry following after, Matt had a horrible sense that he was somehow to blame for Diana's death. He had arrived at Kensington Palace before dawn. He told me, 'I was standing right by the gate, at 4 a.m., because I felt very strongly that I did have a hand in it. This little thing that I did, which I knew was a bad judgement the day after, just turned into this fucking national drama. And you're standing there, and there's a funeral cortège. And little boys standing there, you know? Please don't cry, boys. You're with your dad. And stiff upper lip. And, like . . . yeah.'

Matt Wiessler was born in July 1962 to a German couple who had settled in South Africa's Western Cape. There, certainly in expat enclaves like Constantia, life was still sweet for a prosperous middle-class family, even in the turbulent last years of apartheid. Following school, then four years at the prestigious Michaelis School of Fine Art, Matt thought about architecture, maybe sculpture, as a career, but then in December 1985 he boarded a plane bound for London. There was a buzz about graphic design, with artists on the cusp of switching from pens, card and glue to what seemed like the infinite possibilities offered by new computers. In television the excitement was maybe greatest of all and in 1986, coincidentally the same year that both Bashir and Spencer also entered TV, he was hired by the BBC as a graphic designer.

His first big assignment was a project lasting four whole years, helping devise the graphics for the 1992 general election on BBC1. He told me, 'We had to plan different scenarios for all the individual constituencies, 14,000 different permutations. And on the night the producers could line it all up to tell the story live, digitally. Never been done before, anywhere.' One of his innovations was the famous 'swingometer' wielded by presenter Peter Snow. His work was lavishly praised, winning the Royal Television Society Award that year. Next, the plum posting for an ambitious designer was *Panorama*.

The producers on that show always needed something arresting, and stylish, and more often than not they needed it *now*. It meant late nights, working up to the wire, on a

THE CROOK, THE EARL AND THE WHISTLEBLOWER

programme often still being edited minutes before transmission. Pressures like that built strong bonds, a trench
camaraderie which could begin to feel like friendship.
Wiessler remembers working on at least five different *Panorama* films with Bashir, assisting with the text-based visuals
but also planning and shooting sequences of drama recon-
struction. He told me, 'I really wanted to be a director. So I
started directing stuff, and that was huge, you know? It led
me to having a very close working relationship with Martin.'

The possibilities offered by computers, to create something which didn't exist in reality but which looked very much
as if it might, was tempting for producers and reporters, on
Panorama especially. Often, dry-sounding but crucial passages of narrative needed bringing to life, though it wasn't
quite clear where the line should be drawn. Was what the
viewer saw on TV *real*, or was it not? Twice Matt Wiessler
found himself uncomfortably straddling that line. In a film
looking at the finances of former England football manager
Terry Venables, an authentic-seeming document appeared
on-screen. The figures in it were accurate, verifiable, but the
computerized version was a construct. Another film, in July
1994, made serious allegations about London police officers,
once again showing what appeared to be incriminating documents. Accurate, but computerized.

On this occasion Wiessler was credited as having provided 'special effects', which led to a nervy confrontation
when detectives showed up a short time later at the *Panorama*
offices. Matt recalled: 'In there sat two men who were just
terrifyingly clever, who interviewed me for quite some time
as to how I went about making these documents.' In neither
case had he done anything truly wrong. What appeared on-
screen *did* exist, kind of, just not in the way that had been

suggested. These two near misses would prove crucial, per-haps the gateway drug, when Martin Bashir came along soon after, asking for documents which didn't exist at all.

Scrapes like these were a part of the bonding which hap-pened at *Panorama*, unlikely bonds formed in adversity. Bashir wasn't a friendly figure, Tom Mangold told me: 'Nobody really knew him, he didn't seem to have many friends on the programme.' But Bashir and Matt Wiessler began taking their lunches together, playing squash. Bashir calibrated his banter for what he imagined would put him nicely on a level with Matt, one of the programme's players, he being a reporter, and a gentleman, though one day he got it badly wrong. Matt was seeing a *Panorama* secretary, Lucy Noble, to whom he has now been married for thirty years. He recalled to me: 'I started dating Lucy, and he sort of saw it unfolding, from his little cubicle. And one morning I was in for a meeting, and he says, "Had a nice time with Lucy did you last night? Fucked her up the arse?" And I was like . . . And then he walks away. He wasn't looking for my reaction.'

If only Martin Bashir had lingered, to see Matt's reac-tion, it might have saved him endless grief later on. Because that bit of tackiness illuminates everything that came after. Matt Wiessler was very much primmer than Bashir had supposed. When it came to creating forgeries – not just harmless, computerized mock-ups, but 100 per cent dis-honest *forgeries* – Bashir imagined Matt would join him in, what, a bit of shit-bagging? But Matt's disgust reared up the moment he understood what had actually transpired. And thus he became a whistleblower.

There is a coda to this chapter, a story which has always seemed to me so extraordinary that it would be wrong not to share. In a narrative filled with bizarre events, this ranks among the strangest of all.

In August 1998, three years after the *Panorama* interview, and exactly a year after Diana's death, Martin Bashir was by then still basking in universal fame. The BBC had, by that point, cast out whistleblower Matt Wiessler, blacklisted him. But he was nevertheless enjoying a pleasant Sunday afternoon on the Thames, just downriver from Hampton Court. He had hired a boat, with his mother-in-law Penny, his new wife Lucy and one-year-old son Oscar, and joined the armada of pleasure-seekers, rowing happily on the sparkling water. Then something caught Matt's eye: 'I spotted a man in a full three-piece suit, standing by the edge of the water. And he walked right into the water, holding his hands out. Sort of like Jesus? And we instantly thought, "Right, this is not good intent." By the time I'd rowed over to him he'd disappeared under the surface. As my boat drifted past I saw his face deep under the water.'

Matt's mother-in-law could see there was no time to waste: 'She shouted, "Get in there, get this man out!" She pushed me. I fell in the water, swam round, grabbed him. I swam to the edge, pulled him out of the water, and he was sort of half lying on top of me. Then he started crying, crying, crying. Then he got this wet wallet out. And in it was a photograph. And I was gobsmacked. I was looking at Martin Bashir's face!

'And he goes, "This is my son. He is very famous." And he said, "I haven't seen my son in many, many years. Because I'm just a janitor, at a hospital in Tooting." And something about being estranged from him.' Within minutes the police arrived. Matt says one of the officers took him aside. 'He said, "This guy's got lots of previous attempts to say goodbye to the world." I got his address, which was Tooting. And so I sent him a postcard afterwards saying, "I'm very glad that I managed to save your life. I hope things go better for you." '

They did not. In 2021 Bashir spoke to the *Sunday Times*, the only interview he gave in response to the damning verdict of the Dyson report. Bashir told the newspaper, 'In 2001, I had to identify my father's body because he took his own life. His body was dragged from the River Thames.'

PART TWO
The Takedown

'The only qualities essential for real success in
journalism are ratlike cunning, a plausible manner
and a little literary ability.'

– Nicholas Tomalin, journalist, 1969

5. Forgery by Night

Martin Bashir and Charles Spencer first met, briefly, on Tuesday, 29 August 1995. After his phone call and letter of 24 August the BBC reporter had finally pinned Spencer down, for not much more than 'hello' and a handshake, at the end of the day at the earl's work-base, the NBC News offices in Holborn. But it was agreed that Bashir would drive up to Althorp for a 10.30 a.m. sit-down that Thursday, 31 August. Spencer was by no means hooked, though the bait was in the water.

Exactly what happened over these few days is still confused today. The account provided in the Dyson report offers no final certainty over dates and places, but that is understandable. It was thirty years ago, the written records are patchy and, as we will see, one of the two principals, either Spencer or Bashir, had to be lying through his teeth. As Lord Dyson would put it in his report, at one crucial point: 'Either he is lying or he is telling the truth. There is no scope for innocent mistake here.' And so a small question mark still hovers over the *exact* date on which Bashir asked Matt Wiessler to prepare for him two forged documents. *How* the forgeries were produced is not in doubt. Wiessler told me the story: 'I came home from work and I've got a message. Martin was trying to get hold of me urgently. The next thing, I've got Martin on the phone. He needed to see me. Chop-chop.'

By the summer of 1995, Matt Wiessler's status had changed. His career was on such a high that, after nearly ten years as a BBC staffer, he had quit, gone freelance. He and another BBC graphic designer, Patrick Bedeau, had decided to gamble, scrape together every penny they had and set up a graphics house of their own. They would be independents, Bedeau & Wiessler they called it, tiny at first but hoping to take on the giants in no time. Matt told me, 'We had a very nice office, in Bond Street, opposite Asprey's jewellers. First floor. It wasn't in the post-production part of town, though we could look out of the window, see rich people passing by.' When Bashir's call came through that night the new company was still no more than a half-empty office, dusty desktops, computers and monitors still waiting to be unpacked, plugged in. They wouldn't be ready to take on a new graphics commission for maybe a couple of weeks. No problem, Bashir said. You've got a computer at home?

Matt did have his own computer. Nowadays it sounds an extraordinary question to ask, but 1995 was a different world. Hotmail wouldn't appear until the following year. Google would not be invented for another three years; Facebook, nine years. Wiessler's little Macintosh Performa, with a fourteen-inch screen, hooked up to a printer, in a spare bedroom, was something of a novelty. It was close to 11 o'clock at night when his phone rang again: 'Martin calls, says, "I'm on my way, there in ten minutes." He arrives, very smart, in a suit, walks in. He's got an A4 notebook, one of those black ones with the red spine. And he says, "I need this doing. Because it's just the biggest story!"'

It seems odd that Wiessler did not ask more questions when Bashir arrived at the door of his Camden apartment, late at night, asking him to create a set of mysterious but convincing-looking documents, from some figures in his notebook. But that is the sort of thing that could happen on *Panorama*. This was investigative journalism, where the good guys battle the rogues and sometimes need to cut corners a little. The cloak and dagger was all part of the fun, no harm so long as the good guys and the rogues stayed well apart. Matt recalled, 'He said he couldn't tell me why he needed it. Or who he was showing it to. He said he just needed to prove something? I said, "Have you got a photocopy, of the real document?" He said, "No, no. You've got to do it from scratch." I said, "Well, can you do me a sketch?" He said no. He wouldn't write anything down.'

So Matt thought, 'Let's just do it.' He started taking notes, Bashir describing exactly what he needed, how the documents about to take shape on the computer should look: 'He kept referring to his notebook, holding it close to his chest, looking as though he were solving the answers to my questions as we went along.' The documents Bashir required were to look like bank statements, two of them, both for a bank account in the name of Alan Waller, Earl Spencer's former security chief, at a NatWest branch in North Street, Brighton. The first statement, Bashir said, should show a payment of £4,000, made on 8 March 1994. The money would appear to originate from News International, the company which owned both the *Sun* and its then tabloid stablemate the *News of the World*. The second statement was to show a payment of £6,500, on 4 June 1994. 'OK, paid by who?' Wiessler asked. There seemed to be a problem with this. Bashir paused but then gave the name Penfolds Consultants. Wiessler: 'When he mentioned Penfolds, I remember going, "Penfolds? Are you sure?"'

It seemed that Penfolds Consultants couldn't be right. Matt remembered the name from the *Panorama* film he and

Bashir had made, just a short while earlier, on Terry Venables. The document Wiessler had created for that film had Penfolds Consultants in it too. Matt told me, 'I remember him being short with me, saying, "Just do it, just use that information. That'll do." And I thought to myself, *What do you mean, that'll do?*' But it was nearly midnight now and Bashir was anxious to leave: 'He said, "I'm going to organize a courier to pick it up. Ring the transport office when you're nearly ready?" I said, "Fine."'

Bashir left. Wiessler went back to the bedroom, to study the notes he had scribbled down. It was crazy that this company, Penfolds Consultants, was somehow linked to both Charles Spencer *and* Terry Venables, England's former football manager. How could that be? And this was the moment, a critical moment as it turned out, when Matt realized he was about to produce a thoroughly fake document. A *forgery* would be the uglier word. But then the important thing would be what Bashir did with it once it was in his hands. Matt could only hope for the best. He said, 'OK, I did smell a rat. But then I'd done five programmes with him. I was going freelance. I'd got a mortgage to pay and I needed to get these jobs in.'

For the next five hours Matt tinkered, and tweaked, to build something which, when complete, looked wholly unremarkable but was in every respect a work of art, a stunning piece of craftsmanship, the more so because it was done on a computer which today would be in a museum. He had found a picture of the NatWest bank logo: 'I was lucky. It was really just three black blobs. I did them in Illustrator.' He used the primitive graphics software which was all his little computer could handle. He pulled out a genuine bank statement of his own to get a feel for the fonts which a bank might use. He studied the way the columns were laid out. How the text in one place needed to be just a tad fainter than another. An hour or so in, he realized that the figures Bashir had given him didn't actually add up. He called the reporter. 'Make them add up,' Bashir said. And so he did.

Matt recalled, 'Eventually, about 5 o'clock in the morning, I was happy. I'd done two or three different versions, printed them out on my little dot-matrix printer. And I chose the best ones. I could only do black and white. The real thing would have had pink on it? Or red? But he said that wouldn't matter, this was supposed to be a photocopy. I put them in an envelope that he must have provided, 'cause I wouldn't have had one. I made my phone call. And a motorcycle courier came along.' The courier was one of those used regularly by the BBC, booked through the central transport office. The location for the delivery, the handover, had already been notified. Bashir would pick up his forgeries outside the Sock Shop, Terminal Two, Heathrow Airport.

There is a cosy precision about where the forgeries were bound but a question mark over the exact date of their journey. Bashir would later say this must have been sometime in October 1995. But October would suggest a date long after he had first been introduced to Princess Diana. When questioned later, Bashir referred to the bank statements always simply as graphic 'mock-ups', something he had just required for his personal research file. He said he had really just shown them to Spencer as an afterthought, out of interest. But then why all the urgency? The working right through the night? The motorbike? A little under halfway through the Dyson report, following his six-month inquiry, Lord Dyson delivers a damning line: 'In a credibility contest between Earl Spencer and Mr Bashir, Earl Spencer wins convincingly.' Where the two accounts differ by a mile, as they so often do, Dyson is happy to accept that Bashir is the liar. And the divergence over these bank statements, produced in either August or October 1995, whether they were forgeries or mock-ups, could not be clearer. The fact that they *did* exist is plain. And the fact of their existence underpinned the entire scandal. As Bashir would put it, face-to-face with Lord Dyson on 1 March 2021, a little forlornly, 'In retrospect, if those two bank statements had never been constructed, or reconstructed, we wouldn't probably be here.'

If Dyson is right, and Bashir is the liar, what happened is that the forgeries were produced by Matt Wiessler at the earlier date, at the end of August 1995. The most likely date of all becomes the night of Wednesday, 30 August, with Bashir stopping by Heathrow on his way to Althorp, eighty miles away, exit 16 from the M1. Maybe an hour and a half if the traffic is reasonable.

6. Forgeries R Us

I followed the same route that Bashir must have taken a little over a quarter of a century later. This is a good place to explain my dealings with Charles Spencer, to show my working, because it will help you form a judgement about what you are reading. The exact circumstances of how we came to start talking are described in a later chapter, but when I began to drill down on my investigation of Bashir and the BBC in 2020, Spencer initially brushed aside my request for an interview, just as he did the hundreds of others he receives each year. But then suddenly it became apparent that things I was finding out were of huge consequence to him. As you will see, the Bashir scandal only came to light at all when I managed to get hold of a certain BBC document, one that had been kept secret for twenty-five years, and showed it to Spencer. Everything else followed from there.

What then happened is that Spencer, my source, became in effect a partner. Spencer started out as a journalist, one who had very good reasons to hate sections of the media, the paparazzi in particular, but a journalist nonetheless. And so two journalists were looking at the scandal, one of them, me, the outsider. The other one learning things of profound personal significance for his family. How what the BBC did had affected his own life, and of course the life of his sister, Diana. Although I have used the word 'partner' I am experienced enough to know that you cannot find yourself cheering for one side. I believe Spencer's criticism of the

BBC is justified, that what he has done over the years has been done more in sorrow than in anger. Remember who Spencer's sister was, what happened to her, and you can see why this would matter so much. He summed it up to me this way: 'It still rankles with me hugely that there's been such a sustained and pointless cover-up. Like you I remain a huge supporter of the BBC, but there were bad people there. And they've been enabled by getting the truth of this matter stymied now.'

And so, when I arrived at Althorp I was treading in Bashir's footsteps but there for a very different reason. I sat with Spencer in the library of the grand house, its huge windows overlooking the deer park off to the west, the same room where the BBC reporter had sat on 31 August 1995 to begin unfolding his complex strategy of deceit. Spencer remembers that Bashir was wearing very shiny brown shoes. He also produced, by way of an introductory gift, a tiny electronic device which he had probably picked up in one of the spy gadget shops on London's Tottenham Court Road. Spencer said, 'I've still got it. It's a little two-way earpiece that you can put in your ear for telephone conversations. We're talking about technology a very long time ago but you plug it into a tape recorder so you can tape what someone is saying to you on the phone.' Bashir explained how the little gadget worked, saying that it could help Spencer keep tabs on any suspicious phone calls he might receive. 'He was trying to make me paranoid. It was all sort of, "You're in really dangerous waters here and I'm your friend, Martin. I'm going to make it all OK. Here's a gimmick that'll help you." '

Spencer remembers that the two of them sat either side of the library fireplace, Bashir with a briefcase and a notebook which he would consult from time to time. Bashir's first line of attack had nothing to do with bank statements; they would come later. Instead he began to talk about Spencer's then wife Victoria, the thirty-year-old mother of their four children: 'He went into this whole litany of bizarre ramblings. He said he knew that Prince Charles loathed me, and my wife Victoria. Now, to be brutally honest, Victoria's a completely inoffensive figure who I wouldn't even expect Prince Charles to have recognized in a line-up of three. But Bashir told me that he knew Prince Charles wanted her dead.'

It is the forged bank statements which Bashir next produced at that meeting, the ones made by Matt Wiessler in his spare bedroom in Camden, which would come to play a defining role in the history of the scandal. But at the time, as far as Spencer was concerned, they were only of marginal interest in what they had to reveal about his former head of security, Alan Waller. Spencer said, 'It was just very peculiar really. He told me that he had proof that Waller was working for "very dark forces".'

Spencer has a handwritten note of that August 1995 meeting with Bashir. At the top he has written: '£4K – News International. £6.5K – Penfolds. Waller. Can disappear very easily.' Then lower down: 'M – been working on this for 9 months.' Spencer asked if he could keep the bank statements; Bashir refused. But although what Spencer was hearing was mildly intriguing, it wasn't altogether unexpected since he had *suspected* that Waller was selling stories to the tabloids. No evidence has ever emerged to suggest Waller was guilty, but in 1995 Spencer firmly believed that was the case. The bank statements were not something he'd pick up the phone to Diana about, but: 'It was the breadcrumb towards the trapdoor. So that was clearly their purpose.' The irony is that these two forged bank statements, produced in the dead of night, for thirty years at the very centre of the scandal, were not important in the least in terms of what they said. They were banal. But it was a falling out about their provenance which tipped the whole scandal into the public domain.

Bashir's origin story for the bank statements is much different from Spencer's. The reporter claimed that when he arrived at Althorp it was not him who had bank statements to display but Spencer himself. Here is how Bashir told the story, in an account he provided later for BBC bosses: 'Following Waller's sacking, private mail for him continued to arrive at Althorp House. Earl Spencer opened a particular letter, which was a bank statement. Earl Spencer gave me a copy of that bank statement.' Bashir said the only value of the document Spencer gave him was the raw data it provided: branch address, account number, the correct spelling of names and so on.

But as regards the *figures* in the statements, and who paid what to whom, where did all that come from? Bashir would say, 'The Princess of Wales is the one who had said those figures were paid.' So Diana was the tipster? Surely, to accept the truth of that seemed to defy logic. Because Bashir would agree that he did not meet Diana, at all, ever, until September 1995. Yet Spencer had notes of how he had been shown the forgeries on 31 August 1995. Roughly three weeks *before* Bashir says he met Diana for the first time.

Bashir's story grew odder still. He would claim that the information he got from Diana, his supposed new contact, did not come from some hurried briefing, a whispered phone call. Bashir would unfold a remarkable tale when he provided testimony to the official Dyson inquiry: 'I remember that she called by telephone and asked if we could go for a drive out of London during the afternoon. Since my wife needed the car for work I had to hastily organize a rental car. I believe we drove to the New Forest and back, which took around five hours. During the trip, I mentioned the allegations her brother had made concerning Mr Waller. She described Mr Waller as one of brother Charles's pet hates, and said that she believed the Prince of Wales' private secretary, Richard Aylard, may have set up a fund to pay Mr Waller.'

Bashir claimed that as the chat continued, Diana became more specific: 'She suggested that a Jersey-based trust fund had paid him money. She also said that she knew the precise amount which had been paid by News International.' But then, having painted this picture of a day trip down the A3, the story got much cloudier, yet cosier. He said Diana for some reason pulled back on her story about Waller, Aylard, Penfolds, etc. Bashir's testimony to the inquiry went like this:

BASHIR: I was cooking in Kensington Palace, we were chatting about various things, and she said, 'Oh, by the way, I was wrong about that,' and her source was wrong, and I said, 'Fine,' because, you know, at that stage, I wasn't planning on doing anything with those documents. So it was just, 'OK, that bit of information was wrong.'

DYSON: I'd just like to understand, though, what she was saying was mistaken. So it was the sums of money. You'd been given these figures of £4,000 and £6,500?

BASHIR: I think, my recollection, sir, is that she was basically saying, you know, the whole thing was not true, and, you know, 'I'm sorry, I made a mistake.'

So where did Bashir get the basic information which he had asked Wiessler to build on? The bank account number:

00414301. The branch address: National Westminster Bank, 155 North Street, Brighton BN1 1ON. Here, Bashir stuck to his guns. Yes, he had played fast and loose with some things, including inserting the name Penfolds Consultants. But the rest was right. He said to Dyson, 'The account number, details, those came from Earl Spencer, absolutely. Because I could not have got that information from anybody else.'

Or maybe, could he? After all, *Panorama* was in the business of investigative journalism. An episode which had aired only a short time before the Diana interview in November 1995, an edition called 'Secrets for Sale', had made a huge splash. The journos in that case had struck a deal with several people in the public eye, in particular a famous and fiery trade union leader, Rodney Bickerstaffe. What could they secretly discover about these characters, with what is now called 'blagging'? I spoke with the journalist who was programme researcher for that particular *Panorama* episode, Dan Chambers, who told me, 'We approached various private detectives, who advertised in the Yellow Pages, saying we were making a TV profile. They were able to get hold of bank statements, tax records, medical records, criminal records, ex-directory phone numbers. For a few hundred pounds it was possible to get hold of a full set of confidential records on almost anyone.'

Dyson, sounding rueful, put the question, 'So how was Mr Bashir able to give Mr Wiessler the correct details of the [Waller] bank account? The information obtained by the Investigation does not enable me to answer this question.' But it does seem as though Bashir might have had the tools. They had worked very well for his colleagues in the *Panorama* office.

All said, Bashir's famous forged bank statements were a

disaster. Of course for Diana, but also for Bashir himself. They worried Matt Wiessler enough that, ultimately, he would turn whistleblower. And though they sounded well dodgy, they were not dodgy enough. Spencer did not call Diana right away, as Bashir had hoped. Two days after their meeting at Althorp, on 2 September, Spencer was scheduled to fly to Argentina, for NBC. While he was away, Bashir was working on two new forgeries. And on the scale of dodginess, this time it would be ratcheted way up. Spencer had not bitten first time round. But was that the faintest twitch at the end of the line? Spencer said, 'I think Waller was a very easy in to me. That I was effectively groomed, for the second hit. When he had hooked me in, then he played his ace.'

On Thursday, 14 September 1995 Bashir made his second drive north to Althorp, the weather gloomy, still raining when he pulled up to the north facade at 6 p.m. As Spencer walked his guest from the entrance hall to the library Bashir seemed nervous. Spencer said, 'The awkwardness of Bashir at this time has stuck in my mind.' But perhaps that was the effect of the alarming news that Bashir had to deliver. Bashir had phoned Spencer to say there was something that he needed to know. Something Diana *had* to know. He had been told, by whom he could not say, that two senior officials in the royal household were being paid money, big money, from another mysterious bank account. And, once again, he had bank statements to prove it.

Spencer noticed that something else was different from the time Bashir had sat across from him a fortnight earlier. Then the reporter had been happy to hand across his documents, the ones which Matt Wiessler had laboured so long over. Spencer could not *keep* them, but he could *hold* them. This time Bashir wouldn't let the paper go. Spencer said,

'I remember that Bashir did not release it from his hands. He held it at all times, and he appeared to be agitated. Bashir held it with only the top part, and the bottom part, with various transactions visible. The middle part was covered over . . . the whole sheet was, essentially, folded like a letter, with top and bottom on show but the middle shielded from sight.' But what Spencer *could* see was startling. This was more than some disgruntled ex-employee taking bungs from the tabloids. This was two pukka players, right at the heart of the action, both ex-Navy men: Commander Richard Aylard, private secretary to Prince Charles, and Patrick Jephson, also an ex-Navy Commander and since 1988 private secretary to Diana. And both on the take for tens of thousands of pounds.

The Wiessler statements have been preserved for all time. These new statements have never been seen, as far as is known, by anyone but Spencer and Bashir. In his testimony to the Dyson inquiry Spencer said, 'I clearly remember, when being shown the Aylard/Jephson bank statements, that I pointed out to Bashir that this bank account was based in the Channel Islands. I also clearly remember Bashir answering, without missing a beat, that this was because Aylard came from the Channel Islands. Secondly, I remember the size of two sums that were recorded as being paid . . . £10,000 and, separately, £30,000.' Who got what was not specified, but the narrative became clear from Bashir's briefing. Anonymous payments to these two senior flunkeys could only mean one thing. They were being funded, and in a serious way, by what Bashir called 'dark forces'. What worried Spencer was that Patrick Jephson was said to be on someone's secret payroll. Maybe newspapers? Or with that opaque, sinister Channel Islands connection, more likely spooks? MI5, MI6, GCHQ?

And so what would Bashir, when challenged, say about this meeting? On 5 March 2021, in testimony to the official inquiry, he came out fighting. Everything that Spencer said was a lie. He said the first whisper he had of these so-called Aylard/Jephson statements was when Lord Dyson actually mentioned them to him: 'I was not clear until Lord Dyson explained in my interview with him that Earl Spencer was alleging that there were two sets of bank statements.' Were they now saying that he had a second forger on tap? 'As I understand it there has been no suggestion from Mr Wiessler that he mocked up more statements than the ones in Mr Waller's name at my request. I do not understand whether Earl Spencer alleges I asked another graphic designer to mock up a different bank statement?' Again, he said, where on earth was he going to find names and numbers? 'Where would I have obtained Mr Jephson or Mr Aylard's bank details from?' The whole thing sounded ridiculous to him: 'The suggestion that a bank statement would show payments from security services sounds absurd to me. How would a bank statement show that? Would it list "MI6" as a payer?'

Bashir said he would put his hands up for at least *some* of the blame on the first set of bank statements. But as regards another set? This was too much. Simply didn't happen. And so once again Lord Dyson had to judge between two conflicting stories, this time with much less wiggle room than the last. Either Spencer was inventing an elaborate tale, about peculiarly folded pieces of paper and big numbers, or he was not. Dyson's verdict was unambiguous: 'Earl Spencer has given me a very detailed account . . . I do not believe that Earl Spencer has invented these details. He had no reason for doing so and it would have been extraordinary if he had done so.' Bashir, again, had been caught lying.

What happened next indicates that, in September 1995, Spencer believed he *had* truly been shown something shocking. These new statements had done the trick. This time he *did* pick up the phone to Diana.

7. A List of Lies

Two weeks had slid by after Martin Bashir presented his first set of forgeries, on 31 August 1995. But when Spencer saw the second set, on 14 September, the reaction was immediate. Spencer remembers calling Diana soon after Bashir left: 'When I told Diana about Jephson and Aylard, she was absolutely intrigued, and wanted to learn more as quickly as possible.' The bait scattered on to the water at Althorp had been snapped up right away by Diana in Kensington Palace. Diana's friend Richard Kay told me, 'Diana was extremely keen. I know this because she spoke to me and said that she'd had a conversation with her brother, Charles, Carlos, as she called him. She said, "Carlos has spoken to a man at the BBC and he has told him all about what I'm going through, people spying on me." At last, she said, someone in my family knows what it's like to be me! So Diana was hooked at that stage.'

The brother and sister had used their pet names since childhood. Charles was Carlos; Diana was Duch. A note which Diana sent to Spencer makes it plain just how excited she was:

Darling Carlos, I so appreciated the contents of our telephone call this morning – it all makes complete sense to what is going on around me at this present time. 'They' underestimate the Spencer strength! Lots of luv from Duch x

This was a Thursday. Spencer agreed to get Bashir back to Althorp three days later, to meet Diana once brother and sister had had a catch-up. He said, 'I arranged for her to join me for lunch at Althorp at 12.30 p.m. on Sunday, 17 September, and organized for Bashir to join us at 2 p.m. However, for some reason this fell through, and I then arranged for me to introduce Diana to Bashir in London on Tuesday, 19 September.'

What Diana heard from her brother must have shaken her. As Patrick Jephson told me, 'I was her private secretary, her most senior trusted adviser. We had been working together for nearly eight years. Bashir told her that I was in cahoots with her enemy, her husband's private secretary, that I was gaining from this financially. And at the same time that I was spying on her for the British security services.' The source was critical too. Here was Diana's brother, a journalist himself, a journalist with a deep suspicion of most reporters. Yet what he had been told had come from the BBC, the most trusted, the most august, the most boring-in-a-good-way news outfit in the world. The BBC man had documents too. The news Carlos had to share *must* be true.

But why paint Patrick Jephson, in particular, as a traitor? In Jephson's view: 'Bashir may have seen me as the principal obstacle to his ambition of getting the interview that interviewers all over the world were competing to get.' Jephson had always been Diana's media gatekeeper: 'The world's most prominent TV figures all wanted her. Barbara Walters, Oprah Winfrey, David Frost. She was always very courteous, but always said no. Or more to the point, I used to say no on her behalf.' Wiping Jephson off the board would be essential to get Diana in front of a camera. But when it came to the day of the meeting, the following Tuesday, Jephson would later discover that there was much more to Bashir's game plan: 'It wasn't just about me. It was a whole cast of characters that he was suddenly laying out for her, like some kind of a thriller.'

The meeting began at four in the afternoon, on 19 September, in the Knightsbridge apartment of one of Spencer's old friends, writer Samantha Weinberg. Spencer said, 'I was there first, Diana arrived second. I had set for Bashir to come just a bit later. I vaguely briefed Diana face-to-face because I'd only spoken to her on the phone.' Their host Samantha withdrew into the kitchen, to watch *Countdown* on a small TV set. Diana, Bashir and Spencer got down to business. Spencer told me, 'I had an NBC notebook. I'm a nerd with notes, and I just took notes throughout because that's what I did. I don't think Bashir looked at me once during that whole time. He was transfixed with Diana. And I just sat there, jotting everything down.' The eight pages of notes Spencer compiled are less like a thriller than a scribbled dream diary, pulled out of the naughtiest reverie of a tabloid hack:

Escort girls . . . divorce . . . scum . . . Fergie . . . C's in love . . . Queen . . . lines being tapped . . . bugs on car

Some targets leap out from Spencer's notes:

Jephson dangerous – money . . . Jephson used to do flying lessons in Jersey. Used to go to Jersey for weekends – hasn't been this year

There was Jersey again, the home of Penfolds Consultants from the Matt Wiessler forgeries. Also the source of the money in the second set of home-made forgeries, unveiled at Althorp five days earlier. Bashir seemed set on making Jersey the home of dark, unknowable wickedness. But remarkably there were tiny glimmers of truth. And for Patrick Jephson, deeply disturbing ones: 'He'd studied me. He found out where I spent my holidays. That I was taking flying lessons. This is quite cold bloodedly, forensically taking my life apart. That it makes me feel angry doesn't begin to describe it. I'm also creeped out by it.'

Other trusted figures in Dianaland were fingered too. The *Daily Mail* reporter whom Diana liked the most, Richard Kay, was said to be in cahoots with Prince Charles's man.

Richard Kay + Aylard had dinner in Riverside Room of Savoy, 3 weeks ago. Kay entirely untrustworthy

Kay said to me, 'He claimed that I had set up three shell companies. Now, I don't know much about company law, but the implication is that you're doing something fraudulent? Hiding income from the revenue? He claimed that I was paying off an informant at the Chelsea Harbour Club, which was the gym the princess used. He maintained that I was having an affair with one of the princess's friends, a married woman. Again, completely untrue. Someone I barely know. It was quite clear that this was all an attempt to undermine the princess, to appeal to her paranoias, if you like. But also to insert a wedge between those she was most comfortable with, her friends and close circle, and make her think that she couldn't really trust them.'

So, another traitor. And another dig at his dining partner.

Aylard has no conscience. Very weak + cowardly. Probably having an affair

According to Richard Kay, 'This would have resonated with Diana. Richard Aylard was her enemy-in-chief, if you like. He once worked for Diana, in fact, as her equerry. And then he'd gone to work for her husband and had risen to the very top and become the private secretary. She viewed him as someone who was making her life difficult. And the very idea that he would be in collusion with her own senior aide, Patrick Jephson, would have triggered alarm bells with Diana.'

Spencer noted down specifics, which Bashir claimed to have, on how Diana was under surveillance.

3 lines at K.P. bugged; mail read
   D. followed twice in car recently

Kay told me, 'Bashir maintained that her phone lines at Kensington Palace were tapped. Her car phone was tapped. Bugs had been placed in her car to track its movements. He maintained that twice, quite specifically in the previous week, she had been followed, not by paparazzi but by members of the security services.'

Then the talk veered on to Diana's in-laws. An astonishing claim about the then thirty-one-year-old Prince Edward, at the time unmarried:

Edward has AIDS? Royal Marsden Hospital

Another claim, preserved in just six words scribbled in Spencer's notebook, would have caused Diana to wonder how soon she might be asked to wear the crown:

Queen ill: heart . . . Eats for comfort

Patrick Jephson has sought to imagine Diana's reaction to the extraordinary barrage of information coming her way. He told me, 'There was an enormous volume of new information that she was having to process. There's a principle exploited by propagandists through history that the bigger the lie you tell, the easier it is to believe. Once you have broken down one wall of scepticism, then the rest tend to go down more easily. If you're clever about it, and I suspect Martin Bashir was, you can't stop believing one without disbelieving the lot.'

One story which emerged that afternoon does seem to stretch credibility to its limit:

special present for William 3 weeks ago – bleeping Swatch.

Richard Kay: 'This was possibly the most extraordinary claim of all. Bashir claimed that William had received from his father a watch. In fact, he even named the manufacturer. It was a Swatch, very popular in the mid-1990s. Bashir claimed that it contained a recording device, and he was therefore recording his mother. The very idea of the then thirteen-year-old Prince William doing any such thing. It's beyond unsettling.'

Just over a quarter of a century later, on Monday, 1 March 2021, Martin Bashir faced a video camera, his two lawyers beside him, Lord Dyson on the screen in front of him. And so, James Bond watches? A prince with AIDS? By this stage in the inquiry he had already had to deal with some tough questions. Matt Wiessler's forgeries on 31 August? Yes, but they're not as bad as they look. Another set of forgeries on 14 September? Didn't happen. Now Bashir squared up once again. The eight pages of notes which Spencer had produced? Bashir said, 'I do fear that this is a collation of material which probably was written sometime later, or even possibly last year.' Bashir was adamant. The back-and-forth between him and Lord Dyson that afternoon soon became testy.

BASHIR: It is possible that I could have said some of these things. There's a second category, where I think it is highly unlikely I would have said these things. And there's a third category, where I would never have said some of these things.

MI6 taped C . . . 'in endgame' – D told Aylard what she thought of him, + that she wouldn't divorce

BASHIR: That suggests that it is the Princess of Wales who is saying that. That's not me saying it. If I'm sitting in front of the Princess of Wales, am I telling her what she's told Aylard? It doesn't make any sense.

Difficult relationship with William for D

BASHIR: How on earth would I be sitting there at a meeting telling the Princess of Wales about her relationship with her son? It doesn't make any sense.

DYSON: You keep saying it doesn't make any sense. I take it that, by that, you mean you did not say it?

BASHIR: Well, I did not say it, absolutely.

Then there is this reference here:

Edward has AIDS?

BASHIR: Again, it's being alleged that I'm sitting in my first meeting with the Princess of Wales and her brother and I'm making an allegation about a serious, chronic, potentially fatal illness that may have afflicted her brother-in-law. If I were to say that, surely one would accept, if I was the originator of that idea, it would be very easy to check the provenance of that claim?

DYSON: Are you saying that you just don't think that any of this was said by anybody at this meeting?

BASHIR: I'm saying, Lord Dyson, that I cannot possibly have said the things that are being attributed to me because they are so utterly outlandish and so easy to check that, had I said any of these things, the Princess of Wales could have rung Buckingham Palace and said, 'Has Prince Edward contracted HIV?'

bleeping Swatch

BASHIR: It was alleged that I had said that Prince William had been given a watch that was somehow a device. Well, if I'm sitting in a meeting making an allegation that the princess's son has a Swatch which is in some way being used for bugging purposes, would it not strike you as perfectly obvious that all she would need to do is go and see her son, ask him for the watch, and I would be immediately discredited as an idiot and a fool and somebody not to be trusted?

DYSON: There is no doubt that an awful lot of

things set out here were fantastic. The question is, whose words are they? Spencer says that they came from you, and that he thought you were a fantasist, and that your motivation might have been to frighten Diana. Can you offer any explanation for this? Are you saying this is pure invention on the part of Spencer? Or what are you saying?

BASHIR: I can't speculate on what Earl Spencer's thinking was. What I'm saying to you is, I don't know who said these things, or whether they were said, but I am confident that in the vast majority of cases I could not possibly have said these things.

Dyson's patience was clearly wearing thin that day. Once again, as with the forgeries, two stories were being offered, describing two differing realities, with no overlap in the middle. But Bashir did seem to offer an intriguing further possibility: that Diana had pitched in with wacky ideas of her own.

BASHIR: One other thing I think you need to know, Lord Dyson, and you may already know this, that the Princess of Wales had a number of relationships, and they included clairvoyants, mediums, mystics, various other people, who provided her with support, consolation, and so on. What I'm saying to you is that . . . it is perfectly possible that some of the material in here are things that she had garnered and she had said and, as I say to you, there are so many occasions in here where I couldn't possibly know the details.

So is that how it was, a free-ranging discussion where some of the weirder stories came from Diana herself? Not according to Spencer. In his testimony to the inquiry he said, 'I am a note taker, but I think I particularly took them to make sure I could remind Diana of what had been said, you know, if she progressed things.'

DYSON: What was her reaction to all of this?

SPENCER: Well, she didn't say much. I remember Bashir sitting there with an A4-sized notebook and he sort of went through them. I don't remember her contributing really.

Spencer recalls that as the meeting went on he grew more and more concerned about whether he had done the right thing calling Diana at all: 'It was a very big deal for me. I had never introduced Diana to a journalist before.' He had spent several hours with Bashir, at Althorp, but some of the things he was hearing now simply did not seem to add up. Indeed the very first note he took down had set off an alarm:

4 months ago, 3 men met him – MI6

Spencer knew that there is a big difference between MI5 – the UK-based security service who look after things like counter-terrorism, or catching spies on British soil – and MI6 – by and large foreign-facing, the James Bond characters who lead a much more glamorous life. So MI6 would hardly be the ones tasked with spying on his sister. That would be the *other* lot, MI5, whom Spencer remembered Bashir had name-checked in their previous discussions at Althorp. Then there was:

Wharf (scum) – escort girls in Langham Hilton

Inspector Ken Wharfe was Diana's police bodyguard, said by Bashir to have been up to no good in a five-star hotel, coincidentally just 100 yards from the BBC HQ in central London. But Spencer had heard Bashir make the same allegation about an entirely different person during their last meeting: 'He had said exactly the same thing when I spoke to him earlier about a *Daily Express* reporter. So I thought it was very unlikely. When I say the small details caught him out, that was one. Because I thought it's so unlikely two people would be doing the same thing in the same place. The straight fact was that the things he had told me during our meetings at Althorp did not fit with what he was telling Diana now.'

Spencer, the chap who had been a reporter himself for nearly ten years, longer than Bashir in fact, had the strong sense that what he was hearing was, crudely put, crap. He had sat back, saying little, carefully noting where the briefing led, a number, circled, around each new claim. Number 32 was a story about Diana's hired security expert.

Graham Harding, Fergie's contact, has swept Ken. Palace recently. Cdn't do telephone lines. Didn't do it thoroughly

Spencer wrote '33' and circled it, ready for more. But there was no thirty-third story. The meeting wrapped up, Spencer bemused but content that he had marked Bashir's card. Spencer said, 'I felt that I was listening to a man who was not telling the truth. He was overexcited, but also shifty. That's why I consigned him to history at the end of the meeting.'

And Spencer thought Diana had the same queasy feeling. He told me, 'Bashir left first. And I said to Diana, "I need a word." I said, "Look I'm really sorry. I've wasted your time because I think the bloke's full of crap actually." And she didn't for a moment dispute that. She didn't say, "Actually, no, I think he had a point." She just said, "Don't worry, Carlos, it was lovely to see you. It doesn't matter at all." And so I really did think that was the end of it.'

The problem was, Diana had been watching a different movie that afternoon, or at least the kind where two friends, brother and sister even, can leave the cinema and say, 'Actor X – wasn't he great!' 'Great? He was hopeless!' But then they both hug and head for the Tube. What happened in Knightsbridge that afternoon was much more serious. Bashir was in.

8. Team Diana

That afternoon Princess Diana's world had become a completely different place. Someone who saw her soon after the short journey back from Knightsbridge to Kensington Palace said that she was elated, walking on air. Because she knew the score.

Diana was delighted to know, at last, for definite, that she was indeed surrounded by spies and traitors. That there was a whole tribe of people who wished her harm and had fiendish electronic devices, including a secret watch, in order to do it. Thus far there had only been questions. The chap I had a thing for, Barry? Murdered? That phone call with James Gilbey? A radio ham, or GCHQ? Clicks on the line? Paps when I leave, paps when I arrive? For years, well-attested horror stories that would keep anyone awake at night had been sprinkled with the cruellest kind of wicked-fairy dust. Diana might be wasting her time worrying. They might just be stories. They might *not* be true. Now she knew that they *were* true and she wasn't crazy after all.

Diana's sense of relief, of triumph, will have been like the person with a tiny, nagging pain, who will not shut up, who exhausts the sympathy of every friend and relative, but then finally gets their diagnosis. 'Yes. And who listened?' What is remarkable is that Diana very quickly dealt with the diagnosis, and in pugnacious fashion. She would have the treatment, the surgery, whatever it took, and she'd start right away. From 19 September, when she met Bashir for the first time, to 5 November, when the interview was recorded, when she came out fighting on camera, there were just forty-seven days.

So why did Diana see one movie, her brother Charles quite another? For two hours that afternoon Diana had listened intently as Martin Bashir peered into his A4 notebook, delivering one extraordinary revelation after another. Here was a sober-suited fellow with gold-rimmed glasses, someone who had already shown scary-sounding documents to Charles. *Bashir was the BBC*. And not merely the gold-standard copper-bottomed *10 O'Clock News* BBC. The A-team when it came to digging out state secrets: *Panorama*.

Thirty years ago, before internet news, before the collapse of trust which Bashir himself helped bring about, if BBC *Panorama* said that is how it was, then that is how it was. Diana wasn't a regular viewer, though she knew its reputation. Patrick Jephson too: '*Panorama* was the gold standard. *Panorama* was what you watched. I can remember when I was little, my mother would let me stay up long enough to hear the introductory music because it was so captivating. She knew that it was a favourite of mine. So from that age we had grown up to hold it in the highest regard.'

Charles Spencer was a fan of *Panorama* too. But something about Bashir still didn't gel. Their third meeting had been on 19 September. For maybe six hours in total one experienced journalist had been able to size up the working technique of another. Spencer had quibbles over Bashir's wandering account from one meeting to the next, but deep down he felt that Bashir was simply a chancer. Jonathan Maitland, the colleague who watched Bashir at work for six years, told me, 'There are two sorts of people in this world: those who fall for Martin's charm and those who don't. There were plenty

who'd be like, you're a bit weird and I don't want anything
to do with you. There were others who bought it and were
really burned by it.'

Spencer wanted facts, and from someone he could
believe. Bashir told Lord Dyson how Diana liked 'clairvoyants, mediums, mystics'. One of the people Diana went
to for counsel, at exactly this time, who describes herself
as an 'energy healer', was able to witness Bashir's impact
at first hand. Simone Simmons, aged thirty-eight when she
and Diana met, offers what could be described in a catch-all
phrase as 'New Age therapy'. Yes, there were crystals and
Tarot cards, but the greatest succour she offered the princess
seems to have been just a friendly ear. Simmons told me,
'I was recommended to Princess Diana for healing at the
end of 1993. And over time, we became very close friends,
even though we did have massive arguments. Because I was
very blunt with her, and she didn't always like the things
I said.' She has a powerful memory of the exact moment
when Martin Bashir arrived on the scene in September 1995:
'Diana was terribly excited. Really. You could see she was
floating. I mean, she was on one of those clouds that you
couldn't get her down from.'

In her small north London flat, with scented candles,
wind chimes softly nurdling, a sheaf of letters and cards
provides evidence of an intimate, girly friendship: 'Diana
was an amazing lady. She wasn't worldly wise, but she was
highly intelligent. She always said, you know, if you're sitting at a dinner party, you have to pretend that you don't
understand what people are talking about, especially if it's
important things. That way people ignore the fact that you're
there. And that is the best way to be kept in the loop.'

On 19 September 1995 Martin Bashir was the second

life-changing character to enter Diana's orbit in the space of just a few days. On 1 September, a Friday, Diana had visited London's Royal Brompton Heart and Lung Hospital, a low-rise, functional-looking building in the heart of Chelsea. But this was a private mission, a 10 a.m. meeting with another of her less-than-conventional acquaintances, Irish-born Oonagh Toffolo. This sixty-six-year-old woman, part of Diana's inner circle since 1989, is usually described as the princess's acupuncturist, but her extraordinary life history suggests a deeper spiritual role. After twenty years as a nun, including time with Mother Teresa in the slums of Calcutta, Toffolo left to become a nurse, eventually working in Paris, where she tended the Duke of Windsor, the former Edward VIII, through his final days.

On this occasion it was her husband, Joseph Toffolo, who was in need of medical care. He had undergone triple heart bypass surgery and Diana wanted to wish him well. Simone Simmons recalls, 'I was actually in hospital, having a hysterectomy, and she was going to come and see me. And instead of her coming I got a room full of flowers. And a phone call from Diana saying, "I'm sorry, I can't be with you, but I have to tell you something. I went to see Joseph Toffolo yesterday. And I think I've met my Mister Wonderful."' Toffolo's operation had been conducted by the world-renowned surgeon Sir Magdi Yacoub. Assisting him in theatre was a thirty-six-year-old senior registrar, Hasnat Khan.

Oonagh Toffolo would say later, 'I hadn't noticed anything about Hasnat Khan except that he was a very kind man, with lovely eyes and beautiful hands, and that he was a caring surgeon. But after he had left the room, Diana said to me, "Oonagh, isn't he drop-dead gorgeous!" That was how it started. I think he made a huge impact on her. I suppose she fell in love with him at first sight.' For Diana this was the beginning of what has been documented as a breathless romance, an escapade, with part of the thrill Diana's ability to keep her unlikely new romance a secret from the media.

To go to a cinema, like any normal couple, Diana invented disguises and seemed to relish her tradecraft. Simone Simmons recalled one remarkable success: 'She had a long dark wig, completely different clothes to what she'd normally wear, glasses sometimes, different make-up as well. When I went to the palace, the boys were there. And this woman came downstairs, and said, "Her Royal Highness'll be seeing you upstairs in her little room." I said, "OK," walked up the stairs, walked in. And the boys were there. They burst out laughing. I said, "So what's so funny?" They said, "You didn't recognize Mummy! Clap, please!"'

Hasnat Khan was born the eldest son of a wealthy family in Jhelum, Pakistan, drawn to London for his PhD studies under Professor Yacoub. Simmons says he had a patent lack of interest in celebrity, and principles that even thirty years ago seemed somehow antique: 'Until the divorce was finalized he wouldn't lay a finger on her. He was a perfect gentleman. She said he was the only man in her life that didn't want anything from her, except for her. You know, when his exhaust broke down, she said, "Do you realize we're going to be arrested because of the noise this car is making? Let me pay for a new exhaust." He said, "I'm a man. I'm working. I earn a decent salary. Please, I will do it myself." And he wouldn't let her pay a penny. And he's the only man who didn't want anything from her. All he wanted to do was give, to give her emotionally what she needed.'

Martin Bashir seems to have been quite clear what he wanted from Diana. He had already driven to Althorp twice, lying solidly, inventively, for four hours to her brother solo, another two hours to Charles and Diana as a pair. Charles wasn't sold but Diana was in, right away. Could it be that the coincidence of Bashir's ethnic background was a part of the magic? Jonathan Maitland said to me, 'Timing? The Greeks say, you know. Kairos? The confluence of events? Martin was pathologically, compellingly charming, ruthless. And he culturally, obviously, had a huge amount in common with the man she was in love with. So I have no doubt he would have been able to capitalize on that. It's highly plausible.' Simone Simmons is more definite. She says that as Diana's unlikely infatuation developed, Bashir also oftentimes became her secret conduit to the handsome doctor. She told me, 'For Diana, Martin Bashir was the obvious choice of go-between, because they're from the same place? Pakistan? And for quite a few months Martin was the go-between.'

And so that was how the world was for Diana, come September 1995. The thrilling intensity of a new relationship, a new *kind* of relationship with the modest, cerebral medic, one that would sustain, it is said, up to the time of her death two years later. Plus the incredible news that *every one* of her deepest, darkest fears had been entirely validated. Patrick Jephson witnessed it all first hand. He said to me, 'Think of the world that she was living in at that time. You don't have to watch *The Crown* to see that life in the royal family can be a pretty high-drama business.'

Now Diana 'knew' that Patrick Jephson was a spy. Her chauffeur was a spy. Her police bodyguard too. Her car and her phones were being tracked and tapped. She was Truman Burbank, in the movie where a whole world had been constructed to follow her every move. But now Bashir had explained the premise, and together she and the man from the BBC would exult in spoiling the plot. She and Bashir would be a team. They would fight back. And for the young woman who was at the very top of their hit list: *be afraid.*

9. Enemy in Sight

During that afternoon meeting on 19 September at the apartment in Knightsbridge one name kept recurring.

Tiggy. C's in love with her

Tiggy, properly Alexandra Legge-Bourke, nicknamed since childhood after Beatrix Potter's lovable hedgehog, was the thirty-year-old woman appointed by Prince Charles to help with childcare following the marriage separation in 1992. She would be assigned a critical role by Bashir in the game of human chess which he secretly directed throughout the month of October 1995.

With Charles's London base at St James's Palace and weekends at Highgrove in Gloucestershire, Tiggy took on something close to a mothering role for those times when William and Harry were not with Diana at Kensington Palace. She was a nanny but an extremely well-connected one. Her mother was lady-in-waiting to Anne, the Princess Royal, her younger brother a page-of-honour to the queen, the family home a 6,000-acre estate in mid-Wales. In fact a background remarkably similar to Diana's own, if a few notches down the nobility ladder.

Where they differed was that Tiggy was a real country girl. Fishing and shooting were her thing – the country pursuits which Diana shunned – but exactly what little boys like William and Harry, eleven and nine when she was appointed, appeared to love. And the tabloids loved it too, carrying photos of the three of them splashing through Highland salmon rivers, tramping across wind-scoured grouse moors, whereas Diana's days out with the boys would more likely take in a theme park such as Alton Towers. Patrick Jephson was a witness to this contrast in style: 'Tiggy gave William and Harry what boisterous teenage boys want. She was in charge of fun time. And when they came to Diana there was nothing but old Kensington Palace, which was a dreary place. McDonald's and movies.'

The photos suggested bracing, handmade fun versus manufactured modernity: Barbour versus Barbie. Richard Kay witnessed the effect they had: 'I know, because Diana told me, that it did irritate her. The way that Tiggy was so hands-on with her children. It came as no surprise really that a mother would never be entirely happy to see those photographs. And there were lots of them in the press, of William and Harry having great fun with Tiggy.'

But it went much further than a media battle over photo ops. Charles Spencer believes Bashir was cleverly, continually, refining his allegations for his audience of two on 19 September, carefully developing a thread where need be. He said, 'I feel that he was playing Battleships. Seeing what he could hit. He was scattering these things widely, to see where Diana bit. And she did bite at Legge-Bourke.' Bashir's unfolding account began to dwell not so much on Tiggy as a playmate for the young princes, but for their dad. He could sense that Diana was itching to hear more about an affair between the nanny and Prince Charles. The degree to which Tiggy had her claws in the man, as well as the boys.

And, crucially, the evidence shows that the hatred kindled that afternoon would dictate everything that happened from here on. Spencer told me, 'As my notes show, he did realize he had hit Diana's battleship with Tiggy Legge-Bourke. Diana was very concerned about Tiggy generally. A mother resenting another woman getting so close to her sons, you know? And hearing salacious things about her. Out of everything at that meeting, that would have been the headline Diana took away from it.'

By that point in history the tabloids had provided plenty of gossip for some inspired, low-level mischief-making. A welcome hug by Prince Charles here, an air kiss from Tiggy there. But Bashir's narrative was much more complex.

Carling publicity broke on day C + Tiggy went away for 2 weeks

Note number 11 in Spencer's list purported to show how Team Charles had deployed a highly embarrassing leak about Diana – speculation that she was a little too close to then England rugby captain Will Carling – to grab headlines on the day that Charles and Tiggy departed for a romantic getaway. This charge is likely to have made Diana seethe. Subsequent evidence suggests that the princess and the sporting hero were indeed much more than friends at this exact time, having met at the Chelsea Harbour Gym, prompting a fling which brought public condemnation from Carling's furious wife Julia. But the suggestion by Bashir was that Diana's outing was not the work of Fleet Street muckrakers. Instead, a perfectly timed stiletto thrust by the 'dark forces'. Diana had been shamed only *because*, and precisely *when*, Charles and Tiggy needed cover themselves.

Note 7 suggested that a temporary falling out with William was also part of the nanny's masterplan.

Difficult relationship with William for D, because of Tiggy

Note 17 told how even Richard Aylard, Prince Charles's private secretary, and the man supposedly in charge of taking Diana down, was cowed by the temptress in tweed and wellies.

Aylard terrified of Tiggy – she's v. powerful

This same note has an intriguing addition, significant because in the eight pages of script this is the sole reference to the woman who by then in the popular mind, the tabloid orthodoxy, was the key player, the woman who had broken the royal marriage apart and was keeping it broken.

Camilla: depressed, but quiet for time being

There is the sense of the club's once star striker, now a few miles on the clock, on the bench, maybe injured, maybe just sulking? Maybe ready for transfer? We cannot know whether Bashir's scenario was fully mapped out at that time; Spencer believes it was trimmed and shaped as the critical few weeks went by. But Camilla's place on the park would be defined, and in a remarkable way, before long.

The meeting on 19 September proved critical in netting Diana while at the same time repelling Charles Spencer. It is one of the tragic footnotes of what happened in those autumn weeks that, in a way that not even Bashir can have planned or imagined, his pitch was so perfectly tuned to separate brother and sister at this most critical moment. Spencer had assumed that with his post-meeting apology to Diana she had read the signals exactly as he had. Regarding Bashir, he said, 'I didn't know if he was a liar or a fantasist, but I knew he was bad news, in my opinion, and that was the end of him for me.' Spencer never saw or spoke to Bashir again after they parted on that Tuesday evening. But Bashir was not to know what the effect on the brother had been, demonstrated seven days later when a remarkable document rattled out of the fax machine at the Althorp Estate office.

26 SEP '95 15:36
Charles,

There is about to be a concerted fightback by Miss Legge-Bourke. Rumours have been circulating about recurring intimacy between her and a particular individual. One aide witnessed outdoor pursuits of a different kind.

She is keen to divert such attention. Hence a decision was taken last night to authorise a friend who will say the following:

— her weight loss is not due to her feelings for a particular individual, and his desire for a waif-like figure, but a gluten intolerance which means she cannot eat wheat or any bread substance,

— she has been repeatedly bombarded by nuisance messages on her radio pager. There will be a strong implication that these are coming from a disgruntled source. There can be only one obvious culprit . . .

Following Sunday's successful pre-empting of the visit to Paris this appears to be stage two of the latest strategy. I think you should inform your sister asap.

If you wish to discuss further — at home or on bleep from about 8:00pm tonight.

With all good wishes,
Martin

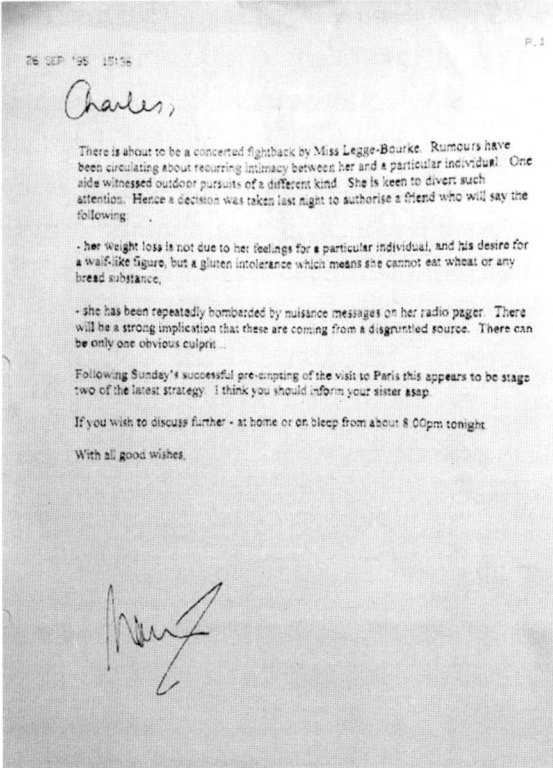

26 SEP '95 15:56   P. 1

Charles,

There is about to be a concerted fightback by Miss Legge-Bourke. Rumours have been circulating about recurring intimacy between her and a particular individual. One aide witnessed outdoor pursuits of a different kind. She is keen to divert such attention. Hence a decision was taken last night to authorise a friend who will say the following:

- her weight loss is not due to her feelings for a particular individual, and his desire for a waif-like figure, but a gluten intolerance which means she cannot eat wheat or any bread substance.

- she has been repeatedly bombarded by nuisance messages on her radio pager. There will be a strong implication that these are coming from a disgruntled source. There can be only one obvious culprit ...

Following Sunday's successful pre-empting of the visit to Paris this appears to be stage two of the latest strategy. I think you should inform your sister asap.

If you wish to discuss further - at home or on bleep from about 8.00pm tonight.

With all good wishes.

As someone who has pondered the details of this scandal for a very long time, this seems to me the most valuable, most crucial piece of evidence we have of Martin Bashir's thoroughgoing duplicity, his wicked intent. It also provides the strongest possible clue to how events truly unfolded prior to the *Panorama* interview, the story which ought to have been revealed by the Dyson inquiry but has not been. A later chapter looks at ways in which, in my view, Lord Dyson failed in the most important task he had: to serve the public interest. That this document was not even mentioned by Dyson, much less interrogated, seems remarkable.

The fax, signed by Martin Bashir and sent to Charles

Spencer on 26 September 1995, a week after the Knights-bridge meeting, is important not just for its content but because it is the single piece of *documentary* evidence which, beyond dispute, makes Bashir a villain. Regarding every other accusation, Bashir offers either denial or excuse. As regards the Matt Wiessler forgeries, the first two bank state-ments presented on 31 August, Bashir would say that the raw data came from Spencer, the specific details from Diana. As regards the forgeries targeting Patrick Jephson and Richard Aylard, shown to Spencer on 14 September, Bashir would say that the entire incident was fiction, confected by the earl. As regards the thirty-two allegations made at the Knights-bridge meeting, Bashir would say Spencer most likely faked the notes which he offered to Dyson as proof.

But even if we were to accept his argument on every one of these points, what does he say about this fax, which we know he did write, and then sign? This vital piece of evidence was retained by Spencer, a copy of the original document, pictured on previous page, sent by him to me. By the time of the Dyson inquiry its existence was no secret, the *Daily Mail* having even quoted lines from it in a story of 3 November 2020.

But Dyson did not question Bashir at all on the content of his fax, on what exactly he was intending to convey to Spen-cer in a story, delivered in a nudge-nudge-wink-wink tone, that seems to begin as *Carry on Camping* before veering closer to a dark, creepy *Bridget Jones's Diary*. What Bashir wants Spencer to know is that a servant has happened upon Prince Charles and Tiggy Legge-Bourke, more than once, having sex, in the open, what he portrays as 'recurring intimacy . . . outdoor pursuits of a different kind'. In a field in Gloucester-shire? In Hyde Park? Perhaps both? Bashir's coded reference to 'weight loss' is designed to suggest that Tiggy has recently had an abortion, the result, presumably, of earlier incautious 'intimacy'. Bashir warns of plans to spread false rumours that Diana has been nuisance-calling Tiggy, Diana described as 'a disgruntled source. There can be only one obvious culprit.'

Bashir's fax seems laughably, almost charmingly inept. The fact that the document exists at all suggests either a new swaggering confidence on Bashir's part or perhaps an impatience to keep things moving at a critical moment. When Bashir commissioned the first pair of forged bank statements, Matt Wiessler noted that Bashir had been careful to write nothing down himself. When Spencer asked to keep them, on 31 August, Bashir refused. When Bashir flourished his second set of forgeries on 14 September, Spencer remembered they had been presented to him just so; again Bashir was careful to leave nothing behind. Here was a document filled with the most astonishing allegations, all of them false, signed by the BBC man himself.

Spencer ignored the fax, not doing as he was urged: 'inform your sister asap'. Still, it provides a priceless window into Bashir's thinking at this time. Most important of all it surely provides good evidence for what Bashir was urging *Diana* to think. Implicit in the text is the suggestion by Bashir that he either has a spy actually within the Tiggy/Charles camp or that someone surveilling the prince and the nanny from *outside* is keen to share their intelligence, via Bashir, to assist the princess. And since Bashir's purported new information has come in *after* the Knightsbridge meeting, only seven days earlier, things are now really moving along.

The question arises: why should Spencer be invited to brief Diana on these vital developments, rather than Bashir do it himself? Perhaps the fax to Spencer was designed to give the story of Tiggy and Charles being spotted in the bushes added oomph, by being passed on by a third party? In any event it is fair to assume that whatever lurid tales Bashir told Spencer, urging him to act as messenger, he would also be willing to tell Diana himself when the chance arose.

A narrative structure, with a secret abortion one of the key plot points, began to be drafted by Bashir at least from 26 September 1995. In the month that followed, the story would blossom in extraordinary fashion.

10. Fear and Loathing

For Princess Diana, October 1995 must surely have been the most thrilling, perhaps the most frightening, certainly the plain weirdest month of her life. An account which seems to me reliable says that she attended the Brompton hospital, where the husband of her friend was convalescing, for seventeen days in succession, proof of her desire to snatch moments in the company of the man with whom she had become recently besotted, Hasnat Khan. Diana's therapist and confidante, Simone Simmons, told me, 'She was very naive, extremely so. Diana was very innocent in so many ways, because inside of her was like this thirteen, fourteen-year-old girl.'

There is a charming vignette in the otherwise sombre testimony presented in January 2008 at the inquest into Diana's death. A close friend, the colourful forty-seven-year-old Argentinian man-about-town Roberto Devorik, tells how he arrived one day, unexpected, at Kensington Palace. Diana was taken by surprise but could not resist showing off her new, down-to-earth, wholly unflashy boyfriend. Devorik said, 'The moment she opened the door, this gentleman faces me. And I look at him. And he was, with all my respect, he was not a kind of Brad Pitt or something of the sort . . . and that was my brief encounter with Dr Khan.'

As the princess and the eminent doctor ventured out on their first dates, Diana in heavy disguise, to the cinema, several times to Ronnie Scott's Jazz Club in Soho's Frith Street, in another compartment of her life a plan was taking shape to spectacularly take down the woman she had grown to despise. The difficulty is that the precise shape of that plan has to be pieced together from only fragments of evidence, a single vital document illuminating the whole on 30 October 1995, the rest assembled from those who can offer either first-hand witness testimony or credible detail of some other kind. Martin Bashir has never provided an account of what passed between him and Diana in the crucial weeks leading up to the recording of the *Panorama* interview on 5 November, nor is one remotely offered in the Dyson report.

In the report the narrative simply expires on 19 September 1995, the day of Bashir's first meeting with Diana. As to what happened *after* they met, Lord Dyson writes only, 'There is no doubt that, following the meeting, Princess Diana agreed to be interviewed by Mr Bashir. That is not surprising. By this time, she was very keen to give an interview, probably to the BBC. Mr Bashir was a charming and empathetic person who would immediately appeal to Princess Diana.' As a service to legitimate public interest, a service to history, Lord Dyson's words here seem to me astonishing, dismissing the need for any serious inquiry with the wholly untested claim that Diana was desperate to be on TV, with Bashir just the sort of chap who might help. It seems impossible to reconcile this lack of curiosity with the first and third of his Terms of Reference laid out in the report:

What steps did the BBC and in particular Martin Bashir take with a view to obtaining the Panorama interview on 20 November 1995 with Diana, Princess of Wales? This will involve a consideration of all the relevant evidence.

To what extent did the actions of the BBC and in particular Martin Bashir influence Diana, Princess of Wales's decision to give an interview?

A later chapter will look at the areas where, in my view, Dyson's near insouciance has left a serious mark on proceedings. Here the issue is to try to determine what actually happened to Diana, how she was inveigled, railroaded, into the extraordinary double act that she and Martin Bashir performed on 5 November 1995.

Diana's butler, Paul Burrell, has written extensively about his time with the princess – for some professional Diana-watchers much too extensively and sometimes too colourfully. With that proviso, his account of smuggling Martin Bashir in and out of Kensington Palace, avoiding the security checkpoint with the reporter hidden on the back seat, seems entirely possible. Burrell would write, 'To anyone looking on, I was alone in the car, heading as normal to my workplace. "Where are we now? Have we gone past the police post yet?" asked a muffled voice from under the rug. "No. Stay under. I'll tell you when," I said impatiently, keen on sticking to the strict instructions from the Princess to "keep him hidden on entry".'

We know from the best source of all, Diana herself, that she and Bashir certainly *did* spend time together. Remember the note which she sent to Bashir on 21 November 1995, soon after the *Panorama* broadcast:

Apart from the fact that you're able to produce a mean pasta in my kitchen, you have other extraordinary qualities of which I have seen and 'worked with' during the last months . . .

In a heavily redacted email from Bashir, dated some twenty-five years later, 23 October 2020, and obtained by me under Freedom of Information law, there is another intriguing reference to the Kensington Palace kitchen. Writing then, Bashir says, 'I may yet tell the story of my relationship to Royalty and produce all of the documents that prove there was no deception. Indeed, I was writing her speeches and cooking pasta in Kensington Palace for her long before she sat down to talk about the three people in her marriage. But that's for another day.' On 1 March 2021, in his testimony to Dyson, Bashir again invokes the kitchen environment. He told the inquiry, 'I was cooking in Kensington Palace, we were chatting about various things . . .' And in the same testimony he offers his strange account of his excursion with Diana: '. . . we drove to the New Forest and back, which took around five hours . . .'

So we can take it that they were chatting. But what about? Patrick Jephson, Diana's secretary, painted as a spy during the 19 September meeting, says that at exactly this time the woman he had worked with for seven years began to show visible signs of fear. And at the same time she started to freeze him out. He told me, 'It does explain why my relationship with my boss suddenly underwent a transformation. I could almost put dates on it now. In fact, I got my old diary out to have a look. Things started to go badly wrong, and I didn't know why.'

I should explain that the relationship I have been able to develop with Patrick Jephson is closer than the usual polite exchanges between a journalist and his source. The former naval officer, sixty-five years old at the time of writing, spent eight crucial years with Diana between 1988 and 1996, at her side almost every day in this country and overseas. As her private secretary he was her confidant, her adviser and a witness to all that went on as Diana's relationship with her husband withered and died. But what Patrick could not know is exactly *why* Diana turned on him in the autumn of

1995, culminating in a vicious confrontation described later in this book. It was the story which I was eventually able to uncover, in 2020, which provided those answers, which have made it much easier to handle the bitter memories of that six-month period thirty years ago.

Apart from Patrick, the best evidence for Diana's state of mind at this precise moment comes from the princess herself, in another remarkable note, undated except for the month, October. To whom it was addressed is unclear. Butler Paul Burrell took possession of the document, in circumstances which are still today a little murky. Investigators who interviewed Burrell in 2004, as part of Operation Paget, the Metropolitan Police inquiry into Diana's death, said, 'He stated that the letter left by the Princess of Wales was more accurately described as "a memorandum or note as there was no addressee"; it was just left inside the blotter in his office at Kensington Palace for his attention.' Diana had written:

> *I am sitting here at my desk today in October, longing for someone to hug me & encourage me to keep strong & hold my head high – this particular phase in my life is the __most__ dangerous – my husband is planning 'an accident' in my car, brake failure & serious head injury in order to make the path clear for him to marry Tiggy. Camilla is nothing but a decoy.*

In their analysis of the note, the police recorded, 'Paul Burrell stated that the Princess of Wales believed that Barry Mannakee . . . had been deliberately killed in a motorcycle crash . . . the Princess of Wales never wavered from this view and this may have influenced her thinking when writing the note.' It seemed that the fear that Diana had nurtured for more than eight years, since she first heard about the mysterious death of her ex-bodyguard in 1987, had returned now in vicious form.

A close friend of Diana's has marked the autumn of 1995 as the period when Diana became most afraid. Rosa Monckton, then aged forty-two, was comforted by Diana when a pregnancy ended in stillbirth in 1994. In May 1995 Monckton gave birth to a daughter, diagnosed with Down syndrome, to whom Diana became godmother. Monckton would write, 'When I look at the timeline . . . I see that it was in September that Diana first met Bashir. In late September I received a letter from her to say that she had had to change her landline number at Kensington Palace, "due to some very strange things". I could never understand the sudden change in her behaviour towards the end of that year. Diana changed from being very concerned with day-to-day matters, just like any normal friend, to suddenly becoming obsessed with plots against her.' Monckton asked Diana to explain what was wrong. Her reply was deeply troubling: 'She was obsessed with the idea that Tiggy Legge-Bourke was having an affair with Prince Charles. At a later meeting, she told me that Tiggy was pregnant with his child.'

And this is the time when Patrick Jephson began to hear terrifying specifics from his boss, including fears of assassination: 'She told me, for example, her car brakes were being tampered with. That she was afraid somebody was going to shoot her, in Hyde Park. These were all things that she said she had been told, on good authority. Obviously I checked with the police to see if there was any real risk to her life at that time. I checked with her driver, about anybody possibly tampering with her car. And all these inquiries came up blank. And yet she persisted in believing these things, that in her normal self, the Diana I knew, would have dismissed, but which suddenly for some reason she was giving some credibility to. It was a period of extraordinary uncertainty. It was unsettling.' He did try to find out who was behind the tip-offs: 'I would try and corner her on it. And she'd be vague, and say, "Oh it's GCHQ. Or MI6." I'd say, "They're two different things?" She'd say, "I know. But I can't say too much because he'd lose his job and he'll be in trouble." And so this person who was giving her the information was under threat themselves, which made it all the more secret.'

Today Patrick Jephson wonders whether during this key period he was actually being used as a patsy, double-bluffed, being fed snippets of conspiracy data to see whether he would traitorously pass them on to his supposed pals in the 'dark forces'. Jephson told me, 'As we now know Bashir had gone to work on my reputation. So with hindsight, maybe she thought I was already a traitor and she wanted this to get back to Buckingham Palace? Maybe it was a test, and she did this to see where it popped out? It wouldn't have been surprising if she had included me in this, to see if I was reliable.'

Jephson's life certainly threatened to spin off into a place that was darkly bizarre. The daily round of fixing visits, handling correspondence, all the work of an experienced private secretary, now included checking that assassins had not sneaked in to the palace garage, making phone calls to puzzled police chiefs: 'Spotted any snipers at all? I gather there's one about.' He needed a second wise head, another pair of ears to listen to a tale that was becoming daily more weird. And so another character joined the cast, one who would shortly play a critical role in these dramatic events.

Diana's legal affairs had for years been handled by the giant, super-smooth, purrs-like-a-Rolls legal practice Mishcon de

Reya, the name itself sounding like a whispered confidence, its hundreds of lawyers elegantly gathered in a giant, marble-pillared palazzo in Holborn. Oddly for a firm selling its skills to the very rich, the man at the top, Diana's man, Lord Mishcon, was a lifelong socialist. Eighty years old at the time of these events, Victor Mishcon was the son of a Brixton rabbi, climbing always – inside the legal world, inside the Labour Party, rising to shadow Lord Chancellor in the 1980s. Aside from top-tier politics he had delicate and famous cases to win too, successfully lawyering for two notorious wrong 'uns: Tory politician and perjurer Jeffrey Archer and champion fraudster Robert Maxwell. It may not have been something he dwelt on with Diana, but Mishcon had also represented Ruth Ellis, who forty years earlier had gunned down her feckless lover and became the last woman in Britain to be hanged. For Patrick Jephson, Mishcon's decades-long experience of paddling through politics and villainy became invaluable: 'I was actually talking to him on the phone several times a day at that point. He was something of a father figure for me. I was thirty-six, he was old and wise, a statesman. Given the situation that I was in, I was keen to find somebody who I could trust. Somebody had been pumping this stuff in, and I wanted guidance, some sort of reference points.'

Tales of gunmen in Hyde Park and severed brake cables perplexed Jephson yet only half convinced him. So why did they land so much better with Diana? Andrew Morton maintained good contacts with the princess and her inner circle. He has often pondered how Bashir was able to ensnare Diana, when so many others came not even close enough to cast their net: 'How did Martin inveigle himself into her life to a point where she, and I'm quoting from one of Diana's confidants here, was "terrified, horrified"? Martin's technique was twofold. One was the gift of the gab. Secondly, place. He would give a sense of drama to everything that was going on.

'So on one occasion, for example, Diana and Martin met in an underground car park. They're sinister places at the best of times. When you're predisposed to think that some-body is going to bump you off, you're in a climate of terror and fear. And this is what happened. Diana was transported from a world of suspicion to one of morbid fear and terror. On one occasion he said dramatically, "They're going to wipe you." That is to say, "They're going to kill you." And that's his genius.'

Bashir's skill was presenting not just the problem but the solution too. He could offer Diana a lifeline, perhaps the only one available. Far from some vague hankering to talk to someone on TV, anyone, about something – as weakly sug-gested in the Dyson report – here was a *specific* response to a *specific* life-and-death question, posed by Bashir, with just one goal in mind. Diana must make a powerful, public statement. On *Panorama*.

11. The Sting

I have come across fascinating evidence that Bashir's focus, once he had won Diana's trust, was at first not on an interview for *Panorama* at all but on something entirely different. He imagined himself following the example of Andrew Morton by using his relationship with Diana to write a best-selling book and earn for himself, as Morton was able to do, a fortune. The story was revealed to me by Roland Philipps, a writer and a well-known figure in London's book world, and in 1995 the thirty-four-year-old publishing director of the eminently respectable Hodder & Stoughton.

In late September 1995 Philipps took a call from Bashir, requesting a meeting. Philipps told me, 'He said he had chosen Hodder because he was most impressed by the religious books in our catalogue. That was what brought him to us.' With discussion of religion out of the way, Bashir got down to business. Philipps remembers that at their first meeting Bashir produced a folder containing what seemed to be thirty or forty letters. Bashir said he had been given them in the strictest confidence. They were private correspondence, between Diana and her father-in-law, the then seventy-four-year-old Duke of Edinburgh. Philipps said, 'He wouldn't let me read the contents, but I could see from the greetings and signatures that's what they seemed to be. I remember I was struck by Diana's letters to Philip. She called him "Darling Pa", in that distinctive handwriting.'

Bashir said the letters were proof that Diana had empowered him to write her authorized biography. The book would be a sensation, and Bashir wanted to know how much it would be worth. Philipps was in no doubt about the BBC man's sense that vast riches may be in store: 'He was very insistent that I give him a figure. He kept pressing. Obviously a book like that would be a blockbuster worldwide and so eventually I said, "Ball park? Certainly seven figures. Let's say, at the very least, one and a half million pounds?" Bashir seemed happy with the amount.' And, from Philipps' side of the table, this would be the kind of coup every publisher dreams of. Signing a deal for the first truly *authorized* biography of the world's most famous woman, the most celebrated and controversial personality at the very top of the A-list, would make him an industry legend overnight.

With mounting excitement he and Bashir kept in close touch by phone. Over the next six weeks they met three times, to discuss details of the upcoming book, at Hodder headquarters on London's Euston Road. Philipps began to be swept up, awaiting only confirmation from the princess herself: 'Bashir said to me that Diana was very excited. She'd given her blessing to the project, as a way of getting her story out there.' But his last conversation with Bashir came on 14 November 1995, the day the forthcoming *Panorama* interview was publicly announced by the BBC. Philipps: 'I watched the interview go out. A day or two later I tried to ring him but got no answer. I tried again of course, but that was it. I never heard from Bashir again.'

To this day Philipps is bemused as to what had really happened. Was Bashir touting a genuine prospect of becoming

Diana's biographer, and somehow the project fizzled? Or was the BBC reporter using the link he had made with this ever-so-upright publishing house – responsible for the Teach Yourself books and volumes by Winston Churchill – to bolster his own credibility with Diana? Philipps has never been quite sure, nor has he ever quite shaken off the feeling that he had so nearly made the biggest deal of his life.

There will always be huge doubt about exactly what conversations took place between Martin Bashir and Diana in October 1995 as the interview drew inexorably closer. Of the only two people present for the key meetings, one of them is dead, the other a habitual liar. When you are building a circumstantial case it is important to cling to whatever hard evidence exists. We can say with certainty that Bashir lied four times to Charles Spencer: on 31 August 1995, 14 September, 19 September and again with his fax on 26 September. As we will see later Bashir lied three times to his bosses at the BBC: in 1995 and 1996. Twenty-five years after that, on 1 March 2021, he would lie at least three times to Lord Dyson in his description of earlier events. Now on each of those occasions there will have been many individual lies, specific falsehoods, but taking just the macro view we can say that Bashir lied ten times: four times, as it were, on the way up, trying to make his plan work, and six times on the way down, trying to escape detection.

All that being the case, is it then more or less likely that he would have lied to Diana when just the two of them were together? I think he would, and there is evidence that the biggest lie of all, the nastiest lie, the one which nudged the needle on an interview from a quivering, wavering, sagging will-she-won't-she to a leaping 'HELL YES!' was a lie told probably on Saturday, 28 or Sunday, 29 October 1995. The reason those dates flash up is because of the way the interview finally came about. Diana sat in front of the BBC camera one week later, on Sunday, 5 November.

Martin Bashir's main aim was of course to get Diana to say she would be interviewed, but once that happened he needed to sort the practicalities. He needed a cameraman, one he could trust to undertake this super-secret mission. He needed someone special, and he found it in Tony Poole. His testimony is important, the *way* he was hired a likely clue as to how the interview was secured. At the time of writing Tony Poole is aged seventy-five, retired, looking back on a career like many another ex-BBC cameraman, a trooper, a pro. His career is like so many but unlike them all. It was Tony who lit the lights, who clipped the mic on to Diana's lapel, who pressed the button on the camera which shot arguably the most momentous footage the BBC has ever recorded, or will ever record.

Tony gives a fascinating account of what happened on the night. For now what is significant is what happened during the preceding ten days. He told me, 'Initially, when I got the phone call from my agent she said, "*Panorama* want you next Sunday." And I said, "Elaine, I don't work on Sundays, it's my family day." She said, "Well, I think you might want to do this, it's a royal. I think it's a big one. Would you mind if Martin Bashir called you?"' The booking was for the evening of the following Sunday, 29 October: 'Martin phoned and said, "I will mention the name only once. It's Diana, at Kensington Palace."' Already, cloak and dagger. 'I'd worked with Martin. I always thought he was an operator. Likeable guy, but an operator. Right from the start there was a paranoia that the phones might be tapped.'

The fact that a Sunday had been chosen confirms Diana's input. This was more than Bashir *hoping* that he *might* have landed her, getting a camera guy on standby. Diana knew that a Sunday was the day to choose to keep everything under wraps, with butler Paul Burrell on his day off, the evening a time when she would often feed herself, from the fridge. It meant busting his weekend but Tony was intrigued, excited. He had shot famous people before, lots of them: Elton John, Nelson Mandela, Tony Blair, Stevie Wonder, his favourite. He had filmed the queen, for heaven's sake, while she'd sat for a portrait. But Diana? At home, at night? He had barely rejigged his Sunday-at-home plans when, he told me, 'It was cancelled. It was quite quick. Went away, nobody said why.'

Diana had said yes, plans were made for 29 October, and then she just as abruptly said no. But why? Was this just a schedule glitch, or last-minute cold feet? The BBC's own internal records describe what happened next this way: 'Specifically, HRH agreed to be interviewed at a meeting over the weekend of 28/9 October.' So what was said at this meeting, on the Saturday or Sunday, which finally convinced Diana that she must give the interview to Martin Bashir?

There is a principle which journalists sometimes have to use, to take information 'off the record'. Confusingly it simply means that the *source* cannot be identified. What they say is absolutely *on* the record, but their name cannot be. There could be any number of reasons why, but often the fact is that the information would not be divulged at all without such a guarantee being given. It is then a matter of judging: is the information true? And second: is the reason the source wants to remain secret a valid one? Of course the net effect is slightly unsatisfactory, the whole a bit more slippery than would be ideal. But in this case I am entirely confident that I have been told the truth, the source having a distinct, verifiable reason to maintain anonymity – in fact, a reason closely bound up with the way the information was gained in the first place. The question I put to this source was: 'So, during that weekend meeting, what was it that finally pushed Diana over the line?'

Diana was shown a document, another forgery by Martin Bashir, which at last provided concrete proof for one of her deepest, darkest suspicions. My source says that he showed her a letter, effectively a receipt for an abortion which Tiggy Legge-Bourke had just had, the operation paid for by Prince Charles. It had happened, and Charles had paid for it. Imagine the disgust, the contempt, the roiling bloody anger which that bit of paper kindled. Oh yes, she knew about them anyway. She knew about them, and what they were planning. The note she had written a few days earlier said it clear enough: '. . . to make the path clear for him to marry Tiggy'. When he marries Tiggy, what do William and Harry become? Stepkids. *Her* kids.

Martin Bashir's fax of 26 September to Diana's brother had slyly hinted at rumours of an abortion – 'her weight loss is not due to her feelings for a particular individual' – but now Diana had been shown proof, and once again proof presented by a representative of the British Broadcasting Corporation. It sounds so horribly scandalous, but then, is it more scandalous than knocking up a piece of paper purporting to prove that two ex-Royal Navy Commanders, Patrick Jephson and Richard Aylard, had taken £40,000 in backhanders, as Bashir did on 14 September? Events covered in the next chapter show that Diana certainly believed at this time that an abortion *had* been carried out, that she talked about 'a certificate' which proved it. And jumping forward six weeks in the timeline, Diana made crystal-clear what she *believed* to be true, that she was confident enough to make a horrible accusation in public.

On Thursday, 14 December 1995, at the Lanesborough Hotel at Hyde Park Corner, staff had assembled for the Christmas lunch laid on for Prince Charles and Diana's people. Richard Kay described to me what happened: 'Diana marched up to Tiggy and said the words, "So sorry to hear about the baby." And Tiggy burst into tears. The implication was that Tiggy had become pregnant, and had either had an abortion or had lost the baby. And it was deeply distressing, unpleasant and untrue.' Tiggy fled the room in tears. Patrick Jephson said, 'When she snuck up to Tiggy at the Christmas lunch and whispered this to her she absolutely believed it. And was proud of it. That's what she told me: "I'm dealing with it. I'm confronting this. I'm not running away any more."'

Here, again, the Dyson report signally fails to shed light on what was the crux of Bashir's deception campaign. Dyson actually notes the abortion rumours but sweeps the issue aside. He writes: 'Suspicions . . . have been expressed by Ms Pettifer (formerly Legge-Bourke) that Mr Bashir was the source of hurtful remarks that she says Princess Diana made to her in December 1995 . . . The question of whether Mr Bashir made the alleged untruthful and unwarranted comments to Princess Diana clearly falls outside the scope of my Terms of Reference.' On the contrary, the question of whether Bashir told the abortion lie, as my source assures me he did, would be central in answering the question at the very top of Lord Dyson's list.

By the night of Sunday, 29 October Princess Diana had made up her mind. She would record the BBC interview in seven days' time. And in the intervening period she would put into effect a plan. A plan that was brilliant, as she saw it, but heartbreakingly daft in reality.

12. The Real Deal

Diana took part in two interviews in the space of seven days, both at Kensington Palace, the first on Monday, 30 October 1995, then on Sunday, 5 November when she sat down for *Panorama*. Easily the most significant, the most truthful from Diana's point of view, was the first of these. Of the five people present on that extraordinary occasion only two are still alive. Patrick Jephson can never forget hearing Diana's words: 'What she said is like a last will and testament. Those are the words of somebody who thinks she might not be around much longer.'

Two of the others present that day were women who would become frequent visitors to Kensington Palace, not clairvoyants or acupuncturists but lawyers, Maggie Rae and Sandra Davis. Newcomers on that Monday afternoon, they would soon be looking out for Diana in the increasingly fraught divorce negotiations with Prince Charles's people. Both women were big fish in the London legal pool, partners at Mishcon de Reya, the place to go for a princess desperate to untangle herself from her royal in-laws. But the delicacy of the situation, the watching paparazzi, meant that the lawyers would always head for Kensington, rather than Diana traipsing across town to Holborn.

The three women would soon be on first-name terms, having what Sandra Davis would describe as 'girly lunches'. Maggie Rae, in particular, would become almost a pal. After Tony Blair became Labour Party leader in July 1994

it was Rae, a leftie since student days, who later introduced the princess to the smiling young politician. Diana
would slip over to Rae's house in Hackney for clandestine
suppers with Blair, his wife Cherie and other star-struck
members of the New Labour ascendancy. But the first
meeting of these three women, on 30 October, was business only. It had been fixed, at least so they supposed, to
introduce them to Diana for the divorce battle ahead. The
princess's legal business had so far been handled by the top
man, Lord Mishcon, but as Maggie Rae would recall, 'By
that stage Lord Mishcon was quite elderly. I think he had
intimations of his own mortality. He wanted to make sure
that, in the event that something happened to him, her case
would be properly handled, and he chose Sandra and I as
his successors.'

Elderly yes, but Lord Mishcon was still a lively and colourful figure in his own right. He knew the stab of matrimonial
discord too – his fourth marriage was dissolved in 2001
when he was eighty-six. Patrick Jephson recalls how Mishcon
pulled up in the palace courtyard at 4 p.m., at the wheel of
his rakish, gold-coloured Jaguar XJ6, Rae and Davis already
upstairs in the first-floor sitting room. Diana joined the party,
the five of them gathered at the end of a long table. With
teas and coffees barely sipped, the princess had something
to say. Lord Mishcon had heard many chilling tales over the
decades but this was unmatched. A princess crying murder.

Mishcon carefully noted down in longhand Diana's list
of astonishing revelations. They would be neatly typed the
following day, becoming a note so incendiary that it was
immediately locked in his safe, hurriedly pulled out days
after Diana's mysterious death for a single top-secret briefing, then locked away for a further seven years. Maggie Rae

admitted, 'I didn't even know about the note. He was a man of few words, Lord Mishcon.'

Referring to Diana as HRH, Her Royal Highness, Mishcon's note began:

> *HRH said that she had been informed by reliable sources whom she did not wish to reveal (they would speedily dry up if she broke her promise of confidentiality) that*
>
> *(a) The Queen would be abdicating in April and the Prince of Wales would then assume the throne and*
>
> *(b) efforts would be made if not to get rid of her (be it by some accident in her car such as pre-prepared brake failure or whatever) between now and then, then at least to see that she was so injured or damaged as to be declared "unbalanced".*
>
> *She was convinced that there was a conspiracy and that she and Camilla were to be "put aside".*
>
> *She had also been told that Miss Legge-Bourke had been operated on for an abortion and that she (HRH) would shortly be in receipt of "a certificate".*

Here was Lord Mishcon, scribbling in his notebook the most extraordinary-sounding catalogue of events promising wholesale national upheaval, an abdication there, a murder or two here. Although, of those present, only Diana could make the connection that it seemed remarkably to mirror the occasion just six weeks earlier when Charles Spencer had noted down the thirty-two fantastic stories offered by Bashir at their meeting in Knightsbridge.

Then the queen had been described as suffering from heart disease, and eating 'for comfort'. Now that had hardened into a decision to abdicate, and in just six months' time. The story of lethal brake-tampering was a familiar one now, touched on by Diana in the note left for Paul Burrell. Evoking again the Knightsbridge meeting, Camilla Parker Bowles gets only a passing mention, this time an indication that she is to be cut from the cast altogether, a casualty alongside Diana herself. And the one who emerges triumphant, newly post-abortion, is Tiggy Legge-Bourke. Diana had underlined that what she had to say on that score was beyond challenge, as her 'certificate' would prove.

For Patrick Jephson the marshalling of the stories was new, though he had heard them emerge singly before in more or less the same form. For that reason he sat a little less taken aback than Rae, Davis and Mishcon. Sandra Davis would later say that she remembered Diana's words regarding abdication and succession slightly differently. In testimony at Princess Diana's inquest on 15 January 2008 she said, 'She believed that Prince Charles wouldn't inherit the throne. She thought a jump in the succession was going to happen and that Prince Andrew would be Regent until Prince William came of age.'

But did Diana *really* believe the extraordinary things she was saying?

COUNSEL: In relation to . . . her fears that she might be killed, as far as you were concerned, you were clear that she was in fact deadly serious about that?

DAVIS: I thought she was serious, yes.

COUNSEL: You got the impression that the 'reliable sources' that she was talking about . . . that she had somebody 'on the inside'?

DAVIS: That was the impression that I got from what she said at that meeting. I seem to recall that her body language, and what she said at the time, made it clear that she was not going to be pressed on the identity of the person or persons who were giving her the information.

Maggie Rae was asked for her recollection too.

COUNSEL: When she spoke of being 'put aside' . . . what did you understand her to mean by that?

RAE: I was very clear in my own mind that she meant that she thought she was going to be killed.

Mishcon, the octogenarian, privy to many a whopper from the mouths of the great and not-so-good, was more circumspect. His note continued:

I told HRH that if she really believed her life or being was threatened, security measures including those relating to her car must be increased. I frankly however could not believe that what I was hearing was credible as to this alleged conspiracy and sought and obtained an opportunity of a private word with Commander Jephson who surprisingly said that he himself "half believed" in the accuracy of what HRH had said as to the risks to her safety.

Patrick Jephson told me, 'When we got back downstairs, Mishcon, in the equerry's room, said, "Well, Commander, these are grave allegations. Do you believe them?" And I said, "Well I half believe them. Do *you* believe it?" And he said, "She's my client, I have to believe it." I thought, "Well, I'm in the same situation. I have to believe what she tells me until I can disprove it."'

The remarkable note concludes:

*HRH in answer to a question I put to her said that in her view the
happiest solution for the future of the monarchy was for the Prince of
Wales to abdicate in favour of Prince William and that without any
malice whatsoever she wished to put that view forward in the interests
of the Royal family and everyone.*

   *She was disappointed that the Prime Minister had not been
to see her or got in touch with her for a very considerable time. I
offered to pass this on to the Lord Chancellor on her behalf and did
so later that afternoon in a private meeting I had with him. I told
him no more.*

These final paragraphs seem to betray a plan that is fully
thought through, something more than the hapless crime
victim briefing a cop, or the pupil setting out someone else's
naughtiness for the headmaster. Diana has a definite plan for
who should become the next monarch. Not only that, she
lets it be known that she would like a word, and soon please,
with John Major, then the prime minister. And she knows
Mishcon is the very man who can make that happen. The
meeting at Kensington Palace began at 4 p.m., Mishcon indicating that by maybe 6 p.m. that same day he was face-to-face
with Lord Mackay, then Lord Chancellor, the government's
most senior law officer, the sort of person whose calls to 10
Downing Street are answered right away. It is a remarkable
thought. From an invented fantasy to the prime minister's
ear with only one, maybe two brief halts in between.

   Patrick Jephson has tried to make sense of what he heard
that memorable afternoon. From Diana's point of view, he
says, it does not sound crazy at all: 'She was in fear for her
own life and, entirely rationally, decided to tell her lawyer
about it. So that if she turned up in the Thames one morning, he and I would tell the world, and Maggie and Sandra

would tell the world what was going on. She wanted this to go straight to Mishcon, so there was no possibility of it being misunderstood or doubted.'

Intriguingly, Jephson suspects that Diana was drawing directly from her own experience, her own childhood, and the bitter divorce battle lost by her own mother. Might Prince Charles be granted custody of William and Harry because Diana would be judged unfit to cope? Jephson said, 'In her mind I can see it all rolling together. That Tiggy would marry Charles and take away the boys. And they would have her "put aside", maybe by saying that she was crazy, an unfit mother. Which had happened to her mother. You don't have to be a psychiatrist to work it out.' Charles Spencer believes that is a theory worth considering. He told me, 'My father won custody of us when we were very young, and then re-won it a few years later. And so yes, that makes sense. That would have been very important to Diana.'

At this point, roughly halfway through our narrative, it is useful to stand back for just a moment to consider quite how bizarre, how bonkers, our plot has become. To reflect that these events are more than the drug-fuelled scribblings of a B-movie scriptwriter. They really happened, and the principal characters – bar one – are still alive today. The British Broadcasting Corporation, the world's most saintly source for truth, had cleverly managed to convince the woman set to become Queen of England that her husband was plotting to murder her. Indeed not just *her* but his ex-lover too, in order to marry a young servant. And so to set the dual assassination off track, Princess Diana would make an audacious knight's move. An announcement before millions that she would *not* be pushed around, climaxing with a declaration that her murderous husband was not fit to become king.

Considering the shimmering sense of not-quite-reality which attends everything which the royals do, plus the passage of three decades, let us bring the same scenario up to date, with characters who are rather more meat-and-two-veg. Let us say that the BBC has managed to convince Lady Starmer, wife of our current prime minister, that *she* will shortly be murdered. Why? Because Sir Keir is enraptured by a shapely intern. And the only way for Lady Starmer to keep herself alive is to call out the plotters. On *Panorama*.

Now *that* is a story.

In October 1995 Princess Diana was the unwitting heroine of the extraordinary drama sketched out for her by Martin Bashir. Now, to counter the plot against her, all that remained was for Diana to make her bold and brilliant knight's move. And with that, *checkmate*.

13. Fireworks Night

The night on which Diana and Bashir came together for the *Panorama* interview could not have been better chosen: Guy Fawkes Night, or Fireworks Night, the night when we remember conspirators who wanted to destroy a king. In 1605, Guy Fawkes and his crew were collared moments before they could light the gunpowder to blow King James I skywards. But in 1995 they were not caught, at least not right then.

Diana had worked out a plan. A Sunday would make it much easier to get the job done in secret. Paul Burrell recalled, 'I remember the princess said to me, "Paul you haven't had a day off this week. Why don't you go home and play with your children?" I thought, "Odd. Odd that she should just dismiss me."' Diana had said the BBC crew must total no more than three, including Bashir, and that they must declare themselves to the police at the security barrier as salesmen, coming to demonstrate a new hi-fi music system. All the kit for the interview would be stashed inside giant cardboard boxes. Tony Poole, the cameraman, could manage one of Diana's stipulations easily enough. He had actually kept the boxes from his own last hi-fi purchase and dragged them down from his attic that Sunday morning. The other requirement would be harder to meet.

Having just three people along – Bashir, producer Mike Robinson and himself – meant that for Tony the whole of the technical side of things became his problem. As he put it to me, 'I was spinning plates.' Nowadays documentaries are often shot by a single operator but thirty years ago things were much different. The cameras were so much heavier, everything altogether clunkier, and in 1995 a cameraman would expect to have a specialist sound recordist, a specialist lighting technician as well. Given the demands of the night, the ultra-high profile of the interviewee, the BBC would normally have sent six people, maybe more.

But they had just three. The producer, Mike Robinson, is one of the shadowy characters in this story. I have met him during my BBC career but never worked with him, or for him. Like Bashir he has never talked publicly about how the interview was won, or shot. Robinson walked onstage with Bashir in 1996 to accept a BAFTA Award for the interview, but even though he was credited as producer, even though he was one of just three people in the room with Diana that night, there is no evidence that Lord Dyson gained, or indeed sought, anything useful from him. He was not interviewed. In the whole of the Dyson report his name appears just once: 'On 2 August 1995, Mike Robinson, a BBC producer, wrote to Commander Jephson asking whether it would be possible to meet Princess Diana "to discuss an idea that would involve Her Royal Highness".'

No evidence has emerged suggesting blame should attach to the producer, Robinson having been drafted in by *Panorama* editor Steve Hewlett at a late stage to provide practical assistance. In getting Diana to talk, Bashir acted alone, managed only by Hewlett himself, in a way that has itself never become entirely clear. Hewlett died from cancer in 2017. Veteran *Panorama* reporter Tom Mangold says the lack of oversight was crucial, saying to me, 'All reporters are supposed to have a producer. The producer is the BBC's policeman, if you like. Martin worked directly to Steve Hewlett and because it was top secret nobody knew about it, which turned out to be a fatal mistake.' Robinson's career did blossom after the Diana interview. He was himself appointed *Panorama* editor in October 2000 and held the job until 2006. But the BAFTA was handed back, in 2021.

The interview would need two cameras, one looking at Diana, the other at Bashir to capture his questions and reactions. Tony owned his own camera, an Ikegami HL-V55, in 1995 a top-of-the-range piece of kit costing then more than a modest house, around £40,000. He hired in the second camera, a Sony, at £300 for twenty-four hours. But even the best cameras in that era, recording on to videotape cassettes, had a habit of mangling the image periodically, what Tony would call 'drop-out'. And so Diana's image would be recorded simultaneously, independently, in case the main camera should glitch. He said, 'I had a standalone recorder. So I would plug the main camera into that, recording Diana's output as a backup.' Two cameras and a separate recording machine to worry about.

That was just one of the headaches Tony knew he would have to encounter as he approached the Kensington Palace security barrier a few minutes before 7 p.m. that Sunday evening, already the sky over London glittering and whooshing with flying rockets. But they passed the police post without a hitch, Diana having rung down to say, 'Expect my hi-fi men.' Tony parked his Vauxhall Omega estate in the courtyard and the three of them got out. According to him, 'Martin knocked on the door. Diana answered. Martin said, "Hello, Captain! These are the boys. Tony and Mike." And she said, "Oh, nice to meet you, do come in. Call me Diana."'

The four of them walked up the stairs to the living quarters.

Normally in a situation like this, an interview with a public figure, the crew would ask, 'Where do you usually do it?' then follow a well-worn path. But of course here there was no 'usually', or indeed 'ever'. It was Tony's job to choose a spot, to decide the setting which would forever define Diana during this momentous hour in her life. He found the place. Not the biggest room, somewhere they called 'the boys' sitting room'. Nice fireplace. Curtains thick enough to stifle the crack and whistle and boom of the night. Plug sockets. Sorted.

The impact of the interview lies mainly in the words, of course, but there was such a haunting look about it too. Inasmuch as he instantly magicked an image which will live for centuries Tony Poole is our Holbein. Bashir and Diana went into the kitchen, where they would remain for the next one and a half hours. Holbein and Mike Robinson headed back down the stairs to begin hauling up those huge boxes. Cameras, tripods, lights, lighting stands, tapes, microphones and oh so many cables. The two of them shifted chairs. They hauled over a low table and arranged on it a few of Diana's framed photographs, all precisely aligned so as not to throw back a reflection from the massive lights soon looming overhead.

They were aiming to start shooting at 9 p.m. Tony felt the pressure, doing three people's jobs: 'I lit it. And then thought: *Bugger! I haven't put any microphones out!*' So he got the mics, tiny, with a thin cable, laid them on the arms of the chairs, ready to be clipped on to Diana and Bashir. Then with his headphones on he checked that the mics were working. Holding his breath for absolute silence. There, in the background? Some kind of low graunching? A hum? Diana's fridge. Tony knocked and asked, 'Could it go off?' He put his car keys inside the fridge. Thoughtful. Some cameramen wouldn't care, yoghurt and lettuce could go to hell.

A little after 9 p.m. Tony was ready. There was a feeling that something rather extraordinary was happening. The secrecy, of course, but also the minimal crew. There was a delicious frisson of need-to-know, an indie feel which would spill right through into the intimacy of the footage, secrets shared.

And for Diana too. No dresser, no stylist, no make-up lady. Those thin dark rings around her eyes were all her own.

It was Tony who decided to frame Diana just so, an inch or two *below* our eyeline. Because of that we look down slightly on Diana, but benevolently, the parent over the cot, not haughtily. To her right, just determinable, that massive fireplace surround and a dark pool of nothingness. To her left an occasional glimpse of a table lamp, a hopeful light. What we see for most of the fifty-four minutes is Diana's face, gliding a little closer one moment, pulling wider the next. When it seemed the subject matter was becoming especially personal Tony would ever so slightly touch the rocker switch on his camera. And Diana's face would glide closer still. At some moments the lower half of her face is out of shot altogether. Those eyes. This was something Tony had thought about: 'Previous February I think it was. We interviewed a guy who had a brainstem stroke, so he was immobile. Gurgling. Dribbling. But he could communicate by blinking. And so I framed him very tight. So it might bring him some dignity. I still get emotional about it. Best film I've ever shot, to be honest.'

Tony looked at Diana, gliding softly in, and then out again. The second camera, pointed at Bashir, that one just ran, nobody looking through the viewfinder. The backup recorder churned away. The tapes in each camera ran for thirty-two minutes and so roughly every half hour everything had to stop for a tape change. They recorded ninety minutes of material, nine tapes total. When it was all over Tony had a sense of relief. He had caught the odd snippet of course, but he was listening for glitches, not history: 'I wasn't aware of the "three of us in this marriage" stuff.' Bashir and Diana went back into the kitchen while Tony packed up, kit back in the boxes, table back against the wall. Diana came in with a bottle of champagne and Tony's car keys from out of the fridge. He could accept one of her offerings but sadly not both. He said, 'I couldn't drink of course. I'd got a forty-mile drive.'

It was half past midnight when Diana waved them off. For the police at the security barrier, five and a half hours those hi-fi blokes had been there. The plan was that Tony would drive the three of them to the home of the *Panorama* editor Steve Hewlett, three miles away, to drop off the precious tapes. Tony recalled, 'Steve was wetting himself, up past midnight and he hadn't heard anything at all. "Have they been arrested?"' They called from the car. The news Bashir had to impart to his fretting boss was good beyond imagining. Hewlett, who had spent the earlier part of the evening at a bonfire party, would later recall, 'I can't tell you the sense of elation. We've got this interview! The world and his wife wanted this interview. And we've got this interview with the Princess of Wales. In the can!'

And so, nine tapes. They had begun at 9 p.m., finishing at midnight, three hours, recording for only ninety minutes. The maths suggest a very leisurely pace, roughly half the time spent in conversation, off camera. And if ninety minutes were recorded, and only fifty-four minutes broadcast, that might seem to suggest a large amount of material that was never broadcast. The BBC says not. It is perfectly possible that much of that extra forty or so minutes could be eaten up with technical checks, battery changes, retakes for one reason or another.

I have always been more interested in the time spent when the cameras were *not* turning over, the hour and a half Bashir and Diana spent in the kitchen before 9 p.m., then the hour and a half between nine and midnight. Paul Burrell claims to know that the interview was less a matter of putting questions and having them answered, more a process of delivering prompts for soundbites. He said, 'It had been rehearsed. I know, from a later conversation. The princess told me. She had to get it perfect. They knew exactly what the questions would be, and how the princess would answer them. Princess Diana was coached by Martin, through the minefield of the interview.'

Tony Poole is not willing to go into how those gaps in the recording time were spent, and why should he? 'Of course there was chat, but . . . I have never revealed that. And I never will. That is not of public interest.' His discretion is part of the professionalism developed since he first joined the BBC in 1968. I asked whether, despite the momentous, historic nature of the job he had been called in to do, there was any regret that he had unwittingly been part of something less than wholesome. He replied, 'No. I did my job to the best of my ability. I didn't know about these forgeries and so on. That's it. I was very pleased with the pictures actually. Very happy with the lighting.'

14. 'YES!!'

Even *before* the interview aired it was headline news. On 14 November 1995 the BBC set all of Britain, a lot of the world too, on a giant guessing game with their announcement that Princess Diana would talk for nearly an hour with the virtually unknown Martin Bashir. And so there was astonishment not just about the interviewee but the interviewer too. If Diana had sat down with an eminent figure like David Frost, maybe a famous American like Oprah Winfrey, that might make sense. Or even one of the journalists she was known to trust, people like Andrew Morton and Richard Kay. But Martin Bashir? Here was someone who, as an ex-colleague unkindly put it, was barely a household name in his own household.

Working from tip-offs, or simply guesswork, some papers began to hint that Bashir had got his scoop by playing on Diana's fears. On 16 November the *Sun* headline read **'DI HAD EVIDENCE OF PLOT BY MI5'** and below it said, 'A close friend revealed last night that Diana agreed to tell her story to journalist Martin Bashir after he unearthed evidence to support her fears. The pal said, "*Panorama* does not get involved in heart-rending about Princesses sobbing on their shoulders. They reveal hard news stories."' Certainly the *Panorama* platform suggested that Diana had something to say; this was not a programme which did fluff. In one of the very few public statements he would ever make on the matter, *Panorama* editor Steve Hewlett would say, 'We started off looking at it, genuinely, in a very *Panorama*-y sort of way: Wither the royal marriage? What are the constitutional implications? He's the future king, she's the future queen. And if that marriage is falling apart, then that's a matter of proper public interest. I don't just mean prurient.'

Reporters were desperate to discover the merest whisper of what might have been said, but at the source lips were sealed. Patrick Jephson learned of the interview eight days after the recording had taken place, just before the BBC announced it to the world. He would write, 'We were sitting on the sofa in her sitting room . . . "Patrick," she said, eyeing me nervously, "I've done an interview for TV." "Really, Ma'am?" I said in my most neutral voice. "For which programme?" "*Panorama*," she replied . . . Something in her eyes told me it was lethally packed with dangerous aspects. "It's going out next week." She looked at me steadily. I looked back. *Oh shit*, I thought.' If Diana had said anything remotely similar to what Jephson had heard her tell her lawyer, then . . . what? What on earth *had* she said? ' "It's terribly moving. Some of the men who watched were moved to tears. Don't worry, everything will be all right . . ." "I'm sure it will be." I tried to sound soothing. "But can't I at least get Lord Mishcon to look at a tape of it so that you're protected from a legal point of view?" "No, Patrick. Everything will be all right . . ." '

Jephson and Mishcon, still reeling from Diana's astonishing testament of just a few days earlier, both tried to make the princess spill the beans. Jephson said, 'I drew on all my years of experience of her in trying to get her to reveal more. Her lawyer Lord Mishcon applied every form of persuasion, from avuncular sympathy to dire legal warning.' But nothing would persuade Diana to blab, pre-transmission. Even within the BBC, normally a nest of gossip, rumour and whispered secrets, the content of the interview remained rigidly confidential. Tony Poole said, 'I was working with Tom Mangold. And Tom said, "So Diana's done an interview for *Panorama*." I said to Tom, "But you don't know who shot it, do you?" And he said, "Was it you?" And I said, "Yeah."'

Finally, at 9.40 p.m. on Monday, 20 November 1995, the waiting was over: 23 million people would watch in Britain, an estimated 200 million around the world, in 100 countries. It is hard to believe that many people in the world today have not at least seen a still image from the night, Diana's eyes wide like a hunted fawn. The interview itself will be familiar to many people, certainly its most celebrated exchange.

BASHIR: Do you think Mrs Parker Bowles was a factor in the breakdown of your marriage?

DIANA: Well, there were three of us in this marriage, so it was a bit crowded.

It is a good line and brilliantly delivered, especially since at that point Diana was firmly of the view that the third point in the marriage triangle was not Camilla Parker Bowles at all, but Tiggy Legge-Bourke. In fact, Camilla, as Diana had explained to Lord Mishcon, was in imminent danger of being 'put aside'. Murdered, just like her.

One of the most arresting things about the interview, for anyone viewing as it aired thirty years ago, was Diana's wholly unexpected fluency, the ease and sometimes almost merriment with which she flipped back answers to the questions ping-ponging her way. Where had *that* come from? Almost exactly ten years earlier, in October 1985, Diana had given her only other lengthy interview, thirty minutes with

ITV broadcaster Alastair Burnet. That had been hesitant, smiley enough but each answer delivered through a fine mesh of reticence, the whole amounting to blandness. Her public speeches were good enough, but never sounded more than Words. Being. Read. Out. But here was a performance to match any A-lister on the chat show circuit, great stories emerging, with zingers too:

'She won't go quietly. I'll fight to the end.'

'I'm a great believer that you should always confuse the enemy.'

'I'd like to be a queen of people's hearts. In people's hearts.'

And it wasn't that they were all soft questions. Bashir wanted to know whether Diana had been nuisance-calling an old boyfriend, Oliver Hoare. He wanted to know if she had had sex with another boyfriend, James Hewitt. Astonishing stuff, but most astonishing was Diana's ability to volley back an answer so neat, so lightning-fast that confession and contrition melded instantly into an expectation of our compassion. On Hewitt:

BASHIR: Were you unfaithful?

DIANA: Yes, I adored him. Yes, I was in love with him. But I was very let down.

It was that section, roughly thirty-five minutes into the interview, which did bring proceedings to a temporary halt during the recording. Diana needed a moment to find just the right words. Tony Poole said, 'I remember Diana becoming flustered when he asked about James Hewitt. But she answered very cleverly.'

It was in the last five minutes that Diana delivered the

lines which she knew, and Buckingham Palace knew, were the ones truly intended to matter, where gossip left off and history kicked in. Did Diana expect to become queen? No. Should Charles become king? Well, it's complicated.

> DIANA: Because I know the character, I would think that the top job, as I call it, would bring enormous limitations to him, and I don't know whether he could adapt to that.

> BASHIR: Would it be your wish that when Prince William comes of age, that he succeed the queen, rather than the current Prince of Wales?

> DIANA: My wish is that my husband finds peace of mind. And from that follows others things, yes.

Extraordinary stuff. If it is possible to carry out one's own abdication, *pre-emptively*, then here that had just been done, by the woman history had marked out to be *Queen* Diana. And, in the very next breath, dismissal of the next *king* too. Here it is just possible to imagine the complex scenario which Diana saw unfolding, given what we know she *thought* was true at that time. She believed, thanks to Bashir, that the queen, heart disease, comfort-eating and all, had just six months left on the throne. Queen Elizabeth's abdication, set for April 1996, had been confirmed to Diana, as noted by Lord Mishcon. By that date the queen would have served fully forty-four years as monarch, perhaps earning the right to retire? Yet even so, abdication would still clearly prompt an enormous upheaval, a whiff of revolution in the air, just as when King Edward VIII had handed back his crown in 1936. Hereditary monarch is surely a job for life, or no job at all. If they come and go according to convenience, even doctor's orders, then why not have a president instead, where we all get a shout?

But if Queen Elizabeth herself was prepared to throw out the rule book, would Prince Charles not take the hint as well? Read the room, after all his carrying-on? If so, once the dust had cleared, once it was possible to see where the pieces had settled on the board, we would have *King* William, albeit a king only thirteen years old. No queen, for probably ten years or so. And in that vacuum, the sweet, misty netherworld conjured by Bashir that would be England 1996, the mother of the teenage monarch, Princess Diana, would occupy a place of power and influence far exceeding anything she had known to date. Far exceeding that of Charles too, finding peace of mind, at last, in quiet exile. King of Highgrove, Prince of Losers.

Little wonder that the *Panorama* interview footage is now held by the BBC to be something so toxic that the nine tapes are likely isolated in a vault, only to be approached by staff in full hazmat gear. The current director-general of the BBC, Tim Davie, declaring his horror following the publication of the Dyson report, would say, 'Now we know about the shocking way that the interview was obtained, I have decided that the BBC will never show the programme again.' Prince William, in his statement of 20 May 2021 said, 'It is my firm view that this *Panorama* programme holds no legitimacy and should never be aired again.' That reference to 'legitimacy' identifies the interview for exactly what it is. A piece of cruel fakery, conducted at the expense of the interviewee. Diana's close friend Rosa Monckton would write, 'The most chilling part, in retrospect, was when Bashir asked, "Do you really believe that a campaign has been waged against you?" Bashir was both the inventor and orchestrator of the very "campaign" he had the audacity to ask her about.'

What to do with the material has become a thorny question. Although the BBC may refuse to sell any more clips, and have already handed the £1.2 million earned since 1995 over to charity, the fact that the interview exists, that it was done at all, cannot be denied. Tim Davie said in July 2022, 'It does of course remain part of the historical record and there may be occasions in the future when it will be justified for the BBC to use short extracts for journalistic purposes, but these will be few and far between and will need to be agreed at Executive Committee level and set in the full context of what we now know about the way the interview was obtained.' In other words, the BBC have realized that they are the possessors of a hostage video, a somewhat historic one, but only showable if we are allowed to see the tribesmen and Kalashnikovs too, in wide shot. Of course anyone who wishes to study the full fifty-four minutes, at any point in history, will only ever need YouTube.

How to *feel* about the interview has also become tricky. For a long time the passages where Diana talks movingly about postnatal depression, about bulimia and self-harming, implicit thrusts at the Buckingham Palace machine and indeed any hopeless husband, were taken to be Diana sticking it to the man. But it turns out the man was all the time sticking it to her. Bashir's former colleague Jonathan Maitland, who worked with him for six years on ITV's *Tonight* show, has thought about this, writing a play called *The Interview*. Paul Burrell attended the London premiere in 2023. In Maitland's view the broadcast ban applied to the footage is just one more charge to be laid at Bashir's door. The bad smell that hovers over the interview has robbed Diana of her voice in the segments where she actually did have something very valuable to say. Maitland told me, 'Much of what Diana said was hugely in the public interest. But the chain of causation starts with Bashir and his wrongdoing. He gave them the knife to cut out her tongue.'

As regards the immediate reaction from Buckingham Palace, the closest thing we have to testimony from the late queen herself is the recollection of distinguished theatre director Sir Richard Eyre. Now aged eighty-one, he was at the time of the broadcast a member of the BBC Board of Governors. He recalled, 'I had lunch with the queen, not long after, and she said to me, unprompted, "How are things at the BBC?" And I said, "Oh well fine." And she said, "Frightful thing to do. Frightful thing that my daughter-in-law did."'

Patrick Jephson was on duty on the night of the broadcast, at Diana's side at a glittering charity dinner at London's Bridgewater House. He would describe later how he and lady-in-waiting Anne Beckwith-Smith, their duties over, then hastily rushed to view a videotape: 'We sat on Anne's sofa drinking her whisky. Groans and exasperated laughter rose like nausea to our lips. Then we uttered terse exclamations of horror. Finally we watched in silence until we could stand it no more. Anne switched off the TV and the ghostly face with the smudged, dark eyes faded from the screen. I emerged wearily from behind the sofa where I had taken refuge. "That's it," I said.'

What was the reaction from Diana's own close family? As almost every household in Britain prepared to watch the interview, at Diana's childhood home, Althorp, her mother and brother were also to be found in front of a TV set. Charles Spencer had exchanged only a few words with Diana since that fateful meeting of 19 September 1995, when he had first introduced her to Bashir. He had assumed Diana had heeded his warning about the reporter, but clearly things had been going on behind the scenes.

Spencer told me, 'The first I knew about the interview happening was when it was announced in the media. I didn't know it was happening at all. She hadn't told me.' On the night of the broadcast Spencer was hosting a visit by his mother, the then fifty-nine-year-old Frances Shand Kydd, remarried following the bitterly contested divorce from Charles and Diana's father in 1969. Mrs Shand Kydd had carved out an entirely new life for herself, living 400 miles away on the tiny Hebridean island of Seil, though she regularly returned to Althorp to see Spencer and her four grandchildren.

Diana had given her family no advance warning of what she was about to say, and so the effect was every bit as astonishing as for the millions more watching that night. Spencer told me, 'My mother was astonished, I think, because she came from a rather more old-fashioned way of doing things. But she was sort of proud that Diana had said what she wanted to say.' For Spencer himself it was clear that something had happened to Diana. Something was motivating her to speak in a way she had never spoken before. 'I always see Diana in that interview, it's rather like you read these horrible things about Spanish bullfights, where they attach a cattle prod to the bull before it enters the ring to give it extra pep. And I feel that this is what happened with Diana. You know, she entered the ring having been charged with unnatural forces.

'It wasn't the Diana who would have been interviewed two months earlier, who would have had a different view of Prince Charles. She thought all sorts of bad things about him that weren't true. But she had been told them. She had been told her husband was having an affair with the nanny. These are all very emotive things. And so what came out of Diana's mouth during that interview was not the distillation of Diana's experiences. It was the result of the lies she had been fed.'

The man who had fed Diana the lies, Martin Bashir, watched the show from the BBC *Panorama* office in London's White City, some thirty people in the room, including the programme editor, Steve Hewlett. Only he, Bashir and producer Mike Robinson knew exactly what Diana was going to say, giving the party the curious air of lads' night with the footy to watch, a live game, but three of the lads already aware that their team has won twenty-nil. Someone who was in the room that night has recounted to me the gasps, the shouts, the silences as each of Diana's astonishing revelations tumbled out.

But as the closing music swelled and the end credits rolled the room did not erupt into back-slapping. Instead Hewlett instantly flicked from BBC1 to BBC2. *Newsnight* was already live with the first startled reaction, Jeremy Paxman and guests, including Prince Charles's friend Nicholas Soames, like fugitives in a shelter still being rocked by echoes of a thermonuclear blast. It was only when *Newsnight* began to wrap, with shots of next day's front pages, each one of them carrying giant headlines trumpeting *Panorama*'s triumph, that Steve Hewlett slapped a hand down hard on the table. A big man, broad face, he jumped from his seat, raised both fists high and bellowed, 'YES!!' The coverage made it all so wonderfully *real*. The plan that Bashir had worked at so diligently, that would bring such kudos for the BBC, so many plaudits, awards, career jumps for the bosses, so much money, had gone like clockwork.

The next morning those newspapers sold in their millions as readers sought to pick over the astonishing details of Diana's disclosures. Because all this happened around year zero of the digital age, just before email and the internet, actual pieces of paper were flying everywhere the next day, to Bashir in particular. On 21 November he received that bubbling praise from Diana herself, her note declaring, 'Dearest Martin . . . There are <u>no</u> words adequate to express how I now feel having had my wings returned to me . . .' and signed off, 'Lots of love from Diana.'

On the same day, more love from Tony Hall, then the BBC head of news and current affairs:

21/11/95

Dear Martin,

You should be very proud of your scoop. It was the interview of the decade – if not of our generation. But equally importantly, you handled it with skill, sensitivity and excellent judgement. There were many pitfalls awaiting us – you avoided them all. I also think you have carried yourself during this whole episode in absolutely the appropriate fashion. You have changed the way we report the monarchy.

Thank you
Tony.

This from Hall to Steve Hewlett:

21/11/95

Dear Steve,

Just for the record – congratulations on a <u>brilliant</u> scoop. But my thanks too for the way you handled it. There were many man traps awaiting us, and you were vital in helping us avoid them.

With very best wishes,
Tony.

Hall also wrote glowingly to the producer, Mike Robinson. To the film editor who had cut the interview together, Ian Corcoran. 'Hero-grams' such things were called in the BBC.

There was nothing for Matt Wiessler, the graphic artist who had done Bashir that favour, late one night, at the end of August. But that wasn't something that worried him. He and his girlfriend Lucy, together in Matt's flat in Camden, had watched the *Panorama* interview go out, the two of them curled on a giant sofa in front of his twenty-inch TV. A lot had happened since that crazy all-nighter, making those strange bank statements for Bashir, three months earlier: 'Martin had never said a peep to me. But I remember saying to Lucy, "So is that what he was up to?"' Matt watched Diana, so candid. Bashir, so unctuous. The two of them together, so cosy.

And he began to feel a chill creep down his spine.

PART THREE
Covering Up

'Friends – on my husband's side – were indicating
that I was unstable, sick, and should be put in a home
of some sort in order to get better. I was almost an
embarrassment.'

Princess Diana, *Panorama*, 20 November 1995

15. The Morning After

So what was Diana's verdict on *Panorama*? Because of her death in August 1997, that is a question which can only be answered by looking at the scanty hard evidence, and considering what seems likely to be the most reliable witness testimony. Diana's letter to Bashir, the morning after the interview was broadcast, positively brims over with excitement: 'I never dreamt that such a response was possible and I am immensely humbled by the reaction.' But then it is difficult to see how it could have been any other way.

Patrick Jephson would write, 'She had lived for weeks and even months with the knowledge of what she was doing in preparing the programme. She had built up with delicious anticipation to the moment of emotional release in front of the cameras. The aftermath . . . was an anticlimax followed by bewilderment.' What Jephson saw was the flopped-out, hung-over host of what had been, yes, the funnest party ever, but someone now surrounded by spilled ashtrays, empty bottles, the carpet ruined and the credit card maxed-out: 'She had taken the biggest possible injection of her favourite drug, and now she felt even worse. After *Panorama* there was no way back.'

Diana's therapist, Simone Simmons, was an immediate witness to Diana's post-interview mood. She told me, 'I got a phone call the morning after the interview, seven in the morning. "Simone, are you busy?" she says. "Can you come over right now?" I said, "Can I have a bath and I'll come right over?" Which I did. She said, "What did you think of the programme?" I said, "Oh God, you made a real prat out of yourself. What about the boys there at boarding school? What do you think their friends are going to say now, seeing that you've publicly admitted to having an affair with a man other than their father? Don't think about *you* in all of this. It's *their* reputation with their friends."'

It wasn't what Diana wanted to hear. If Prince Charles could go on television to make his case, as he had with Jonathan Dimbleby in June 1994, then why shouldn't she? Simone Simmons recounted, 'She said, "Well, Charles admitted to adultery." I said, "It's one thing Charles admitting to it. The whole world knows about Charles and Camilla, but no, the whole world didn't know about you." Diana bitterly regretted it. And at one point, she actually said, "Oh my God, I could kill myself." I said, "No, you're not going to do that. What you're going to do is apologize to the boys, apologize to everybody that's involved."'

Many authors over the years have retold a story of how Prince William, thirteen years old at the time, is said to have watched his mother's interview alone, in a room at his boarding school, Eton. Most report that he was in tears by the end, though it is difficult to know how they can be sure. But there is one account which seems to have the ring of truth, mainly because it now also seems so artless. In 1996, before Diana's death, before freelance photographers became demons rather than swashbucklers in the public mind, two of Britain's then top paparazzi published a racy account of their daily hunt for pictures of Diana. The title of Mark Saunders and Glenn Harvey's book gives the flavour: *Dicing with Di*.

They tell how they tracked Diana to Eton, alone in her blue BMW, on Sunday, 19 November 1995, the day before the interview aired. From their hiding place they witnessed, it sounds like, Diana's final fraught attempt to explain to William what was to come the following night: 'The scene that was unfolding across the road was the most sensational I have ever witnessed. William appeared in no mood for conversation, Diana seemed to be pleading with him to talk to her . . . I leapt on to the roof of somebody's Ford Escort and looked through the lens . . .

'And what a picture it was. William was visibly upset. Diana seemed to be trying to explain something to him which he just couldn't grasp. As my camera fired William appeared close to tears. After a few more moments he walked away from Diana, making no attempt to kiss her or say goodbye.' If the talk that day was indeed about the forthcoming interview, then perhaps William's reaction, as he watched the programme go out, was exactly as those authors have said.

The two snappers add an aside which, though they were writing only months after the *Panorama* broadcast, would become horribly relevant when Diana was chased into that road tunnel in Paris the following year. Whatever benefits Martin Bashir had promised *Panorama* would bring her, it is unlikely that he pointed out that for the rest of her life Diana would become, from the paparazzi perspective, fair game: 'If Diana was prepared to bare her soul on television, she would now have to accept she had given up her private life forever . . . she could hardly complain if the press wanted photographs. After all, she was the one who had put herself firmly back on the front pages.'

How Diana's innermost thoughts on the interview wavered in the twenty-one months before her death is difficult to judge, though powerful evidence comes from her close friend Rosa Monckton. The two of them managed to escape press attention for a final holiday together in the

August of 1997, sailing off Greece largely incognito shortly before the tragedy in Paris. Diana's verdict on *Panorama* as shared with this witness at least has the merit of being her final thoughts on the matter. At the inquest in 2007 Monckton said, 'We returned from our holiday on the 20th August, and in fact the princess dropped me off at my home. I last spoke to Diana on the Wednesday before her death.' Monckton was asked to recall the interview:

COUNSEL: On the Martin Bashir interview, did you know that she was going to do that in 1995?

MONCKTON: No. She rang me on the morning that it was going to appear and told me that she had done it.

COUNSEL: When you saw it, what did you think of it?

MONCKTON: That it was a mistake . . . it was undignified and it would not help her boys, just exposing herself in that way . . . It is something that should be done in private.

COUNSEL: Did you discuss the programme after it had gone out?

MONCKTON: Only to the extent of telling her that I thought she had made a mistake. Which, interestingly, in Greece, she acknowledged that she had, all that time later. She wished that she had not done it, she said.

COUNSEL: But why did she wish she had not done it?

MONCKTON: Because she recognized that it was, you know, not a clever thing to have done. She very much regretted having done the programme.

Since Martin Bashir had come into Diana's life on 19 September 1995 her challenge had been how to combat the threats he outlined in such vivid terms, initially in that first meeting but also in those private sessions in the kitchen, in the underground car park, who knows where else. How stressful must it be to have the BBC confirm to you that your husband is conspiring to have you murdered, leaving to one side his affair with the nanny, and her abortion? Diana had responded, first with her secret testimony to Lord Mishcon, then the long hours of prep for the *Panorama* interview, the five-hour recording session on 5 November, the announcement to her husband, her mother-in-law, the world on 14 November. And then came the broadcast on 20 November. Stressful and exhausting as all that must have been, the next two months would be crazier still. Because life in Dianaland was certainly never predictable, never dull. To understand Diana's post-interview frame of mind it is necessary to picture the extraordinary carousel that was her life at this time, greeting presidents and prime ministers, being heckled by a crowd in New York, being threatened by lawyers in London, being ordered to divorce, by the queen, and whale-watching in Patagonia.

On the afternoon of Tuesday, 21 November, the day after the *Panorama* interview was broadcast to tens of millions of viewers in the UK, while hero-grams were flitting around the corridors of the BBC, Diana was already in a limo to Heathrow Airport with Patrick Jephson, heading for Argentina. And there is evidence that death threats were still on her mind. One of those in the travelling party was her friend of fifteen years standing, Roberto Devorik, an executive with Polo Ralph Lauren who would lunch with Diana a couple of times each month. Argentinian himself, Devorik told Diana's inquest how the princess insisted that, while she would use British Airways, he must take another plane, in case hers had been targeted for destruction by a bomb. Devorik said, 'She was concerned about my safety . . . When she said, "You should take another plane," it is because she always said that she tried not to fly with her friends.' In Buenos Aires two days later Diana returned to the same theme. Devorik added, 'She said she was speaking with Prince William. Then she said . . . that everybody was very annoyed in London and she said, "After this, they want to kill me," like, you know, "I really made a big one here."'

Seven thousand miles away in Argentina, Diana was at least able to escape the worst of the press attention prompted by the interview in the UK. But still newspapers and TV stations around the globe registered their astonished reactions, day after day. There were some reasons to be cheerful. A poll in the tabloid the *Daily Mirror* showed 92 per cent support for Diana, published the same day as photographs of the princess in a bobbing boat, off the far-flung coast of Patagonia, watching delightedly as a giant whale broke the surface and flipped its tail. The following day, in Buenos Aires, at the palace where Eva Perón once held court, Diana was welcomed by the country's president Carlos Menem. At only five feet five inches tall he was already five inches shorter than Diana, without heels, but the pictures show the two of them smiling, joy for the nation which only a dozen years before had been in a shooting war with Diana's people.

Then, after four days in the sunshine of the Southern Ocean, back to a wintry London and the brutal reality of life post-*Panorama*. Prime Minister John Major called by Kensington Palace to offer his assistance if Diana should require it. And on Monday, 11 December, back to Heathrow. Diana and Patrick Jephson boarded Concorde this time, for the three-hour flight to New York, where the princess was to be star guest at a gala attended by the city's biggest names, even thirty years ago: Donald Trump, Rupert Murdoch, Henry Kissinger.

Jephson recalled, 'Everything about the trip had encouraged a wistful sense of happier times. There were motorcades, Secret Service agents, adoring crowds and rooms full of rich, powerful and beautiful people to be charmed.' Diana showed the sparky self-possession the world had just seen for the first time in her feisty comebacks to Bashir on *Panorama*. 'During her acceptance speech at the awards ceremony in the New York Hilton, the princess even dealt with a heckler. "Where are your kids, Di?" someone shouted. "In bed!" she shot back, with a coolness that would have surprised anyone who remembered the tongue-tied novice public speaker of only a few years before. It also earned her the biggest ovation of the evening.'

And then back to London. On Thursday, 14 December Diana had her bruising public encounter with Tiggy Legge-Bourke, making her acid comment about abortion before the startled guests at a Knightsbridge hotel. Butler Paul Burrell offers evidence for how this part of Diana's plan instantly turned sour, for although Legge-Bourke had fled the room in tears, they turned out to be a sign of rage, not submission. She hired London's most feared libel lawyer, Peter Carter-Ruck, who issued a statement: '. . . a series of malicious lies are circulating . . . which are a gross reflection on our client's moral character. These allegations are utterly without the very slightest foundation.' At this point the queen herself stepped in, ordering her private secretary to conduct a discreet inquiry. In the closeted world of the royal circle this meant that the task actually fell to Diana's brother-in-law, Sir Robert Fellowes, husband of her elder sister Jane. The queen's man phoned Diana on 18 December. Burrell remembers that Diana was adamant: '. . . during the phone call she reported her allegations . . . that Tiggy had been having an affair with Prince Charles, and she had undergone an abortion. She even furnished the queen's office with a precise date.'

Fellowes established that, yes, Tiggy Legge-Bourke had consulted her gynaecologist twice in recent months but further than that there was nothing to report. A letter arrived from Buckingham Palace telling Diana so. Burrell said, 'The princess opened it with her silver paper knife and shook her head disapprovingly as she read the words. "Typical!" she said. "Paul, look at this." He had written, "Your allegations concerning Tiggy Legge-Bourke are completely unfounded. Her relationship with the Prince of Wales has never been anything but a professional one. On the date of the supposed abortion, she was at Highgrove with William and Harry. It is in your own best interests that you withdraw these allegations. You have got this whole thing dreadfully wrong."'

If what her brother-in-law was telling her was true, then the story offered to her by Bashir, whether supported by a 'certificate' or not, was entirely false. But Diana had not much more than twenty-four hours to ponder that before another letter arrived, one that would shape the short remainder of her life. It came on 20 December, delivered by royal courier from Windsor Castle. Patrick Jephson told me, 'The queen wrote to Princess Diana saying, "You must finalize the divorce."' The queen said that after consultation with the prime minister and the Archbishop of Canterbury it seemed to her that the best solution now was a speedy end to Diana and Charles's marriage. Jephson: 'I remember Diana accepted it, but she noted the irony. She said to me, "Patrick. That's the first letter she's written to me." I thought that was a terrible admission.'

Diana declined the standing invitation to spend Christmas at Sandringham, going to Althorp instead. It is not hard to imagine that Christmas 1995 for the Windsor family was nightmarish. For William, thirteen, and Harry, eleven, seeing Mum and Dad hating each other, and wanting them to stop, will have been ineffably sad.

In January 1996 there was one small piece of personal business which Diana had to conduct – an aftershock to the detonation of *Panorama*, a tiny twitch of the seismograph after the earthquake had long passed. An event that I know was to haunt Patrick Jephson for twenty-five years, until the BBC's cover-up of Bashir's plot finally fell apart. He has written about it eloquently: 'I too fell prey to the Princess's particular style of aggression, which with sinuous dexterity combined a radiant smile with a knife between the shoulder blades . . . It was my turn for execution.'

One evening in the second week of January, as divorce lawyers began to circle around the corpse of the royal marriage, Jephson made his way to Paddington station to begin his lengthy commute home after another testing day in the office. The 18.35 left on time but then an hour later was unaccountably halted just short of his destination of rural Westbury: 'I was sitting in a deserted railway carriage, staring out at a pitch-black Wiltshire, when with an immediate stab of dread I felt the familiar summons of my pager. I fumbled for the button to stop that awful, reptilian vibration. Then I stared uncomprehendingly at the stark letters.'

The Boss knows about your disloyalty and your affair.

The message was anonymous, though Jephson sensed immediately that the sender could only be the woman whom he had served for eight years, the woman he had seen daily, accompanied around the world, and back again: 'I had to read it several times before the enormity of it sank in ... I was practically in tears now, though whether from rage, self-pity or impotence I was not sure.' At that point in time he had no inkling that the inspiration for Diana's dagger thrust must be her confidential source at the BBC.

But the agony was acute, and cruelly compounded, he thought, by the timing. He told me, 'The clincher for me was that Diana knew exactly what time I got home, and the message arrived just as I would have been arriving at my door. But because there was a delay I got it on the train, which was a godsend.' It seems extraordinary that Diana was now not merely set on wounding him, but in a way designed to inflict the greatest amount of damage. Jephson continued, 'I had a newborn back home. I had a four-month-old daughter. I do look back on it and wonder how the hell I survived at all.'

It is impossible to know whether Bashir had freshly topped up his lies about Jephson, or whether Diana was drawing on the stock of falsehoods first unpacked on 19 September. With *Panorama* now a part of history it seems he had little to gain from continuing to batter a reputation that had already been destroyed. Jephson recalled to me, ruefully: 'She really thought I had betrayed her, was continuing to betray her. And I'm reminded of what she said in the *Panorama* interview: "I like to keep my enemies confused. That's my motto." Yeah. Well, if she was thinking of me, I was sure as hell confused.'

The following day Jephson confronted Diana. And then

he submitted his note of resignation. He described the phone call which followed: 'She was hysterical. Her voice lost all semblance of control and expressed instead the raw emotion of a soul in torment. The theme was repeated over and over, in tones varying from the plaintive to the vicious. What had she done to deserve this? . . . Eventually her voice became clipped, flat, cold. "I have to decide what to do about you." There was a click. She was gone.'

By 20 November 1995, by the time the end credits rolled on the *Panorama* interview, Martin Bashir's work was pretty much done. Like a pantomime villain, with a final twirl of the cape, a hiss and a scowl he could retire into the darkened wings. The lies he would tell in the future were not aimed at Diana, but rather to try to keep the hounds off his own trail. For that reason Bashir becomes only a bit player in the remainder of the narrative, the person who had set Diana careering towards disaster but not the person who might have prevented that disaster unfolding. The people with that power were four men and one woman at the BBC.

16. Fools or Knaves?

When I think through the extraordinary narrative of what happened to Princess Diana and those around her thirty years ago, I try to imagine not only how history will look at these events in the future but novelists and dramatists too, the *Wolf Hall* of 2525. It has always seemed to me that the impossibly rich brew of love, betrayal and then tragedy will live for centuries, the names as familiar to future generations as the schemers and plotters surrounding Henry, Cromwell and Anne Boleyn are to us. And because of that I suspect there is a small group of former BBC executives, retired now, whose names will live on in a way which they may find troubling.

The point was illustrated when one of them was summoned before a committee of the House of Commons, on 15 June 2021, to account for his role during the Bashir scandal. The archives record everything very formally, the witness described as 'Tony Hall, The Lord Hall of Birkenhead, former Director-General of the BBC'. After nearly an hour of fielding penetrating questions his face reddened, his voice rose a little and he said, 'I have been a public servant for thirty-five years. At the BBC running news. I then left and did public service running the Royal Opera House, which at that time was in crisis. I rescued the cultural Olympiad for the Olympics in 2012. And I came back . . . in 2013 to the BBC . . . I have done a hell of a lot for the BBC and, I think, for the arts.'

It was more plaintive than angry, a small outburst from which he quickly settled down. But I remember watching the broadcast from the Commons at the time and thinking, 'That is not how history works.' That the death of Princess Diana will probably trump rescuing the 'cultural Olympiad', whatever that was. Hall and his colleagues have written themselves into history alongside the technicolour villain, Bashir. The question is whether they will be remembered as fools rather than knaves.

Lord Dyson's report goes after Bashir full tilt. There is no nuance. He is a liar through and through. As to the people who might have halted the tragic process which Bashir set in motion, who might have caught him at the BBC, Dyson is circumspect. The BBC internal inquiry which Lord Hall conducted in 1996, described later, is written off by Dyson as 'woefully ineffective'. Yet the impression is given that it failed through a series of innocent misjudgements rather than any intention to suppress the truth. There are reasons to be concerned about Dyson's analysis, on this and other aspects of the scandal, dealt with in a later chapter. But since these BBC bosses will play a critical role in the next part of our narrative, the critical role in determining Diana's fate, who exactly are they?

At the very top of the BBC, the director-general at the time of the *Panorama* interview was a man, like Hall, later ennobled, John Birt. As editor-in-chief from 1992 to 2000, during perhaps the worst lapse in the history of journalism, he will certainly always be remembered as captain of the *Titanic*. But there are special reasons to suspect that what happened might *only* have happened under his stewardship, that he helped fashion the iceberg too. Birt came to the BBC in 1987, hired from the commercial broadcaster London

Weekend Television, first as deputy director-general, with a brief to reform the BBC's journalism. Birt's special target, the epitome of what he deemed must be done differently, was *Panorama*. The veteran Tom Mangold would say, 'Birt is a tall man with rimless glasses, a penchant for Armani suits, and a smile that would chill a rabid timber wolf. "My main task," he said, "was to take over the journalism." Never a truer word spoken. Attending a meeting with *Panorama* people, Birt was asked what he admired about the department's recent output. "Nothing" was the bleak reply.'

In a way that is difficult to credit thirty years later, Birt's tenure at the BBC, his widely perceived arrogance and simple unpleasantness, became in the late 1990s a matter of frequent public debate. Birt's style was captured by the country's leading playwright of the time, Dennis Potter, who in a widely reported speech described him as a 'croak-voiced Dalek', adding that 'fear and loathing were now swirling jugular-high' in the corridors of the BBC. The satirical magazine *Private Eye* began a popular, long-running feature, 'BIRTSPEAK', celebrating the BBC man's fatuous management jargon. The man whom Birt would succeed as BBC supremo, Michael Checkland, was to say: 'I don't know why they all think he's so bloody clever; he's only got a third-class degree in engineering.' But Birt managed to survive the jibes, overcome all resistance, all contempt, becoming in 1992 the twelfth person to be appointed director-general of the BBC.

We are lucky to have an extraordinarily detailed record of events within the BBC news and current affairs division at just this time, actually compiled by an anthropologist, Professor Georgina Born, formerly at Cambridge, now University College London, who was allowed access for more than a year to conduct confidential interviews, collect private diaries and simply observe with her expert eye as the turmoil initiated by Birt swept through the organization. When her lengthy study was published she wrote that she had become almost a 'psychoanalyst' for troubled BBC staffers. The corporation was, she says, 'an unhappy place' for many staff in the 1990s.

The anonymity granted by her academic focus allowed for candour, giving a chilling sense of what life was truly like in the BBC corridors of power. An executive in news and current affairs described how Birt's arrival in 1987 heralded a 'night of the long knives' where many of the senior staff in news and current affairs were simply 'booted out'. It was brutal, he said. A coup. But then those empty chairs had to be filled, somehow. The professor's informant says that Tony Hall, a middle-ranker but a Birt favourite, had his eyes set on perhaps becoming editor of *Newsnight*. Suddenly he found himself director of the entire news division. A common theme is the appointment of managers who came laurelled with academic achievement yet desperately short on hard-scrabble reporting experience. But then what story could *not* be chased down by a man thoroughly grounded in Chaucer, or *Sir Gawain and the Green Knight*? Before long, the professor was told, no one knew how to make films for a mass audience.

Birt's cheerless manner, his messianic zeal, prompted complaints at the time that he was Stalinist, which quickly turned into 'Birtist' as the label to identify both the old hands who had thrown in their lot with the new boss and the startled new appointees suddenly granted enormous power. Reporter Tom Mangold described the new regime in vivid terms: 'New flags had been raised to celebrate Birt's revolution. Even the dark Armani suits he and his acolytes wore resembled the uniform of the black-pyjama-clad Khmer

Rouge.' And Professor Born would write of Birt's new managing director of news and current affairs, Tony Hall, that he was widely perceived as 'more Birtist than Birt.' Birt had appointed a cohort of senior managers, their tenure seeming to be mainly dependent upon showing unquestioned loyalty in return.

As Birt himself records in his 2002 memoirs, battles behind the scenes were vicious and brutal. For one of his new appointees, Hall's deputy Samir Shah, in particular: 'All of my colleagues in BBC News and Current Affairs were affected personally at some point by the hostility to the reforms . . . Samir Shah's changes . . . had prompted a continuous stream of contempt, ridicule and vilification aimed at him personally. Once Samir had his bank and credit card statements stolen, and sent to *Private Eye*, who returned them to him, unpublished.' Samir Shah is, at the time of writing, the seventy-three-year-old chair of the BBC board, appointed in March 2024 to this £160,000 a year post. His remit includes the requirement to 'ensure that the BBC maintains the highest standards of corporate governance'.

And so, in the autumn of 1995, the milieu in which Martin Bashir operated was thoroughly chaotic. He was still a new boy on *Panorama*, the once-venerated programme now having been led by five different editors in seven years, where many of the experienced hands had been fired and replaced by people in key positions with, at least according to the anthropologist's study, little of the journalistic nous required to quickly spot a fraudster at work. When they learned that the unknown Bashir had pulled off the scoop of the century no one paused to say, 'Really?' Lord Hall was tackled on this during his appearance before the House of Commons committee in June 2021.

STEVE BRINE MP: Are you seriously saying that
nobody questioned how an interview with the wife of the
heir to the throne was granted to a junior reporter? Did
that not cross your mind, Lord Hall?

LORD HALL: Yes, we asked about how it had come
about, of course we did, but . . . Lord Dyson is very clear
quite high up in his report that an interview would have
happened anyway . . . an interview, according to Lord
Dyson, was very, very likely. In this sense, Martin Bashir
got it first.

It is impossible to pass by this little exchange without
noting how Hall grabs at the easy defence handed to him
by the Dyson report. To say that the interview was 'very,
very likely' is more or less to say, 'C'mon, she was up for it!'
And that is only a smidgeon away from, 'What the hell did
you expect?' Dyson's assertion, offered without the least evidence, allows Hall to pass over the campaign of manipulation
which Bashir carried out before Diana finally succumbed.

Perhaps the most bizarre aspect of the dysfunctional BBC
at this time, and one which profoundly affected the way the
interview with Diana was managed, was a bitter falling out
between Birt, the director-general, and the then chairman of
the BBC Board of Governors. In a story which does not
lack colourful characters, the BBC chairman, Marmaduke
Hussey, Dukie to his friends, is rainbow bright. Then sixty-
two years of age, this six-feet-five-inches tall, seventeen-stone
giant of a man was a hero of World War II. As a twenty-
year-old platoon commander in the Grenadier Guards he
was mown down by machine gun bullets in an attack on a
German stronghold, his right leg was amputated and the left

paralysed below the knee. After the war he embarked on a career in newspaper management, marrying in 1959 a young aristocrat who was already a close friend of the queen and would become her longest-serving lady-in-waiting, her close confidante and in time godmother to Prince William. When Hussey died in 2006 an obituarist said that he had 'turned himself into a caricature of a Wodehousian aristocrat', though mockery was most often tempered by affection.

Appointed BBC chairman in 1986 he started out as a strong supporter of Birt, overseeing his elevation to the top job in 1992. But soon the relationship soured, spectacularly, so much so that Birt would not speak to Hussey at all. Relations between the BBC's senior-most executive and its chairman had to be conducted through a bemused third party. A governor from that era, theatre director Sir Richard Eyre, said, 'I was at a Christmas party just after I joined the BBC, Marmaduke Hussey came up to me and he said, "Tell me, you know John Birt? Strange fellow, won't speak to me at all. Would you see if you could get John to speak to me?" So I called John the next day, and he said, "He's right. I won't speak to him. No point." So that was when I discovered what I'd walked into.'

The row between the two men was bitter; both describe in their memoirs backstairs manoeuvring to try to gather a majority among the twelve-strong BBC Board of Governors, each to eject the other, a battle being waged at exactly the moment when the fateful *Panorama* interview reared into sight. Birt would write, 'As the Hussey crisis gathered momentum, something happened which would have seemed a preposterous plot point in a bad novel: on 31 October 1995 Tony Hall told me that Diana, Princess of Wales had agreed to give an interview to Martin Bashir of *Panorama*.'

Doubt still exists over exactly when senior BBC managers, including Birt, were informed about the upcoming interview. The record preserved in the BBC archives says that Birt was informed not on 31 October but on Friday, 3 November, astonishingly just forty-eight hours before the most momentous interview in BBC history was due to be recorded. *Panorama* veterans like Mangold, who complain that on occasions Birt was so hands-on that scripts would be torn up or rewritten before their eyes, find that official account hard to accept. But whatever the truth of the timing, Birt has confirmed that he was determined to prevent news of the interview reaching the ears of Chairman Hussey. He believed that Hussey would tell his wife, Susan, she would tell her friend the queen, and Diana would receive a royal command to pull out.

Birt would say later, 'Marmaduke Hussey was really loyal to the monarchy. He was a Prince Charles loyalist. He was increasingly concerned about Princess Diana. On a number of occasions, he tried to poison her reputation with me.' Hussey was kept entirely out of the loop, learning of the upcoming broadcast only on the day that it was publicly announced. Birt knew the possible consequences: 'I realized that there would be major difficulties ahead and I said to my wife that I expected to lose my job because of it.' In rather an extraordinary move, shortly after the *Panorama* interview aired, the BBC chairman wrote privately to the queen apologizing for what the organization he led had just done. In his memoirs Hussey recalls, 'I did write to the Queen's private secretary on behalf of "the very many members of our staff who do not believe that this programme was our finest hour". I received a courteous letter in response.'

It is not necessary to take a view on the motives of those involved to say with certainty that had the internal inquiry conducted by Tony Hall in 1996 *not* been 'woefully ineffect-ive' – had Bashir's crimes been revealed while Chairman Hussey was still at the top of the BBC – then Director-General John Birt would have been quickly ejected from his job, the loyalists he had appointed following him through the swing doors. Hussey would have demanded Birt's head, with relish, had his existing fury over Diana's interview been compounded with the knowledge of how it was obtained. But Hall's inquiry was 'ineffective'. And instead of providing the full truth about the duplicity that had been uncovered, Hall presented only a partial account to a meeting of the govern-ors in April 1996, described more fully in a later chapter.

John Birt remained head of the BBC, continuing to over-see the corporation's journalism through its next major seismic event, the death of Princess Diana in August 1997. Birt was knighted in 1998, then moved on after thirteen years at the corporation. In February 2000 Birt received a further honour, taking his seat in the House of Lords, Baron Birt of Liverpool. His motto, as recorded in *Debrett's Peerage*, is *Ad Meliora*: Towards a Better World.

17. Breaking and Entering

In a way that is grimly poetic, the BBC's entrapment of Princess Diana, the lingering stain it leaves on history, was heralded by the discovery one night of a giant floating turd. It was around 7 p.m. on a weeknight in early December 1995 when Matt Wiessler leapt off his motorbike in the small parking area behind his Camden apartment block, skipped up the single flight of stairs to his front door, crash helmet in one hand, the door key already out before he reached the top: 'I remember, I was absolutely bursting for a pee.' Helmet on the hallstand, he rushed up the dozen or so steps to the bathroom. He went in, and there it was: 'This was someone who had not had a bowel movement in six months. That was not my shit. Someone had been in my flat.'

This shocker came at the end of a fortnight in which Matt Wiessler had felt the walls of his comfortable life closing in, contracting in a menacing way. He told me, 'I saw the film go out. I went, "That's gonna bring the royal family down!" And I just thought, "What have I got myself into here now?"' The mysterious forgeries which Bashir had asked him to produce at the very end of August had puzzled him, but not *worried* him exactly. Now they worried him a lot.

Matt was by this time an ex-BBC employee, three months into his new venture as an independent graphic designer. He was no longer a regular in the *Panorama* office and so two days after the interview aired, on Wednesday, 22 November, he phoned producer Mark Killick: '"Hi Mark, Matt here.

I recently did a job for Martin. I did some documents for him. A bit like the ones we did for Venables?" And he goes: "What?" And it then very quickly went to irritation, and he said, "Hold on, hold on, just send me what you did." ' The mention of the Venables film was an instant red flag. It recalled the *Panorama* episode which Wiessler, Killick and Bashir had worked on together a year earlier, investigating the finances of ex-England football manager Terry Venables. That film had required Wiessler to create a genuine-looking document on his computer, perfectly accurate in all the information it contained, yet a construct nonetheless. Why did the interview with Princess Diana require made-up documents at all?

Matt had handed the master copies of the bank statements commissioned by Bashir to the motorcycle courier waiting outside his door early on 31 August. They were long gone. But he had kept almost identical hard copies, rejected for tiny imperfections in the printing process. He faxed these to Killick, who immediately saw something suspicious. One of the payments was shown to have been made by a company called Penfolds Consultants, exactly the same name as had legitimately been used in the Venables film. As Killick told the Dyson inquiry, 'I was immediately suspicious about the veracity of these documents.' He believed the presence of the Penfolds name proved that the statements could not be genuine. In fact the whole thing looked highly dubious.

Killick said, 'The transactions cried out "look at me" in a way that simply would not happen in real life. There was a real possibility that the bank statements may have been used to deceive someone, and the likeliest target seemed to be Earl Spencer, who was widely known as the gatekeeper to Diana.' The next morning, 23 November, Killick went into work determined to confront Bashir: 'We met in the BBC canteen and I showed him the bank statements. I asked him what they were for and he was clearly very angry that I had the documents. He refused to answer my questions and told me that it was none of my business.'

The BBC is no different from many other outfits where knives appear immediately once the back-slapping is over. Steve Hewlett put it succinctly: '*Panorama*? It's a piranha tank.' Exactly who said what to whom, why and when over the next five months is still moot, but the key events can be described. Within four days of that first angry confrontation between Killick and Bashir proof arrived that the story had begun to leak from the piranha tank. The BBC received the first call from an outside journalist, the *Independent*'s Chris Blackhurst. A BBC press officer noted, 'Chris Blackhurst asked if *Panorama* was researching a programme on MI5 when it secured the interview with the Princess of Wales. He also asked if the programme had documents relating to MI5's reported role in monitoring Diana's movements, what her reaction was when the programme showed them to her, where had *Panorama* got them and how did we know they were authentic?'

Fleet Street was showing a definite interest, and a degree of knowledge. But nothing significant had yet appeared to panic the BBC. A further week passed before, on 4 December, Killick decided to take reporter Tom Mangold into his confidence. To the veteran of more than a hundred *Panorama* films these curious bank statements certainly looked fishy. Mangold told me, 'We went to see Steve Hewlett. He was rude, brusque, told us, "It's none of your fucking business." Killick said to him, "You ought to phone Princess Diana's brother, Earl Spencer. Maybe there's been some terrible mistake?"'

Matt Wiessler, now an outsider, was not aware of the rapidly escalating drama inside the *Panorama* office. He didn't know what to think, though on the evening of 11 December all that would change. That was the night he returned home to discover that he had been burgled. He told me, 'I lived on my own, I was pretty neat and tidy. I went into my bathroom and there's a massive shit down my loo. It's not that I forgot to flush because I did not do that. Panic set in. My heart was racing, thinking, 'Fuck! Who's in here?' I jumped around every room like Bruce Lee.' He rushed into the small bedroom next to the bathroom, the one he used as a study. He was relieved to see that his Mac Performa computer was still there, but something was missing.

Thirty years ago the commonest data storage method was something called a 'floppy disc', a kind of miniature external hard drive. Wiessler was a stickler for keeping his work area neat and tidy, but now there was a gap in the row of small plastic containers where his floppies were stored: 'I had one box with a little blue label on saying "Bash". That's where I kept the work I'd done on the bank statements that night. But it was gone.' Matt went back downstairs, looking to see if the burglar had taken anything else. The box of floppies was the only thing missing from the apartment. He looked for signs of a break-in but found nothing. Located as he was on the first floor, the only practical means of entry was the door he had so recently used. He said, 'The flat had one of those 1960s doors which was solid mahogany with three or four glass panels. That sort of glass you can't smash because it's got wire in it. So it was a really, really sturdy door.'

Matt had been invited to the following day's *Panorama* Christmas party at a canal-side restaurant in Ladbroke

Grove. There, another producer, Peter Molloy, would later tell Lord Dyson, 'Matt looked shocked. He said that his home had just been broken into. He added that this was not a normal burglary because the only thing stolen were the floppy discs that contained the backup to the bank statements he had created for Martin Bashir . . . I strongly recommended that he report this to the police as well as to the BBC.' The first of those suggestions did not seem like an option to Matt: 'I couldn't go to the police. What exactly was taken, Mr Wiessler? Well, these forgeries that I was working on . . .'

But Matt Wiessler was now determined to put his concerns on record at the BBC. He fixed a meeting with the *Panorama* editor but would come away disappointed. He said, 'When I went to squeal to Hewlett, he really didn't want to speak to me. I think he just wanted to see how I was behaving, how angry I was. And he sent me packing. He didn't say, "Goodbye, Matt, thanks for coming." He just said, "It's in hand," and turned his back on me in his office.' And so Wiessler decided to take it up with management. Two current affairs executives, Tim Suter and Tim Gardam, agreed to see him and now they heard about the burglary. They also heard how Wiessler feared that the forgeries he had produced for Bashir might have been used to get to Princess Diana. Suter would tell Dyson, 'He was now concerned that . . . he might now be being "set up" as the fall guy for this, not least because the disc on which he had kept the electronic version of the documents had gone missing, and he feared it had been stolen, and might have found its way to the press.'

Something was going on. And it was at this point that Tim Suter called in Mark Killick. The former producer told me,

'He took me into a side office just off the *Panorama* main floor and said, "Sit down there and write down everything you know." So I did.' Killick remembers that he put together a document of seven or eight pages describing everything that had happened since Wiessler first raised his suspicions over the bank statements. He said, 'The main point I was making was that they had to talk to Charlie Spencer about this, soon as. That was what this was all about. It was obvious to me that he's the person these bank statements were intended for.'

Killick's statement was compiled on one of the computers installed in the small office he had been told to use. He made a hard copy on the nearby printing machine and handed the document to Suter. With the hindsight of twenty-five years it turns out that this was a crucial document, the first indication that Charles Spencer might hold the key which would explain the growing mystery. It is a document which has disappeared completely from the BBC archives and, as will become clear, it is by no means the only one to do so.

Once Killick had left, Bashir was called in. As the record would later show he now deployed the first of many lies to emerge over the next four months, and somewhat similar to one of the lies he would go on to tell Dyson. He said that, yes, he had asked Wiessler to prepare two 'mocked-up' documents, but they were purely for his private research folder. He insisted that they had not been shown to Princess Diana, to Earl Spencer or to anyone else. And he could prove it. Bashir told his bosses that he would provide the best kind of exoneration there was, clearing him, and thereby the BBC, of all blame. Sure enough, three days before Christmas, a courier arrived at the White City building where

Panorama was housed. Inside a small ivory-coloured envelope addressed simply to 'Martin', in just thirty or so words,
Diana ended the possibility that the giant hoax which had
just been perpetrated upon her would be discovered, at least
not in her lifetime.

December 22 1995

Martin Bashir did not show me any documents, nor give me any
information that I was not previously aware of. I consented to the
interview on Panorama without any undue pressure & have <u>no</u>
regrets concerning the matter.

Diana

When Diana received Bashir's request for a note, dismissing the whole idea of forgeries, was the fact that these
suspicions had been raised at all not simply further evidence
of the 'dark forces' at work? An attack on Bashir was surely
every bit as much an attack on Diana herself, the suggestion
that she had been gulled into believing the most outrageous
falsehoods nothing more than an insult to her intelligence.
And of all the disturbing documents which feature in this
saga – the forgeries, fakes, 'mock-ups' and 'certificates' – this
document would have the most malign consequences of all.
It would make Bashir temporarily invulnerable, allow him to
gather his basket of awards, to become a celebrity in Britain, a millionaire anchorman in the US, to have it good for a
quarter of a century.

It would cause his bosses at the BBC either to stumble
ineptly, innocently, through the minefield that had opened
before them, or, from a less charitable viewpoint, to realize that they had been presented with a get-out-of-jail-free

card, just as they feared they might be approaching those terrifying prison gates. Certainly, at this point in the unfolding scandal, it served as a fire-blanket. Reflecting later, one of the BBC executives, Tim Suter, would say, 'We could all now relax for Christmas. We had had a scare, but had got through it.'

18. Whodunnit?

Christmas 1995 seemed to offer very little in the way of joy and good tidings for Matt Wiessler. But at least with work ceased for a while he had plenty of time to ponder his position. The big question was, who broke into his home? The burglary hardly mattered in one sense; the floppy disc would show nothing more than his work in progress on Bashir's fake bank statements. It was the fact that the burglary happened at all that worried him. As he saw it there were three likely suspects. He was well aware how crazy some of it sounded, but he drew up a list.

Number one: some shadowy, unknown figure from the BBC. He felt he could rule this out: by the time the burglary took place the really damaging evidence, the hard copies of the forged bank statements, had already been faxed to Wiessler's one-time *Panorama* colleague Mark Killick. The angry producer had confronted Bashir in the BBC canteen, brandishing his evidence, on 23 November. Bashir would also be fully aware that the floppy could not contain anything of further interest. How could it, since Bashir himself had been the only source of information as Matt laboured away? It seemed sensible to conclude that even if some terrified BBC executive had considered ordering a clean-up, then a moment's reflection would tell him that the horse had already bolted from that particular stable.

Number two: some unidentified, news-hungry journalist seemed possible. At the time the break-in happened Matt

Wiessler's name was already, if not exactly in the public domain, at least known to a handful of reporters outside the BBC. The first phone call looking for him by name came on 15 November, five days *before* the Diana interview appeared on air. That had been prompted by a piece in the London *Evening Standard*, actually written by a former *Panorama* reporter, Michael Cockerell. Though no longer a regular on the programme he was someone with close contacts within the BBC. His article was speculative, yet his background seemed to lend it authority. Cockerell reported that Bashir had been 'specially interested in the notion that MI5 and Special Branch had a hand in bugging the royal telephones and making the transcripts public'.

The piece certainly attracted attention from Wiessler and his business partner, Patrick Bedeau. As Matt recalled, 'Cockerell wrote a piece saying, "Isn't it odd that Martin Bashir did this *Panorama* interview? Bashir's got no royal connection." I remember that was a major discussion point in our little office. Because Patrick goes, "What the fuck is that all about?" Then Patrick got a phone call from someone wanting to speak to me. By then, I'm shitting myself: "Why is the media now showing an interest in me?"' And so the press were on to Wiessler. They knew he had had some kind of role in the upcoming giant scoop. It wouldn't be too difficult to find his address, the three-bedroom apartment he owned in Camden's Woodsome Road.

But even assuming these rival journos would be audacious enough to break the law, to sneak into the apartment themselves, or hire someone to do it, what kind of a story could they print which wouldn't immediately point to themselves, their newspaper, as prime suspects? Just like the BBC, this didn't seem to make sense. Which left the third entity on the list, something you could only really classify under the scary-sounding catch-all 'spooks'.

Stepping through into that looking-glass world required only the same suspension of disbelief which Diana herself had used, so many times. By 1995, after the Squidgygate tape, after Camillagate, it was broadly assumed, and not just by swivel-eyed loons, that some kind of government agency, MI5, MI6 or something so secret it didn't even have a name, was a furtive player in Dianaland. The tantalizing suggestion in that news story of 15 November '. . . that MI5 and Special Branch had a hand in bugging the royal telephones' seemed like just the thing that the spooks *themselves* would be keen to learn more about. Or, at least, learn more about who had spilled the beans on the 'MI5 and Special Branch' team in the first place.

And there was more. Only a week after the burglary at Wiessler's apartment there was another, this time at Mark Killick's home in the south-west London suburb of Chessington. He described to me how he returned home from the *Panorama* office at around 7 p.m. to discover that his study, on the ground floor, had been ransacked: 'There were things thrown around, papers everywhere, but nothing had actually been taken. I looked to see if they'd been in the rest of the house but no, they hadn't.' If this burglar *was* looking for copies of the forged bank statements, they would be disappointed.

Alerted to the possible danger by what had happened at Wiessler's apartment, Killick was already one step ahead. He told me, 'I'd put them in a folder and left them with a mate, just in case. So they were safe.' Unlike Wiessler, Killick did report his burglary to the police. He got his crime number, but since nothing had been stolen there was little interest in taking things any further. So was there a connection with what had happened at Matt Wiessler's apartment? Killick cannot be sure except to say that during five years in that property this was the one and only time he suffered a break-in.

Whether or not this second burglary was mere coincidence it served to convince Wiessler that he was in *someone's* cross-hairs. He had used his skills to produce documents which were extremely convincing forgeries. It seemed likely that they had been used, in some so far unspecified way, to achieve the biggest journalistic coup in modern times. But now someone seemed to be on the case. On *his* case: 'That was my concern. I didn't want to end up in court being told I'm a forger or whatever. I'd been through other *Panoramas* where I'm like, "Hold on, are we supposed to do this?" You know, your imagination can run away with you. And I started getting nervous. And Patrick of course, he goes, "You're fucking in the shit now!"'

Matt was inching from burglary victim to whistleblower. The person who pushed him over the line, now dead, appears only as a peripheral character in our narrative, but is someone without whom the entire story could well have remained under wraps. Michael Hill QC was then a sixty-year-old London barrister with a reputation as one of the toughest and smartest of lawyers. He had prosecuted in high-profile terrorist cases, including the Guildford Four. He had tussled, coincidentally, with Princess Diana's lawyer, Lord Mishcon, on opposite sides in a celebrated courtroom battle involving Jeffrey Archer. At this point in his career Hill was at the very top of his game. He was also an old friend of Matt Wiessler's soon-to-be mother-in-law, Penny Noble. Matt said, 'I spoke to a QC who was a friend of Lucy's mum. Very well known.

He said he hated speaking to me because I wasn't paying! He said, "You know how to get yourself into a mess, don't you?"'

The razor-sharp QC listened patiently as Wiessler explained about the forgeries he had made. How he had raised his fears with bosses at the BBC, but to no obvious effect. How someone had burgled his apartment. And then, free but sage, came the expert's opinion: 'He said, "Get the news out, before the news comes to you." It wasn't inconceivable that when this went off the rails it could end up in court. Martin could end up at the Old Bailey. It's very hard then to say, "Well, I wasn't a co-conspirator." If you weren't, why did you remain silent?'

Stories as lurid as ones involving forgeries, burglaries, possibly spies and a princess are too good to stay hidden for very long. As January 1996 turned into February, then into March, as spring beckoned, this one crept closer to bursting into bloom. Late one night in early March a freelance journalist, Mark Hollingsworth, received a call from a trusted source within the BBC. Though nervous about sharing too much on the telephone his source said that something very bad had happened, that the BBC appeared not to be dealing with it, and the only thing which might prompt some action was publicity in a national newspaper.

Hollingsworth met his contact the following evening at the St Ermin's Hotel near St James's Park. The extraordinary tale of the forgeries, the burglaries, the barely supressed scandal bubbling in a corner of the BBC White City building went into the reporter's notebook. There was just one problem. Someone with an insider knowledge of the London media world might be able to link Hollingsworth and his source from a past experience. And so Hollingsworth passed on what he had learned in a detailed memo to the then editor of the *Mail on Sunday*, Jonathan Holborow. Another reporter should take over. And what they first needed to do was to talk with Matt Wiessler.

Just a few weeks earlier the graphic designer had moved location. The Camden flat had been sold for £80,000, funding the purchase of a quirky single-storey home on Trowlock Island, a tiny dot in the River Thames near Richmond. The island is reached by a narrow footbridge and in March 1996 it had been crossed, many times, by people seeking out the by now highly wary thirty-three-year-old Matt Wiessler. The tabloids were on his case. It came to a head on a Sunday morning with a half-dozen reporters from different papers, photographers snapping away as Wiessler came to the door.

Matt told me, 'I remember the guy from the *News of the World* was just loud, brash, rude. Standing on the island in the little path in front of my house. I open the door and he just shouts this abuse at me: "Are you the forger? You're the forger! Did you sell this to Martin Bashir? What's your involvement with Martin Bashir?"' One of the group carried himself rather differently. The *Mail on Sunday*'s Nick Fielding was urbane and softly spoken, waiting for the clamour to die down: 'Nick Fielding was standing there and he said, "You don't really want to speak to those guys. You want to speak to me." And I said, "Well, in that case, why don't you come in for a cup of tea?" And the others were just like, "Bastard!" and walked off.'

The shouting that morning on bucolic Trowlock Island helped Wiessler understand something profound about the press. In a case like this, even if they have only half the story, they'll do it with you or without you. Nice or nasty. Within days a story was likely to be strung across someone's front page and Matt Wiessler would either be a villain, the forger, or a hero, the whistleblower. The choice was as stark as that, and it was the unspoken starting point as Nick Fielding and Wiessler became acquainted over their cup of tea. Fielding already knew the basics; what he needed now was confirmation and, crucially, copies of the forged statements.

Fielding told me, 'The first thing to do was to try and establish whether the story was true or not. To get this into the paper, and to get it right, it required a specialist. Somebody who knew how to handle this kind of material and would not make a mistake on it.' He proposed a deal, finessed in later meetings, whereby Wiessler would provide a signed statement describing exactly how he had been asked to produce the statements, in a rush, and how they had then been delivered to Heathrow Airport.

In fact, that was all he *could* say. At that point in time Matt had not the faintest idea what Bashir had done with the forgeries. He knew nothing of his meetings with Charles Spencer at the splendid stately home, the meeting with Spencer and Diana together in the fancy Knightsbridge apartment. He knew nothing of Bashir and Diana cooking up pasta, or sitting huddled together in underground car parks. The last thing Matt knew about was that motorcycle courier disappearing into the August dawn light, before he wandered wearily back up the concrete steps to his front door. But the little he did know was more than enough. For the *Mail on Sunday* the mere existence of the forgeries promised to be massive news.

Fielding explained that his paper would make it clear that Wiessler was simply acting under instructions. Yes, the bank statements might be forgeries, but it is what you do with them that counts, surely? Fielding said, 'He was effectively a functionary, somebody whose job was to do what he was told by his bosses. He's not got any input whatsoever into the editorial process.' All that made perfect sense. But when this appeared in the paper, what would it do for the career of a young, newly freelance graphic designer whose main client happened to be the BBC? For the last three months the phone had hardly rung at all. What about the next three, after the *Mail on Sunday* had gone to town?

Fielding knew where the conversation must ultimately lead: 'We were willing to compensate him for that information. Quite often you have to pay somebody a fee because of the risk that they're taking, the loss of their livelihood, all sorts of other reasons which are entirely legitimate.' Matt had plenty to think about. One journalist outside his door had called him a *forger*, a criminal. The one across the table was offering to write a piece which would make it clear he was innocent, a stooge maybe, but an innocent one. He would need a couple of days in which to decide.

Matt needed to speak to two people. The first of them, the eminent, usually very pricey, barrister Michael Hill QC, offered wisdom born of a lifetime's experience in the law. Matt recalled, 'He said no matter what happens, I have to clear my name. Stand up, say it the way it is. That's what Michael Hill told me to do and I thought, "He's an eminent, two-grand-a-day sort of guy."' The second person he needed to talk to was Martin Bashir. 'I phoned up Martin and I said, "Look, I'm going to make a public statement because I think you guys are up to no good and this is your last chance to meet me and tell me what's really going on." So he said, "OK. Where should we meet?" And I said, "Well, what about somewhere in Clapham High Street?" "OK, I'll turn up."'

The venue was a pizza restaurant. Wiessler remembers that it was an intensely cold, frosty mid-afternoon, only a waitress hovering as a sad little scene played out: 'It was the time of day when you could get away with just having a coffee sort of thing. I'm sitting there drinking a glass of water. He comes ten minutes late.

'And he said, "Why are you talking to anyone anyway?" And I said, "Because I don't believe what's going on. And the press is all over me. I've had people at my door."

'He said, "That's all sour grapes." And, you know, "They're just trying to ruin my career. I'm a black guy da da da. And, you know, don't speak to the press any more." And I said, "I'm going to have to make that decision myself." And that's the last I spoke to Martin, ever.'

19. Whistleblowing

Matt Wiessler had an excruciating decision to make, neither option good. The prospect of shame, maybe even criminal prosecution on the one hand. The likelihood of a promising career in ruins on the other. There was one thing Nick Fielding could offer to speed the choice. If Wiessler would provide a sworn statement, and copies of the forgeries Bashir had asked him to make, the *Mail on Sunday* would pay £50,000. And so, cheque-book journalism? Fielding says not: 'He could have got a lot more money from one of the red-tops. In particular, the *News of the World* would have given an enormous amount of money for the story. I don't think this was a story driven by money, let's put it like that. His concerns were ethical questions.'

And so it was that Matt Wiessler decided to become a whistleblower. For Nick Fielding the prospect of holding the BBC to account was enticing: 'We worked on this very hard over a number of weeks. There was an awful lot to tie up because not only did we have to check out that Matt was telling the truth, we had to investigate the information that was contained in these documents. And that opened up a whole new area.'

The BBC realized that Wiessler was talking when on Saturday, 23 March 1996 the *Mail on Sunday*'s executive editor John Dobbie rang BBC executive Tim Gardam to say the paper had confirmation of the existence of the forgeries. He believed they may have been shown to Charles Spencer and to Diana too. It is likely that Gardam had been dreading just such a call at some point, ever since he first heard Matt Wiessler's anguished account of his burglary, shortly before Christmas. He said he would make inquiries. He spoke to Bashir, who repeated his assurance that he had shown the documents to nobody, not Diana, not Earl Spencer, no one. The newspaper was given that response, but they didn't give up. And so late that night Gardam called Bashir again. And this time he crumbled.

Gardam, the sixty-five-year-old former BBC boss, related to Lord Dyson on 16 February 2021 his utter horror on learning that, yes, Bashir had shown the forgeries to Spencer after all. He said, 'I remember absolutely crystal-clear, because, you know, it was one of those moments when you just go cold, and I know exactly where I was standing at the time . . . I actually took a great effort not—to keep temperate, actually because I was absolutely staggered that a BBC journalist . . . could have behaved like this. It would never have occurred to me that a BBC journalist would lie to produce something to deceive someone, and then at the same time lie to his editor and managers.' Horrifying as it was, that crucial piece of knowledge, that their reporter had commissioned two forged documents, passed them off as genuine to Charles Spencer, and then lied three times before admitting it, would remain covered up by the BBC for more than a quarter of a century.

The place that information did *not* appear, most notably, was in the *Mail on Sunday*, a fortnight later on 7 April when the story sweated over by Nick Fielding splashed in large print across the front page: **'DIANA'S BBC MAN AND FAKED BANK STATEMENTS'**. The story certainly raised questions, seemed to hint that something very sinister had taken place. But it was less than a sensation. The BBC had ensured that the information which had so horrified Tim Gardam was entirely absent. A statement from the press office in response to the story, approved by Tony Hall, would read, 'The draft graphic reconstructions on which this story is based have no validity and have never been published. They were set up for graphics purposes in the early part of an investigation and were discarded when some of the information could not be substantiated. They were never connected in any way to the *Panorama* on Princess Diana.'

The intention was clearly to suggest that Bashir's bank statements were materials commissioned for a programme but then later set aside, rather than blatant forgeries passed off to a member of the public. Nick Fielding, who at that point had no means of detecting the subterfuge, told me, 'They gave us a statement saying that they had been "mocked up" for a story which had proved inconclusive, and therefore they had disregarded the documents. That is, in my view, a cover-up. Too many people had too much to lose.'

Journalists from other papers called the BBC to follow up on the *Mail on Sunday* exclusive. One of them was Chris Blackhurst, the *Independent* reporter who had been chasing the story ever since the *Panorama* interview five months earlier. On the morning the *Mail on Sunday* story appeared he put the critical question to the BBC, as recorded on 7 April by the BBC press office archive: 'Blackhurst called again and asked, "Had the statements been shown to Earl Spencer?" . . . said we had nothing further to add.' The key admission, that the forgeries had been passed off to Spencer as *genuine*, was not made by the BBC. Nor, critically, could the *Mail on Sunday* elicit that confirmation from Spencer himself.

So why did Spencer not come forward to denounce Bashir? He told me, 'The reason is very straightforward. What Diana had done was extremely controversial. And I didn't want to say or do anything that would look in any way questioning of her decision. So I left it alone, I just stood aside. Not out of any other instinct except to not rock the boat really, for Diana. I couldn't care less about Bashir. But I felt if I queried it in any way it would add fuel to those who were criticizing her decision.' He says that to have come out as a strong critic of Bashir would have been in effect to paint his sister as a gullible fool. Far better to say nothing than open up a family rift.

When Spencer was approached by the *Mail on Sunday*, asking him to comment on their story, he was guarded. An avowed enemy of the press, at that very time heavily involved in a libel action with the *Daily Express*, he wanted nothing at all to do with Fleet Street. By April 1996 he and his family were already relocated to South Africa, in large part to escape the kind of intrusive media coverage he had come to hate in England. He told me, 'I went to South Africa to bring my children up in a place remote from that. And so I rather consciously turned my back on the media in England. I know it sounds odd, but I never really was that interested in the press coverage of Diana. It was lovely to see her doing good things, but I wasn't slavishly reading *Hello!*. So I think I was in a sort of slightly parallel universe to what was going on over here most of the time.'

In April 1996 Spencer was never informed by the BBC that the documents he had been shown by Bashir were in fact forgeries. Bashir's meetings with Diana, over pasta in the Kensington Palace kitchen, in dimly lit underground car parks, were not something Spencer knew anything about.

When he saw his sister's interview air on *Panorama* on 20 November 1995 he was as astonished as the rest of the millions of viewers. And so the one person who might in other circumstances have lifted the lid on the scandal did not do so, for a complicated set of reasons.

The issue of whether the BBC actively decided *not* to contact Spencer is critical. The BBC say they did try, though exactly how is not at all clear from Lord Dyson's report. Whatever communication there was passed through *Panorama* editor Steve Hewlett, dead since 2017, and, perhaps remarkably, leaving no written evidence on this or any other aspect of the scandal which has survived in the BBC archives. The two executives who took charge of events in April 1996 were Tony Hall, later to become BBC director-general, and the acting head of weekly programmes, Anne Sloman. Of them Dyson said, 'They never even tried to contact him and invite him to answer some of their questions ... I am satisfied that, if approached by the BBC in April 1996, Earl Spencer would have been willing to answer their questions ... His unhappy relationship with the tabloid press did not mean that he would be unwilling to speak to the BBC. Again, he was not asked.'

By an extraordinary coincidence there was one BBC executive who *could* have picked up the phone to Spencer at any time and been assured of a friendly reception. Tim Suter, the first manager to hear of Matt Wiessler's concerns, and in the spring of 1996 working right alongside Hall and Sloman on the developing crisis, had actually shared a house with a young Charles Spencer years earlier. Spencer explained to me how, at the age of eighteen, his final term at public school was spent not inside Eton itself but in accommodation just outside. And there to look after him was a young English

Prince Charles and Princess Diana during their state visit to South Korea, November 1992. Their formal separation was announced the following month.

Patrick Jephson and Princess Diana at the Burghley Horse Trials, September 1989.

Charles Spencer at Althorp, July 1999.

Matt Wiessler, graphic artist and whistleblower, summer 1996. Unknown to him he had already been blacklisted by the BBC.

Princess Diana and Martin Bashir, recording the interview on Sunday 5 November 1995.

Martin Bashir receives an award from the Television and Radio Industries Club, 12 March 1996. Two weeks later he will secretly confess to BBC bosses that he had employed forged documents, and then lied about doing so.

Steve Hewlett, editor of *Panorama* in 1995, who died in 2017.

Tony Hall, in charge of investigating Martin Bashir in 1996. BBC director-general from 2013–20, now a member of the House of Lords.

Tim Gardam, the BBC executive who first learned of Bashir's forgery activities on 23 March 1996.

...ne Sloman, the BBC
...cutive who conducted
...voefully ineffective'
...estigation yet compiled
...ighly revealing record
...events.

...m Suter, BBC executive
...the heart of events, and
...ormer housemate of
...arles Spencer.

John Birt, BBC director-general 1992–2000.

Marmaduke Hussey, Chairman of the BBC from 1986–96.

ony Hall and Tim Davie, together at a Buckingham Palace garden party, May 2024.

arles Spencer and Prince William follow Diana's coffin on the day of her funeral, eptember 1997.

Lord Dyson, whose report was published on 20 May 2021.

Andy Webb and daughter Effie, preparing to face the BBC legal team in court, June 2024.

teacher, what in Eton terminology they called a 'beak', Tim Suter.

Spencer told me, 'At Eton in those days if you wanted to try for Oxford or Cambridge, you had to stay on for an extra term after A level. I was allowed to "live out", it was called, in what was known as a "colony of beaks", little places where bachelor masters lived. And I lived with three masters, one of them being Tim Suter. He was a junior English beak. I lived for thirteen weeks with this bloke. Having breakfast with him every day.'

A career change took Suter from schoolmastering to broadcasting. During his inquiry it appears Lord Dyson was not aware of the long-standing personal connection between Spencer and Suter. But he did pose an important question. Dyson wrote, 'I asked Mr Suter why it had not occurred to him to approach Earl Spencer to ask for his version of events. Mr Suter replied, "I don't think that I would have been the person in the position to take that decision, to be honest . . . it would not, I think, have been for me to pursue a conversation with Earl Spencer."' He did not consider it his job or that he had authority to do so.

It seems to me that, notwithstanding Spencer's generalized loathing of the media, the single journalist in the world who could have picked up the phone and said, 'Hey Charles! Whassup?' was this man who had shared a house with him for three months. After a couple of minutes of pleasant reminiscence might he not have then said, 'Curious thing with one of our reporters. Chap named Bashir. What's it all about?' That kind of coincidental personal link to a hard-to-reach celebrity is something that reporters dream of. But Spencer's phone did not ring.

Dyson, correctly, says that because of their BBC credentials

Spencer would in fact have readily spoken to either Hall, Sloman or Suter. He would have given them a confidential briefing on what Bashir had done. Had they called him, Spencer would also have learned, for the first time, that the documents he had been shown by Bashir were in fact forgeries, prepared by a graphic artist at the BBC. At that point, in April 1996, the whole scandal could have been brought to light, with profound consequences for Princess Diana most of all. Reading the Dyson report one gets a sense that this is the *critical* moment, raising a critical question. Were the BBC bosses, in particular Sloman and Hall, *really* trying to discover what happened, or were they not?

It is important here to say a little about one vital document which will feature many times as the story unfolds. This is an eight-page memorandum, composed by Anne Sloman, dated 22 April 1996. For me, as an investigative journalist, I realized on first seeing Sloman's memo that it was pay dirt. Its value is that it not only provides a record of events from the period in which Bashir first met Diana to the point where the cover-up was in full swing six months later, it also makes frequent reference to *other* documents. Ones which, as we will see, would later disappear from the archives in mysterious circumstances. And so Sloman's memo is like a treasure map. The treasure may have been dug up, but at least her map tells us that it *did* once exist. And also where it had been buried, before being spirited away.

It has often occurred to me that someone doing a thorough clean-up job in the archives would have been far smarter to remove not just the *treasure* but this treasure *map* as well. But that would be to suggest some sinister motive. The BBC, despite being asked by me many times to explain, have never given more than a cursory answer to my question:

'So what happened to the crucial incriminatory documents which disappeared from the archives?' And their refusal to explain has been given a huge boost by Lord Dyson's own lack of curiosity, the BBC's official position now being, in effect, 'Lord Dyson did not ask, so why should you?'

And of course the BBC's reluctance to go into the issue of the missing documents leaves open the possibility of all kinds of possibly *innocent* explanations. Perhaps they simply wafted away, through an open window? Or fell behind a radiator? Perhaps they were eaten by mice? There are all sorts of perfectly innocent explanations for how these documents might have gone missing. But at least the Sloman memo tells us that these vital documents did exist at one time.

The memo is a fascinating document in other respects. It ends with the chilling words, 'The Diana story is probably now dead, unless Spencer talks.' Wow. That is right on the nail. And the author of those words, written in April 1996, appears to have recognized just how ballsy they still sounded twenty-five years later. Anne Sloman, summoned by Lord Dyson on 19 February 2021, said to him, 'It sounds a bit like the mafia, but it wasn't meant that way, I promise you.'

SUMMARY

1.   The Diana story is probably now dead, unless Spencer talks. There's no indication that he will.

An internet search reveals Anne Sloman to be a woman who went from the BBC to serve at a senior level within the Church of England, who has received an OBE, and in 2012 was rewarded by the Archbishop of Canterbury with the Cross of St Augustine for 'exceptionally distinguished service'. She is clearly a person who gets things done. Her encounter with Lord Dyson also seems to reveal someone whose approach to moral issues is pragmatic. When challenged by Dyson on Martin Bashir's repeated lying, there was this exchange:

DYSON: Let's be blunt: he wasn't honest, was he?

SLOMAN: No, not all the time . . . I mean . . . let's be careful before we make . . . a grand moral judgment. We are not all divided into honest and dishonest people. I mean, some people are congenitally dishonest, like criminals and so on, but very few of us who would regard ourselves as being honest have never actually told a fib. Have you never not told a fib . . . ?

I have no first-hand experience of Anne Sloman. But for the veteran *Panorama* reporter Tom Mangold, interrogated by Sloman in early 1996, the memory of her remains vivid. Mangold told me, 'Tony Hall sent a lady called Anne Sloman as his investigator. He sent her into *Panorama*'s offices. She patrolled the corridors and listened in on conversations. She was sent to spy on us. I mean, I've never seen anything so pathetic. It was sad, but it happened. I was marched in front of Sloman and she spent a lot of time trying to find out from me who were the jealous reporters? Who were the trouble-makers? Who was phoning their Fleet Street contacts? Was I one of them who had leaked? And I said nothing. I'd seen a shitstorm coming and I just thought, "I'm going to stay out of it."'

For this long-time BBC foot-soldier the battle raging internally was uncommonly brutal. He told me, 'I've seen the BBC in many crises in my forty-three years with them.

And what happens is that the wagons are immediately circled. You wait for the Indians to stop throwing the tomahawks, and you hope you can come out at the end of it. Things will be as they've always been before. But it wasn't going to happen. There was absolute chaos. It was just a terrible, terrible time.'

In short, Anne Sloman's memo provides by far the most important guide to what went on behind the scenes at the BBC during this crucial period. Recalling that time, Lord Dyson also listened to an account of how Hall and Sloman interviewed Bashir, on Wednesday, 17 April 1996. According to Hall this was a tough encounter: 'We pushed Martin Bashir hard on the details because we were very concerned that he had lied to the BBC . . . my recollection is that by the end of the meeting, Martin Bashir was in tears and came across as completely remorseful.' By the time of this meeting Hall was already aware that Bashir was a serial liar, a fact established by his colleague Tim Gardam three weeks earlier when Bashir had finally confessed to him over the phone. But during the tearful interview Bashir told still more lies. Unfortunately, Hall says, he and Sloman did not spot them. That on *this* occasion they firmly believed that Bashir was telling them the truth.

Summarizing this encounter, Dyson writes, 'In these circumstances, it is puzzling that Lord Hall and Mrs Sloman accepted Mr Bashir's account.' Puzzling indeed. Dyson goes on to offer a suggestion as to why Hall and Sloman, among the most senior and highly paid journalists in the UK, might have responded as they did to Bashir: 'He is a persuasive and charismatic person as Princess Diana discovered during the *Panorama* interview. It may simply be that he successfully worked his charm on Lord Hall and Mrs Sloman.'

Certainly Hall and Sloman remain adamant no form of cover-up was ever intended. And so one is left to decide, was Bashir able to get away with it here because he was such a charmer? A rogue who melted the hearts of a couple of old softies? Were his inquisitors simply too trusting for their own good? And was this gullibility fed by the wave of sackings which would roll through the BBC's upper floors if Bashir was exposed? Who can say?

20. Chairman of the Board

By the time of that tearful meeting on 17 April 1996 it appeared that the small knot of BBC executives charged with managing the scandal had weathered the media storm, just. One of them, Tim Gardam, had actually left the BBC. Tony Hall, Tim Suter and Anne Sloman remained, hoping that by now the worst was over. But one critical encounter was still looming. The final test would be a meeting of the BBC Board of Governors, just one week later, on 25 April. And the task of addressing the twelve men and women – two lords, three knights, business titans, academics – in the ornate council chamber of New Broadcasting House fell to Tony Hall. He had prepared notes for the meeting, which I was finally able to extract from the BBC after a long, drawn-out battle using Freedom of Information law.

These notes show that, once again, as with the BBC's response to the media, the issue was not what to say, rather what to leave out. Hall would not reveal that forged documents had been passed off to Spencer as genuine, nor reveal that Bashir had lied. It was in all respects a remarkable performance, ensuring that the governor watchdogs did not growl, much less bite.

This meeting, beginning at 9.30 a.m. on a cool and slightly overcast Thursday morning, would prove to be the most critical of the whole affair. The moment when the *whole* truth might have been told, but was not. The BBC governors were the people appointed to keep an eye on the men and women who actually made the TV and radio programmes, mostly to nod along approvingly but maybe, just maybe, to raise an eyebrow, to raise the alarm, if someone had sinned. In the whole sweep of the scandal this meeting would be the single opportunity for outsiders to demand an explanation, to demand a remedy.

But by an extraordinary piece of bad timing the one man who might have got to the heart of the matter with a few blunt questions was absent that day. The ten-year term of Marmaduke Hussey as BBC chairman had come to an end just weeks earlier, in March 1996. And so the meeting was led by a new character, Sir Christopher Bland, a familiar – in fact, friendly – face for the head of the BBC management team also present at the meeting, Director-General John Birt. After months of strife with the combative Dukie, peaking dramatically over the Diana interview which Hussey had so bitterly opposed, here was a man with whom Birt could do business.

The appointment of a new BBC chairman was a big deal, tossed around in newspaper columns for weeks beforehand, the decision ultimately being made by the prime minister of the day. As Birt would recount in his memoirs, the fact that he and Bland had previously worked closely together at London Weekend Television might have prevented the newcomer from being given the prestigious post at all. Birt said, 'The main downside of Bland – in the government's mind – was that he and I would be too close, having been colleagues at LWT, and having remained friends.' But any concerns that their friendship might be problematic were evidently set aside. As Birt would write, 'Christopher Bland's arrival as Chairman of the BBC in April 1996 marked the beginning of my happiest period at the institution.'

Birt will clearly have been more comfortable to find himself sitting across from Chairman Bland than his old antagonist Hussey. But he was taking no risks. In the document bundle given to me under Freedom of Information law there is a brief handwritten note, signed simply 'John', addressed to 'Tony', dated 22 April, three days before the crucial Board of Governors (BoG) meeting.

> *22/4*
> *Tony*
> *Obviously we need to be clear before BoG about the matters we have been discussing.*
> *John*

Hall, who at this point knew beyond doubt that Bashir had passed off his forgeries to Charles Spencer as *genuine* documents, had lied about doing so three times, but then been forced to confess, drew up a statement in preparation for the governors' meeting saying not that, but something else instead:

> I have talked to Martin, and others involved, and I am satisfied of the following points: the graphic had no part whatsoever in gaining the interview with the Princess of Wales.
>
> I have talked to Martin at length about his reasons for compiling the graphic: he has none, other than he wasn't thinking. I believe he is, even with his lapse, honest and an honourable man. He is contrite.

Tony Hall then went on to demonstrate to the governors that, having satisfied himself about Bashir's honesty, tough action would be taken regarding someone else. Matt Wiessler would be blacklisted:

> We are taking steps to ensure that the graphic designer involved – Matthew Wiessler – will not work for the BBC again . . . In addition . . . we will work to deal with leakers and remove persistent troublemakers from the programme.

And so what would have been the result, had Tony Hall presented a full and frank account of Bashir's duplicity to the BBC Board of Governors? Sir Christopher Bland, chairing the critical meeting that day, died in 2017. Of the twelve governors present on that Thursday morning three others are also now dead. The youngest survivor, now aged eighty-one, is the distinguished theatre director Sir Richard Eyre. On the day of publication of the Dyson report, 20 May 2021, he said, 'The fact that Bashir lied should have been made clear to us, but . . . it never was. We can see now that the false bank statements were the lever that opened the doors to Diana.' Asked by me what would have been the result had Hall told the whole truth about what he knew, that Bashir had commissioned forged documents, passed them off as genuine to Spencer and then lied about his actions, Sir Richard's reply was unequivocal: 'There is no question that the governors would have insisted on a full-scale inquiry had they been aware of the circumstances.'

The intervention of this former BBC governor is crucial. Here is confirmation that had Hall *not* covered up what he knew in April 1996, then it is inevitable that Spencer would have been alerted to Bashir's duplicity. In turn Diana would almost certainly have received a briefing on the hoax which had been perpetrated, with consequences for her that can only be guessed at. It is that realization which today members of Diana's family find maddening and utterly heartbreaking.

There is another person who says that, just like the governors, he was not told the whole truth. Remarkably, despite his close relationship with Hall, despite the discussion he had asked for on 22 April 'to be clear' about things in advance of the governors' meeting, former Director-General John Birt says that he was not briefed by Hall on Bashir's lying. Summoned before the House of Commons committee on 15 June 2021, Birt would maintain that he was never made aware of the most important aspect of the scandal.

LORD BIRT: It came as a great shock to me when . . . well after Lord Dyson's inquiry started . . . I learned for the first time that Martin Bashir had lied.

JOHN NICOLSON MP: When Tim Gardam wrote his March 1996 memo to Tony Hall saying that Martin Bashir had lied, were you shocked?

LORD BIRT: As I have already made clear, I was shocked when I read Tim Gardam's report but that was only a matter of a few weeks or months ago. It came as a complete surprise to me.

JOHN NICOLSON MP: Tony Hall did not run that vitally important report past you?

LORD BIRT: I cannot find enough ways to say no.

JOHN NICOLSON MP: Yet he did not tell you, and just confirm, about this vitally important Tim Gardam document that showed that Martin Bashir had lied three times. That is clearly something he should have told you about.

LORD BIRT: I think that is something you have to ask
Tony Hall.

JOHN NICOLSON MP: Perhaps Tony Hall was
protecting you by not telling you.

LORD BIRT: As I have said more than once, you will
have to ask Tony Hall about that.

This extraordinary testimony asks one to accept, regarding the single most critical aspect of the scandal, that Birt
remained ignorant of vital matters by then well known to
Hall, to Tim Suter, to Anne Sloman, and of course to Martin
Bashir too. That Hall did not tell him what Bashir had done
and that Birt, often criticized for micromanaging the most
mundane aspects of programming, did not ask. Birt's testimony in this instance is clear, with no reference to a cloudy
memory due to the passage of time. And testimony of this
kind – a peer of the upper House speaking before elected
members – is governed by ancient convention. To knowingly mislead parliament would be a grave misdemeanour.
Yet I have seen documents which powerfully suggest that
parliament *was* misled. In the words of an unimpeachable
source, who was in the room when Lord Birt was briefed on
the scandal: 'It was impossible for John Birt to know nothing
of Bashir's lies.'

From a personal perspective the scenario which Birt
outlines also appears impossible to envisage. During my
fifteen years at the BBC the principle constantly drummed
into employees was that when a difficulty arose, especially a
problem which might spill beyond the confines of the corporation, then 'refer up'. Tell the boss. It was a principle
which promised a dual benefit. The problem might thus

be given consideration by a wiser and more mature head, but it also at the same time shifted responsibility from the character on the lower rung of the food chain to the boss immediately above. In this case, we are invited to believe, Hall did not follow the rubric instilled into every BBC staffer from day one. Having learned the terrifying news that *Panorama* harboured a reporter who was both a forger and a serial liar, we are asked to believe that Hall did *not* tell his boss. He did not refer up.

And while members of Parliament were clearly intrigued by this encounter between Hall and Birt, it appears that Lord Dyson was not. His report does not go into the question of why Hall failed, as Birt insists he did, to brief him on the issue at the very heart of the crisis. As to why he did not, and the likely consequences of his inaction, the Dyson report is utterly silent.

So did BBC bosses, Hall in particular, engage in a 'cover-up'? Hall and the rest are all adamant they were not involved in a 'cover-up' of any kind. The term has no legal definition but the *Oxford English Dictionary* captures the sense pretty well: 'An attempt to prevent people discovering the truth about a serious mistake or crime.' Dyson *does* use the term, but only in a specific and limited way. He describes the BBC's failure to enter details of their own internal inquiry into what he calls the 'press logs', material to be passed on when reporters call, as a 'cover-up' of that information. But since the inquiry was itself 'woefully ineffective' this means very little.

The charge levelled at those who devised and managed this piffling cover-up did not punch through when the report appeared, since Dyson does not identify any sinister, overall attempt to keep the scandal buried. Hall's failure to tell the whole story to the governors, which might have brought the whole affair immediately to light, and his alleged failure to brief Birt are not included in Dyson's assessment. In fact Hall's behaviour before both the governors and Birt goes entirely unremarked.

It is one of the most extraordinary aspects of the Dyson report, so baffling that it is almost impossible to believe there is not some hidden explanation, but this clear instance of Hall's lack of candour in front of the corporation watchdogs seems to have passed by Dyson completely. Amid the 45,000 words of Dyson's report the word 'governors' appears just once. In a detailed chronology of events in April 1996 Dyson analyses events *before* the meeting, and *after* it. The report gives every indication that Lord Dyson was unaware or failed to register that this critical meeting had taken place at all.

It is clear from Anne Sloman's memo, her eight-page document compiled on 22 April 1996, that behind the scenes at the BBC, for five months there was constant fire-fighting as details seemed likely to burst into the public domain. As her record comes to a halt with those chilling words, 'The Diana story is probably now dead, unless Spencer talks,' it seems possible to detect a collective sigh of relief that now, at last, the scandal seems to be under control.

But, of course, life went on outside the confines of the BBC. And wasn't April supposed to be the month when the whole of the UK was plunged into turmoil? The month when, certainly as Princess Diana understood things, the queen was due to abdicate? Diana had assured Lord Mishcon that that would be the case and had made her plans accordingly. So how was all that working out?

21. All Clear

Come late April 1996 those in the know at the top of the BBC must have felt they had raced and tumbled through terrifying rapids for five months but finally, blessedly, hit what seemed to be calm water. So they had, and with all the tearful confessions, burglaries and boardroom fights going on, it must have been easy to forget that at the centre of it all was a thirty-four-year-old woman, a mum of two, a *single* mum soon to be, a woman whom we would nowadays say had been groomed and gaslighted and treated appallingly by men from an institution she had been brought up to trust. But then Diana had no champion for her interests, as those within the BBC ducked and dived between November 1995 and April 1996.

The extraordinary emotional vortex Diana had been whirling through must still have held her in a very troubling place. Her certainty about Tiggy Legge-Bourke and the abortion will have been shaken by the assurance of Sir Robert Fellowes, the queen's private secretary and her brother-in-law, that it was all nonsense. But then his denial was itself unsatisfactory, what any agent of the 'dark forces' would say, surely? A harder thing to get one's head around must have been Bashir's guarantee, first hinted at during the Knightsbridge meeting on 19 September, that the queen would abdicate by April with a consequent shuffling of the royal pack.

It is possible to imagine Bashir as the kind of thunder-voiced prophet of doom who assures his flock that the world will end Sunday midnight but then has to explain how Monday happened. But perhaps he did have answers. The queen, still there on the throne? You and Camilla, not murdered yet? Don't you see, that *Panorama* interview worked just as I said it would! There must have been some kind of April recap, but of the two people who would have had that conversation only one remains alive.

There is evidence that Diana and Bashir did stay close, at least for a while. When his wife, Deborah, entered hospital in March 1996 for the birth of their third child, Eliza, Bashir would say that Diana was excited: 'You must let me know the moment the baby arrives, and an hour later, there was a knock on the delivery room, and in she walked.' Bashir has kept a note which Diana wrote on 10 March, apparently holding out the prospect of even a shared holiday: 'Dear Deborah, I wondered if the idea of staying a couple of nights in Scotland (!) might appeal? I'm so sorry to hear how uncomfortable you've been.'

The holiday plans were not followed through, though Bashir, speaking to the *Sunday Times* in 2021, his only lengthy reflection on events, said Diana did invite his family for lunch at Kensington Palace: 'Prince Harry was there and Paul Burrell was serving. Our eldest and Harry kicked a ball around. It was a very precious relationship and one we treasured.' Bashir has said he could pick up the phone and talk with Diana if need be. In his handwritten confession, requested by Tony Hall on 28 March:

In speaking to HRH The Princess of Wales yesterday evening (2330 hrs 27th March '96) she said that after her brother had introduced her to me – she had never spoken to him about Panorama, or anything to do with our relationship . . . She did not trust him and felt that he might leak information about the interview before she had informed Buckingham Palace.

But the relationship was to turn sour. Paul Burrell has written of an occasion, which he does not date, claiming something said by Bashir over the phone proved embarrassing: 'What she didn't know was that Bashir phoned me regularly, on the hunt for inside information. What he didn't know was that, once, when he rang, the Princess was standing next to me in the pantry . . . she mouthed to me, "Who is it?" Covering the receiver mouthpiece, I mimed back, "Martin Bashir." "Put it on the speaker." She pointed at the button on the telephone. I pressed it, and within seconds, the irreverent voice of the journalist echoed round the pantry. After that conversation, the Princess saw her "friend" in a different light.'

Diana's therapist and frequent companion at this time, Simone Simmons, gave me an account of something she dates from around July 1996: 'He was around a lot. And then in the end she was really fed up with him because, Paul Burrell told both me and Diana this when we were together, he said, "Oh, Martin Bashir's been around. And he was saying, you know, Diana's with Hasnat Khan. And obviously she likes dark-skinned men. And I'm just wondering, you know, I'd like to give her one." And when I heard that, I said, "Oh, God!" And after that we nicknamed him the Poison Dwarf. It was disgusting.'

Like so much in this story the voice of one person is missing because on 31 August 1997 it was silenced forever. It is impossible not to reflect that, from the point of view of Martin Bashir, if even only those transgressions identified in the Dyson report are to be accepted as fact, likely to destroy him at any point over the years, then Diana's disappearance might have been, once the shock had died away, not entirely regrettable.

BBC management, for their part, were able to put aside any lingering misgivings there might have been about the *Panorama* interview, commissioning a celebratory tenth anniversary special documentary film, broadcast on BBC2 in November 2005. Titled *The Princess and Panorama*, this film is an extraordinary piece of work, copies of it now circulated among aficionados like *samizdat* treasure, not something which will ever find its way on to iPlayer but which will be prized by historians for decades to come. The characters who would parade sombrely before Lord Dyson in 2021 appear in much better spirits in this incarnation sixteen years earlier, the interviews occasionally chilling given what we now know. It has the feel of those true crime documentaries where a husband is shown at the police press conference, tearful and distraught, yet we know already that his poor wife's body is under the patio.

The interviews have not aged well. Tony Hall, the man who had known since 1996 that Bashir had commissioned forgeries, passed them off as genuine and then lied three times about it, said in the 2005 film, 'I think Martin is the sort of interviewer who people trust. He works very hard at getting into your confidence.' Well, yes. Tim Gardam, the man who in 2021 said he had almost keeled over when he first heard of Bashir's duplicity, said this of the *Panorama* interview: 'It was the most intense moment of my television career. One was watching something that was history. You had there a piece of television that, in a hundred years' time, would be seen as a really significant historical document.'

Patrick Jephson was also interviewed for the programme,

sounding rather a sourpuss amid all the jollity: 'The woman I worked for was actually very strong, remarkably stable, given the pressure she was under. But the images that I saw on the TV were of a self-pitying and not very coherent person and I felt that that did her no favours at all.'

There is something alarming but at the same time almost endearing in the sparkle-eyed enthusiasm with which the BBC men recall that golden time in 1995 when they got down and dirty, when they mixed it with the red-tops. You had us down as nerds, with our tedious shows about Maastricht and monetary policy, our audiences of 1.3 million? We can do sex, James Hewitt, 23 million too! The disjunction of these men, exquisitely educated – Tim Gardam with an English double first from Cambridge; Tony Hall, PPE, Oxford – recalling their dashing raid into tabloid territory provides a clue to the fatal flaw which most likely underlay the whole *Panorama* project.

Perhaps deep down the whole thing was perceived as a bit of froth. Do we really care what Princess Airhead has to say about the British constitution? And doesn't everyone cut corners down at the stinky end of Grub Street? Gardam shared his bedazzlement, gushing, 'You kept on having to realize that it was real! That all the stories that were picked up in the tabloids and put together, the shards of gossip, the person who really knew about X or Y and the secrets of their lives, that it actually was a story that was true.'

Tabloid journalism was a world where not-quite-gentlemen did occasionally beastly things. Also one where the rookie reporter might deliver the world's biggest scoop because, well, sometimes lovely things just happen to one, do they not? Gardam seemed content not to know more, so long as those lovely things kept happening: 'How exactly he was getting into the palace we didn't know. He said rather mysteriously, "When I go to see her, I do not look as I do now." So, whether it was in a funny disguise or not, we never found out!'

Tim Gardam was the executive who had interrogated Bashir, on Saturday, 23 March 1996, and finally forced from him the confession that he was both a liar and a forger. As Gardam would say at the Dyson inquiry in 2021, 'I remember absolutely crystal-clear . . . I know exactly where I was standing at the time . . . because I was absolutely staggered that a BBC journalist . . . could have behaved like this.' That staggering recollection, crystal-clear as it was, played no part in his contribution to the documentary film in 2005.

Another contributor appears to have been equally guarded. In 2021 the veteran BBC journalist John Ware composed a piece – still carried on the BBC's own website today – in which he describes research he had carried out on his own behalf into the 2005 documentary, especially the part played by *Panorama* editor Steve Hewlett. Ware wrote: 'I understand Hewlett agreed to be interviewed provided he wasn't asked specifically about the forged bank statements . . . The idea that Hewlett hadn't yet suspected that Bashir got to Diana by deceiving Spencer sits uneasily with his careful editorial eye . . . it seems he was troubled by something.'

The decision to make *The Princess and Panorama* seems to have been prompted by an unquenchable desire in 2005 for certain BBC bosses to relive their finest hour. But it turns out it was a rash decision, with consequences still playing out today. Making the film meant ignoring the sinister warning issued by Anne Sloman on 22 April 1996: 'The Diana story is probably now dead, unless Spencer talks.' Charles Spencer, recalling events that took place twenty years ago, told me, 'This female producer wrote to me and said, "It's the tenth anniversary coming up and we'd love you to be a part of it." And I wrote back to her and said, "I cannot believe that you're celebrating such an appalling moment in the BBC's history. The interview was obtained by dishonesty and I have all the documentary evidence to prove that, and I'm copying this to the director-general." I have a photocopy of the letter I wrote to the director-general.'

Spencer has indeed kept that 2005 correspondence, part of the bulky 'BBC dossier' stored in his study at Althorp. He showed me a copy of the now yellowing document. On 18 July 2005 Spencer had written:

> *Thank you for your request for an interview for your proposed documentary on my late sister's appearance on Panorama 10 years ago; but I am afraid I do not wish to take part.*
>
> *Based on the documents I have at Althorp – including notes I took at the time in my own hand – which prove Panorama's role in this matter to have been less than honest, I must register my astonishment that the BBC wishes to revisit this moment in its fine journalistic history.*
>
> *I am copying this letter to your Director-General, so he can learn the truth about Panorama's methods a decade ago, if they are of interest to him now.*
> *Earl Spencer*
> *c.c. The Director-General, BBC*

The BBC director-general in 2005 was Mark Thompson, first-class English degree, Oxford, the youngest of the hotshots brought on by John Birt, at thirty-three years old in 1990 the youngest-ever editor of the BBC *Nine O'Clock News*, editor of *Panorama* two years after that, still only forty-seven years old when made director-general in 2004. So did he see Spencer's letter? Remarkably, following a Freedom of Information request by Spencer himself, in 2022, he was sent a copy of the very *same* document which he had sent to Thompson seventeen years earlier, preserved in BBC archives over that period. The top right-hand corner bears a circular BBC stamp, dated 20 July 2005, and saying 'Governance and

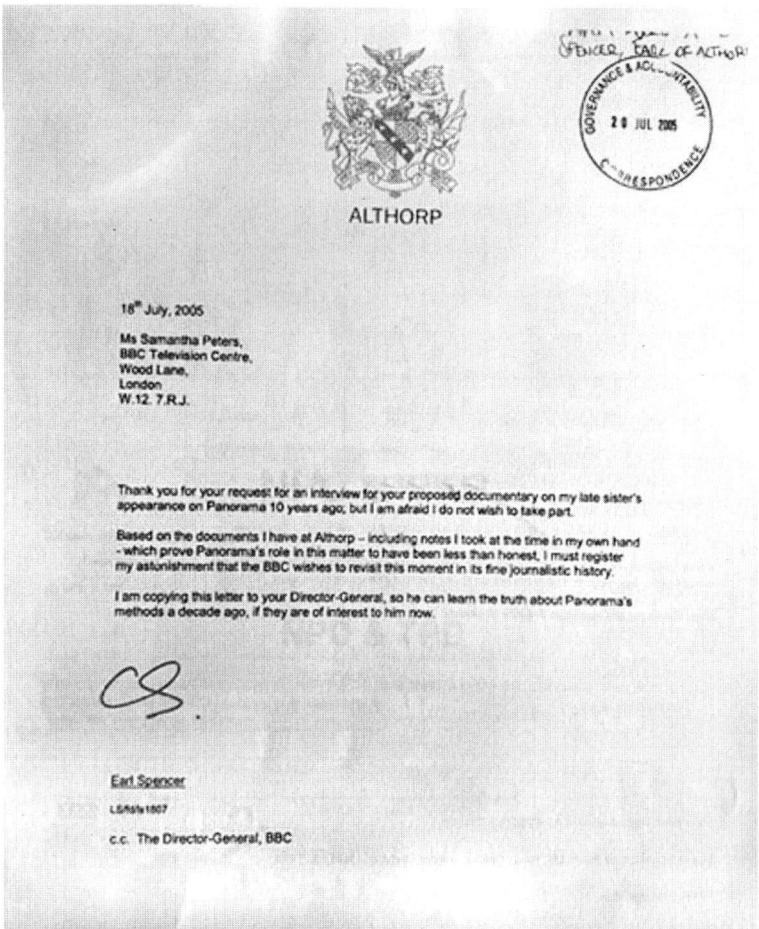

ALTHORP

18th July, 2005

Ms Samantha Peters,
BBC Television Centre,
Wood Lane,
London
W.12. 7.R.J.

Thank you for your request for an interview for your proposed documentary on my late sister's appearance on Panorama 10 years ago; but I am afraid I do not wish to take part.

Based on the documents I have at Althorp – including notes I took at the time in my own hand - which prove Panorama's role in this matter to have been less than honest, I must register my astonishment that the BBC wishes to revisit this moment in its fine journalistic history.

I am copying this letter to your Director-General, so he can learn the truth about Panorama's methods a decade ago, if they are of interest to him now.

Earl Spencer

LS/ns/s1807

c.c. The Director-General, BBC

Accountability Correspondence', indicating that it received scrutiny by those very close to the top.

But would anyone have cared? Ten years after Diana's interview appeared, wasn't all this simply old news? In 2005, despite the impression given by the gushing anniversary film, the potential scandal bubbling around the 1995 *Panorama* interview was at that time still a hot topic of conversation in BBC circles. And it had been so for years. Bashir's transgressions – or at least some of them – were common gossip up and down the BBC, something which I can report because I was there, if by then only in a freelance capacity but still with a wide circle of well-informed friends.

And the gossip had by then also spread way beyond the corridors of New Broadcasting House. It had become much more serious than gossip, with versions of the story even appearing in bestselling books. That is why it seems to me, and to Charles Spencer too, astonishing that this letter of warning – *from the brother of Princess Diana* – should have made its way right to the department of the BBC responsible for 'Governance and Accountability'. And then been completely ignored.

Mark Thompson left the BBC in 2012 after eight years as director-general, where, on a salary of more than £800,000, he had become the highest-paid public servant in the UK. He has pursued a stellar career in America, becoming president and CEO of *The New York Times* and, at the time of writing, is CEO of the news network CNN. But my attempt to seek a response from this eminent lifelong journalist, now aged sixty-seven, and knighted in 2023, provides perhaps a better sense of events than does the response itself.

My email to CNN headquarters in New York was dealt with not by a press officer there but referred instead to the world's largest crisis management firm, Edelman. In March 2025, I received a phone call from the president of Edelman's international division, offering, over forty minutes, 'background contextual information', though with the strange proviso that all of it must remain not just 'off the record' – that is, from an unnamed source – but unreported *in any sense*. Thompson's crisis manager declined to answer specific questions on the handling of Spencer's letter, or the significance of its classification under 'Governance and Accountability'. Nor would he provide a comment on Thompson's behalf *for* the record.

Five months later, in August 2025, Thompson altered his position. Lawyers acting on his behalf *did* now offer a statement. Spencer's letter never reached his office, Thompson said, perhaps because it was a letter merely copied to him, amidst a huge volume of mail channelled through the correspondence unit. The statement went on: 'I regret that Earl Spencer's offer to share information about the Panorama Diana programme was not picked up on at the time'.

Such regret seems appropriate. Here was the *first* occasion when Diana's brother pointed to serious issues concerning the *Panorama* broadcast, confirming also that he had notes to support his concerns. It is beyond doubt that had Thompson or the documentary makers responded in 2005, then the hoaxing of Diana would have been revealed at a much earlier date. The victims of the scandal who were paid very large sums in reparations would have suffered just ten years' anguish, not twenty-five. Had the scandal been revealed in 2005 it would also likely have taken its toll on the careers of several people then still in powerful positions. It would undoubtedly have made Tony Hall's later appointment as BBC director-general – and elevation to the House of Lords in 2010 – very unlikely.

As to that extraordinary bit of filmmaking, *The Princess and Panorama*, the most notable absence in the celebratory line-up is Martin Bashir himself. He had nothing to contribute to the film, although it is beyond doubt that he will have been invited to take part. Having been poached from the BBC by ITV in 1999 Bashir went on to make, in 2003, what would become another notorious documentary, the two-hour *Living with Michael Jackson*, revelatory about the singer's dubious private life but also revealing a great deal about Bashir's technique in first winning the star's trust and then turning on him. The *Sunday Times* TV reviewer A. A. Gill wrote in February 2003, 'Michael Jackson I had had enough of after 15 minutes. It was Bashir who held a cobra-like fascination. It was like watching Ebola hit a journalism college . . . he throws in the most lickspittle, craven ploy of question-couching. He does it as if simply passing on gossip — "Some people might say", "How do you respond to those who accuse you of . . . ?" Oh, for Christ's sake. Have the guts to do your job, man.'

After Bashir's film went out Jackson was arrested on child abuse charges, tried, acquitted on all counts but then struggled up to the time of his drug-induced death in June 2009. The jury is still out on Jackson's reputation but not on the impact that Bashir had on Jackson's life. Exactly as with Diana there is a sense, impossible to pin down, that somehow both their lives might have been much happier, and longer, had Martin Bashir not become their pal.

PART FOUR
Shining a Light

'Did you ever expect a corporation to have a
conscience, when it has no soul to be damned, and
no body to be kicked?'

Edward Thurlow, jurist and Lord Chancellor, 1731–1806

22. The Gathering Storm

A visit to a theatre in London's Covent Garden towards the end of August 2006 would turn out to have a profound effect on my life. I was there to see the opening of *Frost/Nixon*, the first stage play by Peter Morgan, subsequently creator and writer of *The Crown* for Netflix. The play tells the background story of the famous 1977 series of interviews conducted by David Frost, circling around and then nailing ex-US President Richard Nixon, 'Tricky Dicky' of Watergate fame. After its run at the Donmar Warehouse Morgan's play did spectacularly well in theatres around the world, becoming a movie nominated for five Oscars.

One memory in particular remains of that night at the theatre. In the interval I bumped into Mike Robinson, the producer of the Diana interview and one of the three *Panorama* crew who were present on the night of its recording. We shared a drink, chatting about how one of the supporting characters in Morgan's play was drawn from real life. David Frost's researcher for the Nixon project was the then thirty-three-year-old John Birt, ten years before his ill-starred arrival at the BBC. Once the curtain fell I left the theatre marvelling at how Peter Morgan had hit upon a brilliant but simple idea. In painting the background to an iconic television encounter the core drama is already there, just waiting to be repackaged. Perhaps I could do the same?

The first interview which I considered was, of course, the November 1995 encounter between Princess Diana and

Martin Bashir. I began to think about it, as a fascinating moment of social history, to read all I could. But within just a few days I began to wonder whether my perception was somehow skewed. Was I seeing something which everyone else had unaccountably ignored? The first book I turned to for research was a history of *Panorama*, the 2003 *Panorama: Fifty Years of Pride and Paranoia* by the late Richard Lindley, himself a reporter for the programme in its heyday between 1973 and 1988.

Over four carefully sourced and authoritative pages there was a more or less complete account of Martin Bashir's commissioning of forged bank statements, the fact that he had used them, somehow, in the build-up to the Diana interview and what appeared to be a frantic cover-up by the bosses. I next read a 2004 book by Andrew Morton, *Diana: In Pursuit of Love*, a follow-up to his 1992 volume. In this new book Morton has a chapter actually called 'Fakes, Forgeries and Secret Tapes' which provides a detailed account, now let us say 95 per cent accurate, of how Bashir got hold of the forgeries and what he did with them.

It seemed to me astonishing then, and it does today, that this information was so glaringly out there in the public domain and that nobody seemed to care. How had Bashir not been collared? How did he go about, a celebrity of sorts, with these charges laid against him and as far as I could see totally unchallenged? A partial answer to questions like that would emerge when I started to do my own digging. The BBC had swerved the questions put to them in 1996 by the *Mail on Sunday*, putting out a statement that was merely grossly misleading.

A decade later when I started asking questions the BBC

would simply lie, boldly, and in writing. Following up Lindley's lead, describing in particular Hall and Sloman's questioning of Bashir, in April 2007 I put in a request under the Freedom of Information Act. Shortly thereafter the BBC replied:

BBC

Information Policy & Compliance
bbc.co.uk/foi

9 July 2007

Dear Mr Webb,

Re: Freedom of Information Act request – RFI2007000585

Thank you for your Freedom of Information Act ("the Act") request dated 4 July. The reference number for your request is RFI2007000585. You requested:

'minutes or notes taken at any meetings involving Tony Hall, Tim Suter, Anne Sloman, Martin Bashir and others, concerning the Panorama interview on Diana, Princess of Wales....and copies of Press Releases touching on this subject.'

The BBC does not hold the information that you have requested. As this programme was an exclusive, News has confirmed that any paperwork would have been kept to an absolute minimum, certainly before transmission. Much of the communication would have been done deliberately by telephone or face to face to avoid the need for documented records. This will have also meant that any meetings to discuss this particular programme would not have been minuted and the number of people involved in the process kept to a need-to-know basis only.

Dear Mr Webb,

Re: Freedom of Information Act request – RFI2007000585. You requested:

'minutes or notes taken at any meetings involving Tony Hall, Tim Suter, Anne Sloman, Martin Bashir and others, concerning the Panorama interview on Diana, Princess of Wales . . .'

The BBC does not hold the information that you have requested. As this programme was an exclusive, News has confirmed that any paperwork would have been kept to an absolute minimum . . . any meetings to discuss this particular programme would not have been minuted and the number of people involved in the process kept to a need-to-know basis only.

It is clear beyond doubt that the BBC *did* have detailed notes, minutes and reports on all of this, including Sloman's eight-page 22 April 1996 memo detailing the complete process. A copy sits on my desk right now. But if the BBC has decided simply to lie, what can one do? Over the following years I continued to build up a research file, a little bit here, a bit there, but of course I had a busy career too, making documentary films. And I began to be aware of a very curious phenomenon which I am going to call 'protective notoriety'.

Bizarrely, on rare occasions, a famous person can become tainted with scandal but somehow to the *exact* degree that that knowledge itself prevents the rest of the story emerging. Like inoculation, where a tiny dose of smallpox prevents smallpox killing the host. The best and most notorious example would be Jimmy Savile. For years journalists and police would resignedly trade rumours that something was up, something wasn't right, but somehow the widespread knowledge of those rumours meant it just wasn't news any more.

I think Bashir had been thus inoculated. The way the documentary film business works is that a freelance director such as me puts a proposal to one of the broadcasters, maybe ITV or Channel 4. I would pitch the idea of a film about Bashir's crimes, laying out the lurid background, the forgeries, how Diana had been hoaxed into the most famous TV interview of all time. A commissioning executive would exclaim, 'Wow, that's incredible! How do we know all this?' and I would reply, 'Well, it's in a history book about *Panorama*.' The conversation would then go, 'Oh. Right. So it's not new?'

I would explain that the story had been there in plain sight for five years. For ten years. And then for fifteen years. How, come 2016, Martin Bashir had been reappointed by the BBC, becoming, beyond satire, the corporation's editor of religion. As a journalist it was intensely frustrating that such an important story should remain untold, though on every occasion I understood completely where the commissioning executive was coming from. Protective notoriety.

I take the possibly over-optimistic view that as time rolls by, as records emerge, as people die or people simply start to talk, most scandals will eventually emerge into the daylight. And there are two special factors which meant that the Bashir time bomb which had since 1995 been ever so quietly ticking, then hissing, fizzing and spluttering, would burst in a thunderous detonation in 2020. In February 2017 the man who had been editor of *Panorama* in 1995, Steve Hewlett, died of cancer at fifty-eight years of age. Like all those associated with the Diana scoop his career had rocketed afterwards, Hewlett leaving the BBC for a lucrative position with the ITV company Carlton Television. He later became an influential industry pundit, presenting BBC radio's *The Media Show*.

A former *Panorama* producer, Phil Craig, recalled a 2004 late-night drink with Hewlett, a friend and former colleague. The discussion turned to Bashir, and as Craig recalled, 'I came away that night with the very strong impression that he thought there was a chance that one day the Bashir story would cause everybody a lot more trouble, that there was more to come out about the background to the interview, that there was something that hadn't gone away and was still lurking in the shadows.' Birmingham-born Hewlett was widely liked across the small world of TV current affairs documentary making. Although his exact role will probably never be pinned down, it is certain that a documentary exposing Bashir would be a tough programme to have made during Hewlett's lifetime.

The second factor that would lead to Bashir's undoing was breathtakingly simple. November 2020 spelled twenty-five years since the iconic interview had first been broadcast. And so as the date of this quarter-century anniversary grew nearer, three separate production teams found themselves labouring on competing programmes looking at the Diana interview: ITV, Channel 5 and the film I was producing and directing for Channel 4. There are entire postcodes in west London where it is impossible to throw a stone without hitting someone who currently works for or *has* worked for *Panorama*. Channel 5's documentary was commissioned by executive Daniel Pearl, a former deputy editor of *Panorama*. ITV's film was commissioned by executive Tom Giles, formerly editor of *Panorama*. At Channel 4 my film was commissioned by Fatima Salaria, whose husband, Sandy Smith, is a former editor of *Panorama*. My wife, Diana Martin, was in 2020 the *Panorama* deputy editor.

It was a bizarre position, probably not seen before or since, that three of the principal UK broadcasters were working on exactly the same subject, for broadcast at exactly the same time. Meanwhile the BBC, so keen to recount their triumph in 2005, were definitely not going to be part of any celebration this time around. Most definitely not. Emails which I was able to obtain after a long battle using Freedom of Information law show that during the summer of 2020 there was growing tension within the BBC about exactly what might be about to appear on the rival networks. It appears that Bashir was already considering his own defence, alleging racism and jealousy as the motives for criticism. In July 2020 he wrote to the head of BBC history, Robert Seatter:

From: Martin Bashir
Sent: 20 July 2020 16:34
To: Robert Seatter
Subject: Private and Confidential

Dear Robert,

I am sorry to hear that this so-called 'forgery' story has reared its head again. It played no part in the interview but did allow professional jealousy, particularly within the Corporation, to hang its hat on alleged wrongdoing. At the time, it was also apparent that there was some irritation that a second-generation immigrant of non-white, working class roots should have the temerity to enter a Royal Palace and conduct an interview. It would have been so much easier if one of the dynastic families (Dimbleby et al) had done it!

With all good wishes,
Martin

In a situation like this, with three research teams chasing essentially the same story, there is obviously a nervousness about who is going to do best. Who has been able to get the killer interview, uncover the most damning document, find the smoking gun? I knew that I had good material raising tough questions for the BBC. But I also knew that if three documentary films are to appear on the same subject, yours needs to be *first* on air. Quite simply, if the other two are good, then they might have material which you do not and you look a fool. If they are bad, then viewers will be very unlikely to give film number three even a glance. Why would they? Channel 4 executive Shaminder Nahal, in charge of the production at that point, had been a wise and supportive figure but was unable to guarantee that the programme would be given an early transmission date. As the anniversary, 20 November, grew closer I grew increasingly nervous that we might be beaten to the punch. And so it seemed to me that in those circumstances it would be legitimate to gently nudge the conversation along.

It is remarkable how, even in the digital age, with news swirling all around, a newspaper story can focus the attention, reset the agenda. And so if a responsible paper like the *Sunday Times* were to note the fact that *three* TV companies were racing to put the Bashir story on air, it might help my case that we should be first out of the gate. With apologies, if they are needed, to those concerned, my simple stratagem paid off in a spectacularly successful way. The BBC employs among its 22,000 staff many who have witnessed the cover-up of the Bashir scandal over the years and have been appalled. Others were incensed to see how Martin Bashir, a proven scoundrel not just from his earlier time at the BBC but latterly in America too, was eased into a highly paid job for which he clearly did almost no work.

Most people at the BBC are honest, decent and hardworking, and a few of them had begun voicing their concerns, confidentially, to me. On a day which I vividly remember I met with one of these, at an internet cafe in Ealing, and we composed an email to be sent, anonymously, to the *Sunday Times*. It would let reporters there know a little of the three TV films soon to appear, and also something of the disquiet among some BBC staff. It seemed to me a fair-enough bit of tradecraft, saying things that were perfectly true. When a story appeared the following weekend, on Sunday, 4 October, it was clear that my plan had paid off in a way that I could never have imagined.

The *Sunday Times* reporters had succeeded in driving the story forward in a way no other newspaper had been able to do in a quarter of a century. They had managed to get an off the record briefing from Charles Spencer, establishing that Bashir *had* shown him the forged bank statements. More than that, the story made an oblique reference to Spencer having kept 'notes' of his meetings with Bashir. Notes about what? From my position as a fascinated observer this was incredible. Spencer had turned down my request to be interviewed for my film, as he routinely did to documentary makers. But here he was, beginning to break cover at last. The story contained another nugget, buried in the final paragraph, but from my point of view an absolute game-changer.

Having read this far you will know that the story of the forged bank statements can get a little opaque. The BBC had since 1996 ensured that things remained that way, being careful in all that time *never* to acknowledge that the forgeries had ever been shown to *anyone*, referring to them always as 'mock-ups', suggesting graphics material for internal use only. For that reason the final paragraph of the *Sunday Times* story contained twenty or so words which made my heart race. It said, 'BBC records from the period indicate that Martin had explained to the BBC that the documents had been shown to Earl Spencer.'

Why so dramatic? This simple announcement, an official statement from the BBC press office, meant that, no, the bank statements were not graphic mock-ups, ordered for some innocent internal purpose. They *had* been shown to Spencer. The press office did not elaborate, but it followed as night follows day that if documents which were known to be false had been 'shown' to anyone, then there had clearly been an attempt to deceive. They were being used as *forgeries*.

And now, after a quarter of a century, clearly rattled by the intervention of Charles Spencer, the BBC was finally admitting as much.

That crucial fact had been carefully kept from the *Mail on Sunday*, in the press statement devised all those years ago. It had been kept from the BBC Board of Governors in the statement delivered to them in April 1996. If that single, slender thread had been pulled, then the whole fabric of deceit would have unravelled and the ultimate target of the deceit would most likely have begun to perceive the terrible trick that had been played on her.

As a journalist it is the little moments like this which are the most thrilling, which tell you that the path you have been following, in this case for years, is precisely the right one. Those twenty words from the BBC press office also constituted, for me, a confession. Thirteen years earlier, in July 2007, in response to my Freedom of Information request, I had been confidently told that there were no documents relating to the suppressed scandal. But now here was confirmation of 'BBC records from the period' – exactly what I had been seeking. What I had been told was plainly a lie. Nobody likes being taken for a mug. And it was with the most intense satisfaction that, just a short time later, I was able to bring the whole edifice crashing to the ground.

23. Two Lords, Two Tales

One result of the *Sunday Times* story – in fact the only result I had been anticipating – was that the transmission date for my film was immediately pulled forward. Instead of airing on 20 November 2020, the twenty-fifth anniversary of the 1995 *Panorama* programme, it would go out on Wednesday, 21 October. I still could not be sure when our competitors on ITV and Channel 5 would go to air but at least we would not be tail-end Charlies, trying to scoop up the few remaining viewers who hadn't already had their fill of the anniversary.

What the change did mean, for me and the rest of the small research team at Blink Films, the independent production company who had taken on the commission for Channel 4, was that the next seventeen days would be a frantic race. We had to complete our interviews, tie up all outstanding research issues, argue with lawyers about the spiky things we needed to say. And then of course we had to put together a film, to blend all this intriguing but highly complex information about who did what with two bank statements, a very long time ago, into a piece of television which would pass compellingly, beguilingly before the viewers' eyes for forty-five minutes or so. That is always the challenge. Taking a dry-as-dust fact and conjuring just the right wrapping in which to tender that fact, along with the thousand others the viewer will need to understand what on earth is going on. And, of course, to care.

It was the BBC's lack of honesty with me back in 2007,

on the question of whether or not they had records on Bashir's duplicity, which I hoped to leverage in the few days that remained before transmission. The BBC had clearly got themselves into a mess, and a complicated one, as would quickly become clear. As the documentary film had begun to take shape I had decided, in July 2020, to repeat my Freedom of Information request from 2007. I said to the BBC, in effect, 'It is clear that there was an internal inquiry concerning Martin Bashir back in 1996. So what documents do you have on that?' In 2007 the BBC had said there were no documents. This time the reply was rather extraordinary.

The BBC said that, yes, in fact they *did* have documents after all. But they would not release them. The BBC wrote to me explaining how, in their opinion, a particular clause in the Freedom of Information Act meant that materials held 'for the purposes of journalism' could be kept secret. End of story. But now, thanks to that article in the *Sunday Times*, things had moved on radically.

Surely, in that statement from the BBC press office, published on Sunday, 4 October, the corporation had clearly cited these documents, what were referred to in the newspaper as the 'records from the time'? I emailed the BBC on 6 October saying, more or less, 'This is ludicrous. I have been asking for these records for thirteen years. And I want them now.' The BBC reply was a comic masterpiece in attempted opacity.

Dear Mr Webb,

In your email of 6 October you have pointed out that our response to your FOI request in 2007 was that we did not hold the information you asked for, but our response in July 2020 was that the information

requested was held for the purposes of journalism and so exempt from
FOIA, confirming, of course, that we do hold information.
    Now we have looked into this, we have concluded that the 2007
request is anomalous.

Anomalous? The easiest definition: 'deviating from the normal'. Anomalous? No, the response to my 2007 request had been a lie. But this same letter, emailed to me on 19 October 2020, would turn out to be merely a part of the BBC masterplan for dealing with the rapidly escalating scandal. And it would cause the whole thing to explode in the most spectacular way.

In putting together a documentary film like this one, making allegations about the behaviour of certain named people, it is standard practice to offer them a 'right to reply'. It gives fair warning that something damaging may shortly appear, but it is also an opportunity for the target of the criticism to explain their position, to say, 'No, it wasn't quite like that. Here is what happened . . .' In reality it is vanishingly unlikely that the response will be a wholesale denial of the charges: 'No, Mr Smith did not murder his wife, dismember her body and claim £1 million in insurance. Mrs Smith is in fact alive and well.' The documentary team had better be, at this point, pretty damn sure that Mr Smith *is* a murderer because they have a whole film saying so.

In most cases the right to reply is likely to evince no more than a small squeak of protestation, perhaps resulting in a brief caption at the end of the film: 'Organization X says that it was unaware of Y and at all times sought to ensure Z.' It is also possible to judge purely from the *timing* of that response how strong a hand your opponent has. Is there some significant point of fact which you have got wrong? If so, you will hear about it right away. If not, it is likely that the target will hold off responding until the *last* possible moment, in order that the point they *do* want to make slips into that concluding caption without having been properly interrogated.

Making an investigative documentary film, like the one I had so nearly ready to go, really is like assembling a jigsaw, piece by piece, fact by fact, until you look at what is down there on the table and you can say, even though 30 per cent of the pieces might still be missing, 'Anyone can see that is a duck/*Mona Lisa*/Tower Bridge' – or whatever you care to name. Sometimes you wait until you have 90 per cent of the pieces. In very rare cases you might have 100 per cent of the pieces on the table. Sometimes people broadcast films where they have only 15 per cent, and the duck turns out to be not a duck at all, but something quite different, and that is when they get sued for huge sums of money.

The issue of what you *can* broadcast, the final decision on how your film will look, will not be made by me, the director, or even the person who commissioned the film. That decision will be made by in-house lawyers, who will make a hard-headed ruling on whether you have collected enough pieces of the jigsaw, or whether you have not. In this case, looking back with the knowledge I have now, I would say we had 75 per cent of the jigsaw puzzle at the time we went on air. Everything we wanted to say was *true*. We had assembled evidence suggesting that Martin Bashir had used his bank statements to gain the trust of Charles Spencer, and thereby gain access to Diana. That in itself was a dramatic revelation, indicating serious wrongdoing. But we now know that is only a small part of the picture.

At that date, in October 2020, there was of course so much that I still did *not* know. The BBC had *not* revealed the smallest detail of their 1996 internal inquiry, where Bashir lied three times and then finally confessed over the forgeries. The BBC had *not* revealed that there had been that crucial meeting of the governors, on 25 April 1996, at which Tony Hall presented a misleading account of what Bashir had been found to have done. None of this was known to me at the time. What I find disturbing is that the BBC *did* know, beyond doubt, at that very moment, how serious the situation was but decided not to say so, for a complex set of reasons discussed in a later chapter. The BBC knew, in October 2020, that there were documents showing that Bashir was a serial liar but they decided not to reveal that, instead giving every indication that he was an honest individual.

The press office gave us no indication that a dossier of damaging documentary evidence had been collected by the BBC in September 2020, regarding Bashir and also former director-general Tony Hall, seeking instead to convey the impression that everything was above board. That is wrong, and for the BBC it is especially wrong. Journalists understand that press officers are people briefed by their bosses to spin a particular story, that they may not tell the *whole* story, that they may be 'economical with the truth'. The problem throughout the Bashir affair is that BBC press officers have too often spread information which is simply not true. It happened in 1996 and it happened again on this occasion.

Around noon on 19 October 2020 I received an 800-word statement from the BBC, their response to our formal offer of a right to reply. A quick scan of the document showed that there were no serious rebuttals to the points we had raised. The statement was consistent with BBC practice, referring to Bashir's material six times as 'mock-ups' rather than forgeries. That seemed by now merely an annoyance, but viewed with the benefit of hindsight there were also disturbing attempts to mislead. Though its author must have been fully aware that Bashir had lied, repeatedly, during the BBC's 1996 internal investigation, the statement would say now, quite untruthfully, 'At the time, he cooperated fully with the internal BBC investigations . . . had readily admitted his role in the mocking up.'

The press statement went on to say that Bashir was currently too unwell to face new questioning – an issue which would grow in importance later. But by far the most mysterious, the most *dramatic* words were in the first sentence of the statement: 'our FoI team have also written to you separately'. The BBC Freedom of Information team was writing to me? Now? Forty-eight hours before my film was due to go on air? The people who had refused point-blank up to this point to release the documents they were holding? What could it possibly mean?

At 12.58 p.m. on this Monday, 19 October 2020, in the chrome, glass and orange-panelled Zone E on the fourth floor of New Broadcasting House, a BBC employee was poised at their computer keyboard. They had only to press a single key, dispatching a single email, to complete the plan thrashed out by the BBC's top-most managers and lawyers. Charlotte Morgan, head of communications for the news division, knew that what was about to happen would cause a sensation. What she did not know was that this email would plunge the BBC into the greatest crisis in its hundred-year history, tarnishing its reputation worldwide, force the outlay of millions of pounds in reparations and, because of consequences still playing out today, raise major questions about how the BBC is being run.

The email had only to make a seven-mile journey to my office in the attic of a Chiswick terrace, where it dropped silently into my inbox. It comprised a five-page covering letter, but intriguingly also a separate PDF file. Sixty-seven pages of documents, scanned from internal BBC memos and reports a quarter of a century old, many marked 'confidential'. As I began to flip through the documents I was puzzled. The BBC had already, only thirty minutes earlier, emailed to me their 800-word press statement. So what had I now been sent, and why?

It was when I reached page 43 that I stopped dead. What was written there, partly obscured by heavy black redactions, was extraordinary. *It could not be true.* What was said in those few words had first appeared utterly banal, so mundane that it slid by on first reading. But then, as realization dawned, my eyes instantly snapped back to that precise spot on the page:

Earl Spencer told him [REDACTED]. He showed him some documents including this man's bank statement.

This was part of the confidential report which – we now know – was delivered by Tony Hall to the BBC governors on the morning of 25 April 1996, but kept secret since that time. The redactions made it hard to follow exactly what had happened. But what was earth-shattering was the simple phrase 'He showed him . . .' Reading those words made me shiver. The story which I *thought* was true hinged on the exact *reversal* of that proposition. Surely it was *Bashir* who had shown something to *Spencer* – not the other way round?

Two months earlier Charles Spencer had told me, politely, to get lost. I had received a note from Sarah Summers, his executive assistant at the Althorp Estate, thanking me for the invitation to take part in my film but declining the opportunity, oh, and with best wishes for the success of the project. So I had little hope for what seemed the only way out of this. Could Spencer explain *why* he had got hold of a bank statement and shown it to an investigative journalist? Could he deny it?

Surely not. At that governors' meeting of 25 April 1996, Hall had apparently assured twelve of the country's great and good that that is *exactly* what Spencer had done. And now the BBC felt confident enough, in October 2020, to brief me, yes, in a somewhat sly way, but in the expectation that I would in turn let the world know, in my documentary film.

Even so. For the next twenty-four hours – always frantically busy ones as a film nears transmission – I wrestled with the issue. What were the BBC implying here? How serious was the charge they were laying at Spencer's door? Finally, on the evening of 20 October, I decided I must act. I made a screen-grab of the critical passage of Hall's report and composed a note for Sarah Summers at Althorp, saying in effect, 'The BBC have sent me this. Does Earl Spencer have any comment?'

When my phone rang early the next morning – now the day of transmission for the film – I recognized the voice, oddly, since it was one I had not heard since the funeral of Princess Diana more than twenty years earlier. Then, in a speech which became instantly famous, that voice rolled from the speakers set up outside Westminster Abbey, to the 2.5 billion people watching around the world. Now the voice was the same, born from five centuries of lordship, buffed by Eton and Magdalen College, almost languid. But it also had the same combative tone.

Charles Spencer said the BBC was lying.

He had looked at my screengrab, showing Hall's allegation of what he had done. And his reaction was explosive: 'What I saw was utterly astonishing. I was outraged. I had done no such thing.' Then, over the next forty minutes on the phone, Spencer unfolded an amazing story. What seemed then a barely believable story. This is where he would recount to me the astonishing details of Bashir's trickery – now so familiar from the Dyson inquiry – but here being revealed to an outsider *for the very first time*. Quoting precise dates and timings, he told me how Martin Bashir had spoken of a plot by Prince Charles to murder not only Diana but the rest of the Spencer family too. I scribbled it all down in my notebook, Spencer, on the other end of the line, reading from notes he had himself recorded at that extraordinary first meeting between Bashir and Diana, in Knightsbridge, on 19 September 1995.

Much of it sounded utterly bizarre: 'He would not rest until the last of the Spencers was in the ground. Prince Charles said, "We're in the endgame now."' Spencer said Bashir in fact showed him four bank statements, not two. Spencer said Patrick Jephson had been portrayed by Bashir as a spy, working for MI5. I continued to scribble everything down, every extraordinary detail. And then, after the strangest forty minutes in my career as a journalist, we said goodbye.

I was spinning. Because I now had *two* desperately competing accounts of what had taken place twenty-five years earlier, and I knew that only one of them could be true. But then one of the great joys of being a journalist is that rare moment when, even as a no-account nobody, you are called upon to judge the doings of the very powerful, the very famous, the very rich, knowing that the verdict you reach will have huge consequences, and it is your call.

I looked again at the notes I had hastily scribbled down during Spencer's phone call. And I looked at the document sent to me by the BBC, Hall's April 1996 report to the Board of Governors. I had two completely different stories – one from the BBC, and one from Spencer; both were sensational, yet neither accorded with the film which was very soon to air. If Hall's account was true about the origin of the bank statements, the film would have to be radically altered, probably pulled. If Spencer's story was true, the film could at least still be shown on television, in just a few hours' time. The allegations I wanted to make were not in question, though it certainly appeared that instead of a molehill of criminality there was a great towering mountain.

So which way to jump? In those circumstances, as a journalist, you apply a test. What if somebody sues? If the story results in an action for defamation, what do I fall back on? Here, if we went with the BBC version of the truth, Spencer would be accused of something deeply shifty, possibly criminal. But the wrapping that the allegation had arrived in was very attractive. The charge was being levelled by Tony Hall, thought to be a straight shooter. His career path had led him right to the top of the BBC, having himself served for seven years as director-general. He had been elevated to the House of Lords, for heaven's sake. It was also fair to assume that clever BBC lawyers had considered the risk of libel yet still given the greenlight that the information could be made public. And, crucially, this was an allegation made not in a furtive verbal briefing, scribbled in my notebook. It was in a document which had lain in the BBC archives for twenty-five years – given to me freely – a printed copy now lying on my desk.

And Spencer's story? If I went with that, the defamed individual would be one of the BBC's most famous names. Their editor of religion no less. Martin Bashir, now a byword for what it is to be a *disgraced* journalist, was in October 2020 one of the BBC's most senior editorial figures, highly paid and respected, laurelled with awards from a thirty-year career at the very pinnacle of his profession. Yes, I had heard from Spencer an astonishing series of allegations. A fever dream of murder plots, spies and conspiracies. Yet all I had was a few pages of notes, following a conversation with a man I had never met, nor spoken to before.

But there is another test. What does common sense tell you? If Spencer *had* done what the BBC claimed, why not simply ignore my approach, lie low? Why make a fuss? Why invent an extraordinary panoply of lies, with dates, with timings, with quotes? 'We're in the endgame now.' I had not secretly recorded the call, though, from Spencer's standpoint, I might well have done. Would someone in his position risk such a bizarre catalogue of allegations becoming public if they were lies?

I now had two different stories, being proferred by two different lords. And it was because of this second test, little more than a gut feeling, that I decided, now with just a few hours remaining before the film was due to be broadcast, which one to accept.

Earl Spencer's story was true. The story from Lord Hall's report was not.

24. Hold the Front Page

At 8 o'clock that night, Wednesday, 21 October 2020, the opening music which I had heard many hundreds of times before in the edit suite sounded again, on Channel 4. My film, *Diana: The Truth Behind the Interview*, began to play. There is something intensely exciting when a film that you have made goes on air and now millions of people will at last get to see what you have been about. I have never shaken off the feeling that it is rather like having your essay read out in the school classroom, you, sitting there, quietly imagining what you hope will turn out to be universal admiration. Sometimes, it is; sometimes, who knows. In this case, for me, the broadcast was specially significant. As a freelance film director you usually get involved in a project lasting maybe six to nine months. But here was a film I had been desperate to get on-screen for so many years. And the most extraordinary thing was, maybe 90 per cent of the story – the jaw-dropping *what-was-that-he-just-said* elements of the story – were not in the film at all.

Charles Spencer's forty-minute briefing to me over the phone had come on the morning of transmission, roughly eleven hours before the tape started to roll in the Channel 4 transmission suite. The documentary had been pretty much completed, checked and rechecked for all the myriad technical necessities two or three days earlier. The film was certainly punchy, presenting evidence for the first time that Bashir had used his forgeries to get close to Diana, raising questions about whether what he had done with the bank statements amounted to criminal forgery. But Spencer's vivid account of what we now know to have been the 19 September 1995 Knightsbridge meeting, the way Bashir presented more forgeries targeting Patrick Jephson, blood-curdling death threats to the Spencer family, all these remained just in my notebook, not on the TV screen. The thought of beginning a massive overhaul to a documentary film on the morning of transmission would be like grabbing hold of the bride, in the church porch, to switch her wedding dress. It was a bizarre situation, a unique one in my experience, and I wasn't at all sure how to handle it.

I weighed up the options. And then I decided to tell the BBC the whole astonishing story which Spencer had told me. The murder plots, the spies and all. I did it not knowing exactly what would happen. At the very least, surely, the BBC would have to announce an immediate inquiry? If we moved at lightning speed, maybe we could put together another film for Channel 4 which would keep us well ahead of the game? What actually happened next was something quite different, revealed through a remarkable batch of emails, obtained by me under Freedom of Information law, tracking internal discussions at the top of the BBC. I have also seen emails which were simultaneously speeding between those same BBC bosses and Charles Spencer. Together they would reveal how, over seven days, despite the BBC's extraordinary refusal to see the juggernaut headed their way, the collision that had been threatening for twenty-five years finally took place.

On the evening of Wednesday, 21 October 2020, just as my film was about to air, I put together a note which I would send to the BBC News head of communications, Charlotte Morgan. Looking back at it now it bears an uncanny resemblance to the scenario eventually described by Lord Dyson in his report published seven months later. At 8.40 p.m., as my film was drawing to a close, I sent off my carefully worded email.

Dear Charlotte,

Our information is that at an 11.30 am meeting at Althorp on August 31 1995 Earl Spencer was told by Mr Bashir that he, Bashir, had a contact within MI5 who had important information regarding surveillance of Princess Diana. After consulting their notes and diary, this same person has told us that at a second meeting, at 6.30pm on Thursday September 14, at Althorp, Mr Bashir produced two documents which he claimed were bank statements. One of them showed money having been paid from a company based in Jersey.

According to our source's notes, Mr Bashir explained that Jersey was a significant origin for these funds because a man within the Royal Household, Richard Aylard, was a Channel islander. Our source's notes also indicate that Mr Bashir said he had information that Mr Aylard, private secretary to Prince Charles, and Patrick Jephson, private secretary to Princess Diana, were both, as ex-Naval officers, closely connected to the intelligence services and were working on behalf of Prince Charles to report the private activities of Princess Diana.

Our source's notes indicate that at a meeting in Knightsbridge at 4pm on Tuesday, September 19, Martin Bashir was introduced to the Princess by Earl Spencer. According to our source, at this meeting Mr Bashir repeated his claim to have information supplied by a contact within MI5. One of the more disturbing claims made by Mr Bashir was that he also had information that Prince Charles was embarked on a plot to murder the entire Spencer family.

We gather that during the 90 minute meeting Earl Spencer took more than 20 pages of notes. We understand that these notes contain a reference very close to the following: 'Prince Charles said he would not be happy till the last Spencer was under the ground. We are now in the end-game'. You will appreciate that, according to our source, this caused great concern to Princess Diana, who subsequently believed that her life was under threat.

You have earlier pointed out that Mr Bashir's unfortunate illness makes it difficult to check these matters with him. Therefore I will only address questions to you which do not require input from Mr Bashir.

Our questions are as follows:

Given the many conflicting versions of what really took place, and as you have pointed out, the historic importance of the Panorama broadcast, has the BBC given any consideration to a full independent inquiry to determine what actually happened?

I gather that Earl Spencer was both surprised and disappointed that he was not in any way consulted by the BBC during the April 1996 inquiry overseen by Lord Hall, which concluded that Mr Bashir's forgeries 'had no bearing, direct or indirect' on the Panorama interview.

It is also perhaps worth noting that our source feels that, in their words, the BBC 'must now be held to account', and is eager to assist further to ensure that happens, if current BBC management maintain a policy of slowly releasing what the source believes to be somewhat misleading information.

My understanding from this person is that now is the time to be utterly transparent rather than maintain a posture which may do current management little credit when the complete picture emerges, as I suspect it soon will.

I look forward to hearing from you,

Kind regards,
Andy Webb

It was intended to be a shocker. Does anybody make that sort of material up? It seemed to me that the BBC would *instantly* have the same reaction as I had done when Spencer unfolded the blood-curdling details to me. And then someone would pick up the phone to Spencer – and everything would come tumbling out. But no. At 9.17 p.m., thirty minutes or so after my email to her had arrived, Morgan contacted the BBC's top-level crisis group: the director-general's chief of staff, Phil Harrold; the corporation's top lawyer, Sarah Jones; head of news and current affairs, Fran Unsworth. All of them undoubtedly just having watched my film go out. Morgan's email read:

> *What timing. Sorry to disturb your evening's viewing. Channel 4 are not letting this rest. They have a 'source' (who seems very well connected to Earl Spencer), challenging our timeline and calling for a 'full independent inquiry'*
>
> *I mean what can we say beyond that a quarter of a century on, we can only go on contemporaneous BBC records, as we made clear to them previously, and with the testimony of the Princess herself, in the form of her note?*
>
> *Clearly we need to discuss.*
> *Charlotte*

Harrold, the director-general's man, was sanguine. His brief reply:

> *No worries.*
> *I'll arrange a call for tomorrow.*
> *Phil*

What was discussed on their call the following day, Thursday, 22 October 2020, remains known only to those who took part. But my plan to set events in motion had failed spectacularly. On Friday, 23 October I received Morgan's reply. She concluded:

> The BBC does not intend to take further action on events which happened twenty-five years ago.

So what to do next? I could only ponder. But in a series of events which only became clear to me a good while later, things would now happen which were entirely out of my hands. Charles Spencer had had enough. He had revealed the whole lurid story to me, yet not a word had appeared in my documentary film. And so he – quite unbeknown to me – would do exactly the same thing that I had done. He would report what Bashir had done *directly* to the BBC, to urge them to investigate.

As he would later explain to me, 'I thought that would be the clever thing for them to do, the right thing to do, ethically. To say, OK, we do have these high standards. It looks like they've slipped. But we'll get to the bottom of it.' And so on Friday, 23 October 2020 – exactly the same day that Charlotte Morgan had turned down my approach – Charles Spencer composed his own 600-word 'Strictly Private and Confidential' email to BBC Director-General Tim Davie.

It was in effect a summary of all the terrible events which would later be outlined in the Dyson report, indicating Bashir's many forgeries, his death threats, his stories of royal affairs and abortions. Spencer wrote to Davie, 'I have detailed notes of many of his extraordinary allegations, and I have records of many of his calls, as well as notes from him to prove my version of events.' Complaining that the BBC had never yet sought him out, Spencer continued, 'It is also astounding to me that I was not contacted at that time, so that senior figures in the BBC could hear my version of events. Again, it leads me to suspect that the truth was not being sought.'

My own colourful breakdown of the scandal had gone to the director-general's chief of staff at 9 p.m. on 21 October 2020. Now, entirely separately, two days later, there was this from the source himself. And Spencer's email was truly chilling stuff. It was the sort of email to which the only appropriate response is, 'Stay right there. I'm in an Uber!' Instead, Spencer waited the whole of that day, checking the computer at his study in Althorp for Davie's reply. He waited the whole of the following day. Still nothing. When the reply finally came, the day after that, it had the slightly weary tone of the parish council chairman dealing, damn it, for the umpteenth time, with some wretched person complaining about a pothole. On 25 October 2020 Director-General Tim Davie wrote to Spencer:

Dear Charles,

Thank you for the email, I wanted to confirm receipt.
I will get a response back to you over the coming days.

Best regards,
Tim

Over the coming days? Spencer wanted very much more than that. Spencer to Davie at 3.17 p.m. on 27 October:

I would like to know, please, where your thinking is, now? What is being done your end, and what is the immediate time frame, please?

Davie's reply, at 4.39 p.m.:

I'm just consulting colleagues with regard to the detail in your note from Friday, and will come back to you as soon as I can.

Spencer at 5.58 p.m.:

I'm afraid things my end can't wait till the end of the week, so I will deal with this situation as I see best.

It was on the following day, Wednesday, 28 October 2020, that Spencer finally received Davie's response. Gone was the spare but still chummy tone of 'Tim's' previous notes. Countersigned by chief of staff Phil Harrold, this 900-word email bore every sign of having been composed laboriously, intricately, by a sweating team of BBC lawyers. As the phrase has it, it 'smelled of the lamp'. But if it was an attempt to silence the increasingly furious Spencer, it would fail, dramatically. One paragraph above all clinched things. Davie had written:

You say the BBC's sequence of events is incorrect and that Mr Bashir had shown you the documents before you had introduced him to the Princess of Wales. Unfortunately, the account you give does not accord with the account that Mr Bashir gave the BBC at the time.

Excuse me? Was that the same Mr Bashir who had lied to the BBC – not once but three times – about these events in 1996? The Mr Bashir who had lied so much that BBC executive Tim Gardam went hot and cold? It was, but Mr Bashir's story was apparently easier for Davie to swallow than the story being told to him now, by Princess Diana's brother. And for Spencer, that was it.

Now the gloves would come off. Spencer had already written, privately, to an earlier director-general, Mark Thompson, way back in 2005, raising the alarm and offering to share his notes on Bashir. He had now done the same thing again, with another director-general, Tim Davie, fifteen years later. Both times he had been rebuffed. But the BBC had had their chance to deal with the scandal discreetly, in a dignified way. Everything that happened from here on would happen in the full glare of publicity. Spencer said to me, 'It was outrageous. It's absolutely clear that they thought if they could just see me off till after the twenty-fifth anniversary, they could get away with it. When they made it clear they weren't going to help, I thought, "Well, it's got to come out."'

Spencer is a journalist by training, and a well-connected one. He told me, 'I'd always had a fairly fraught relationship with the *Daily Mail*, but I did know the editor, Geordie Greig. His twin sister was a flatmate with Diana when they were younger.' And so it would be the *Daily Mail* which would now deliver the message to the BBC which Spencer's own emails had so signally failed to do.

Since 1927 the BBC has had an official motto, carved in stone above doorways and so on, which reads 'Nation Shall Speak Peace Unto Nation'. In recent years a more apt motto would perhaps be '*Cave Quotidie Litteras*', scrappy Latin for 'Beware the *Daily Mail*'. In a way that is semi-comic, but also deeply troubling, the BBC is held more or less to the path of righteousness not so much by any moral judgement on what is right or wrong, or by any fear of what BBC governors might say, but by the fear of what might appear in, above all, that particular newspaper. Salaries too generous? What will the *Mail* say? Do we dump this star for touching up the staff? What will the *Mail* say? Minicab or limo? Business class or first? *Cave Quotidie Litteras*.

Now the BBC was about to feel the stinging lash of the *Daily Mail* as they had never felt it before. And each stripe would be delivered with extra relish, each one a punishment for the way the BBC had so grossly deceived an earlier generation of reporters back in 1996. With almost a mischievous air, Spencer now emailed Director-General Tim Davie once again.

At 10.07 on Monday, 2 November 2020, Spencer wrote:

Dear Mr Davie,

Thank you for your email of Wednesday.
*   Please see below but one example of what I have in my Bashir/ BBC file at Althorp.*

In that sweet upper enclave of New Broadcasting House where the carpets are a tad thicker, the decor more lovely, the coffee a little nicer, a second or so after Spencer's email dropped there will have been a brisk snap of tightening sphincters. Because attached to the email was a copy of Martin Bashir's outrageous 26 September 1995 fax, signed by the reporter, making hideous allegations about nanny Tiggy Legge-Bourke and Prince Charles.

Davie could savour this damning piece of evidence. And he could also read Spencer's thundering declaration. The email continued, 'I have to leave you in no doubt – because I want to be absolutely clear, not to threaten: this is all going to come out now. I am now formally asking for the BBC to open an inquiry into this matter.' Spencer was not just demanding an inquiry. He wanted from the BBC an apology. And, as he wrote, 'one directed posthumously to Diana, to all who were so grossly lied to, including a global audience; and to me'.

Davie did not have long to wait before the assault began. The *Daily Mail* had prepared a devastating campaign, a series of five successive front pages, the first appearing on Tuesday, 3 November with the giant headline:

EARL SPENCER: BBC'S VILE SLURS TO ENTRAP DIANA

When the early editions appeared, even before midnight on 2 November, panic began to grip BBC press officers. At 9.12 p.m. Charlotte Morgan emailed BBC head of communications John Shield. She'd had a tip-off from an insider:

Just spoke to Paul and he said it looks like it'll be the splash.

Shield replied from his iPhone:

Says pages 2-5. That means they've been working on this for some time.

He was right. The *Daily Mail* had prepared a damning compilation of the evidence Spencer had provided to them. At 11.20 p.m. Morgan screenshotted the newspaper's photo of Bashir's compromising fax and sent it to her shell-shocked comrades. And inside the paper, yes, a further four whole pages. Here at last was the evidence which Spencer had patiently offered to bring to the BBC, time and again, privately, in a grown-up way. First way back in 2005 and again, repeatedly, over the preceding fortnight. Now it was there for millions to enjoy. In their newspapers, on their computers, and on their phones.

And so – at last – the BBC sprang into action. By 11.05 the following morning Phil Harrold, Davie's right-hand man, had composed an email for his boss to send to Spencer. No cosy 'Charles' in the greeting this time. Instead the respectful 'Earl Spencer'. Looking for agreement from the rest of the bosses, Harrold wrote:

From: Phil Harrold
Sent: 03 November 2020 11:05
To: John Shield - Comms; Charlotte Morgan; Elizabeth Grace; Fran Unsworth; Peter De Val; zzKen MacQuarrie-PRIVATE; Graham Ellis-Private; Sarah Jones
Cc: Phil Harrold
Subject: response to Spencer

Thanks John

With minor amends from me – is everyone happy with this as a response from Tim.

I agree that he has to offer a personal meeting so it doesn't look like he won't meet – but I've made it clear that it's not just 1-2-1.

Is everyone happy if we send this around 12 noon?

Phil

Dear Earl Spencer,

Thank you for your latest email.

I am keen to see the information you have; we will of course investigate the issues you raise.

Would you please pass the information on to me.

As you know, Martin is unwell, but we will raise the issues directly with him as soon as his heath allows.

I am also happy to meet with you, along with senior editorial executives who are close to these issues, to discuss this directly.

Best wishes,

Tim

Tim Davie
BBC Director-General

With minor amends from me – is everyone happy with this as a response from Tim.

I agree that he has to offer a personal meeting so it doesn't look like he won't meet – but I've made it clear that it's not just 1-2-1.

Is everyone happy if we send this around 12 noon?

Davie makes an intriguing reference to Bashir's alleged ill-health – as we will see later, hugely significant. But whatever they could say now would be too late to stop the onslaught. Day after day the *Daily Mail* would batter the BBC with fresh front page splashes.

BBC DIANA SCANDAL: SPENCER'S DAMNING DOSSIER

Inside the BBC bunker a virtual group now huddled, linked by email. Harrold, the director-general's man. Fran Unsworth, news boss. Sarah Jones, the BBC's top lawyer. As the press office pinged them each ghastly screenshot of the latest *Daily Mail* horror story, a gallows humour began to develop. At seven minutes past ten on the night of Friday, 6 November 2020 Charlotte Morgan emailed the group to say:

> *These front pages are like a parallel universe where it's still the 1990s.*

But no they weren't. Those terrible revelations about Bashir's entrapment of Princess Diana never did make front page news in the 1990s. Because he had got away with it. The BBC had covered up for him. And so the story still had juice. Lots of juice.

BURGLARY OF BBC'S DIANA SCANDAL FILES BBC CRISIS OVER DIANA VILE SLURS SCANDAL

After seven days' brutal pounding the BBC could take no more. The white flag was hoisted. Buckling under the intense media pressure, the decision was finally taken inside New Broadcasting House that, d'you know what, maybe we should find out exactly how Diana was hoaxed into giving her *Panorama* interview twenty-five years ago. On 10 November 2020 Director-General Davie announced that, yes, there *would* be an inquiry. On 18 November he named the senior jurist chosen for the task. Davie announced, 'The BBC is determined to get to the truth about these events and that is why we have commissioned an independent investigation . . . Lord Dyson is an eminent and highly respected figure who will lead a thorough process.'

PART FIVE
Judge and Jury

'. . . yet gaps remain in the record. Suspicious
historians are bound to turn detective and to
ask what the gaps mean. For the suppression or
destruction of evidence in itself is evidence, and
the challenge is to discover: evidence of what?'

David Fromkin, historian, from
Europe's Last Summer, 2004

25. Blind Justice

The current most widely accepted account of the Bashir scandal is the one developed by the character who has already cropped up many times in this account, Lord Dyson. Historians will inevitably make his assessment of the evidence, his publication of edited transcripts and a selection of documents their first port of call, and they may enquire too, who is this man? Usually judicial figures of Lord Dyson's eminence seem rather unknowable but in this case the opposite is true. In 2019 he published a memoir, *A Judge's Journey*, which offers a fascinating account of the often moving family history which underpins his own remarkable career.

Dyson writes of a cultured Eastern European Jewish family only a step ahead of their murderous Nazi tormentors. His mother, born in Bulgaria, reached England just weeks before World War II engulfed Europe; we learn that many members of his family who did not flee quickly enough were seized and perished in Auschwitz. Dyson's father changed the family name, from the Dytch inherited from his own Lithuanian background. Young John Dyson, fiercely bright, then began his climb from a virtual ghetto existence in Leeds, via Oxford, to the very top of this country's professional and social ladder. Dyson became a barrister, aged twenty-five, in 1968.

Thereafter his experience as a working lawyer was wide, at one point punching on behalf of 1960s rock star Dave Clark, in a battle over money owed, on another occasion fighting to establish the Premier League as successor to the fusty old Football League, to become the generator of billions of pounds in football televised worldwide. Every tattooed millionaire who can kick a ball about and is torn which shade of Lamborghini next to buy has Dyson to thank.

He became a judge, and was knighted in 1983, rising to the Supreme Court and finally to appointment as Master of the Rolls, the second most senior judge in England and Wales. Aged seventy-seven when he was appointed by the BBC to conduct his inquiry, already by then retired from the official legal round, he still offers his expertise as a mediator, levying fees which might appear astronomical to many people but reflect both Dyson's rare expertise and the vast sums of money at stake in the commercial disputes which require his judgement of Solomon. Through intellect and energy Dyson has grasped all the prizes available to a second-generation immigrant grammar school boy. Except, curiously, one.

Because of a late change in the rules, Dyson's appointment to the Supreme Court was not accompanied by a seat in the House of Lords, something he anticipated and a point which clearly rankles. He writes, 'Since all my colleagues were known as "Lord X" or "Lady Y", this made me feel uncomfortable. It was as if I was a second tier Justice. After an unconscionably long time, it was agreed that I would be given the courtesy title of "Lord" Dyson.' He returns to the point of this missing peerage many times – 'I have to confess that I have been disappointed not to be given a life peerage' – so much so that one feels that the wound is deep, and raw: 'I have mentioned the peerage issue not because I am obsessed by it. This is far from the case. In fact, most of the time, I do not even think about it.'

And so, more correctly, 'Sir John' rather than 'Lord'

Dyson. Either way his energy seems undimmed; the photograph on his professional web page suggests less an ossified
judicial drudge than a handsome and smiley leading man not
at all too old to play one more role. And he is clearly aware
of the box office draw of having investigated the Bashir
scandal. Although carried off with all fine taste and gravity,
web pages like his are essentially adverts, touting for business. At the time of writing Dyson places his appointment as
Diana inquisitor at the very pinnacle of a legal career stretch-
ing back fifty-six years. So, a man of huge knowledge and
experience. Is it remotely possible that he could have made
mistakes in this inquiry?

Conducted over the last few weeks of 2020 and the opening
months of 2021, Dyson took twenty-nine written submis-
sions and questioned eighteen people face-to-face; because
of Covid these interviews were conducted over video. Many
of those who appeared before Dyson had a lawyer beside
them. Bashir, he records, had two. Dyson is candid about
the ground rules, writing, 'This has not been a public inquiry.
I have had no powers to compel anyone to write or speak
to me; or to produce documents.' It was also, remarkably, a
single-handed affair. Dyson did not operate with a second
lawyer conducting the examination of witnesses, as is often
the case in proceedings like these. Here Dyson was not only
judge and jury but his own cross-examiner as well.

The inquiry, involving essentially one person with a small
support team, was not astronomically expensive as these
things go but neither, at £1.2 million, was it cheap. If the
process can be said to have lasted from the date on which
he was appointed to the date of completion, we arrive at a
figure not far short of £10,000 for each working day of the
report's gestation. So has such a large investment of public

money, the fruit of 7,500 BBC licence fees, been properly rewarded?

I have been a journalist long enough to develop a proper respect for the judicial process, but also long enough to know that judges can make mistakes, which is why our judicial system allows for ascending levels of re-examination and review. In this case, not in reality a part of the judicial process at all but an informal arrangement between Lord Dyson and the BBC, there is no such option. That is why I believe it is now legitimate to look at the report in detail, bearing in mind Dyson's own promise on page 367 of his memoir. There he writes, 'Judges have to be prepared for public criticism and need to be tough and should try to develop a reasonably thick skin. But the skin should not be too thick. A judge should respond positively to fair criticism and be prepared to admit that he may be wrong.'

There is a style of writing that is so utterly matter of fact that one can read the words on the page in front of oneself and hardly see them at all. If the writer does not consider what is being said to be in any way extraordinary, then why should I? Paragraph 150 in Lord Dyson's report seems to me to be a remarkable example. What is referred to below as 'the document' is what has come to be known simply as 'the Diana note', the crucial handwritten document of 22 December 1995 in which Diana appears to absolve the BBC of blame. Here is what Dyson writes in paragraph 150:

An account has been provided to me on condition of confidentiality of what became of the document between, probably, early in 1996 and November 2020. The person concerned was asked early in 1996 by someone in BBC Management to 'guard it with his life' (or words to that effect). At some point, he took it home for safekeeping and filed it in his study.

The anonymous guardian had been given custody of not just the Diana note, the most significant document in the whole affair, but other, unspecified documents too. Dyson continues:

When he moved house, he took it (and other documents relating to the Diana interview) to his new house. In about early November 2020, he became aware of the news story that the Diana note was missing. He searched for it and found it together with the other BBC documents that he had kept. On 10 November 2020, he informed the BBC's Legal Department. On the same day, someone from the BBC went to his house and collected the Diana note and the other BBC documents.

Dyson's cold prose masks events which more properly demand CAPITAL LETTERS. <u>Underlinings.</u> Exclamation marks!! What did he say? *Who* in the BBC was so determined to get this document off BBC premises? And why? Why was the secret keeper told to 'guard it with his life'? And what are these 'other documents' which Dyson refers to? The failure to ask these questions, let alone answer them, implies a scenario which Dyson understands to be entirely innocent, unworthy of interrogation. But surely this scenario seems instead to reek of guilt, and what is more a determination that this guilt will never be exposed. Diana's note must, in 1996, have spelled extreme peril in the BBC wargaming of where the scandal might go. Of course it *might* be needed, at some point in the future. But only in circumstances where everything had already gone belly up. And so it was vital to retain it, perhaps for decades, but just as vital that its existence must never become known. The note promised to be a get-out-of-jail-free card. But the downside of employing it would be the admission that the BBC had been in jail in the first place. If historians or anyone else learned of the note's existence, at some date even decades in the future, they would clearly ask, 'So what exactly were these documents which the princess was being quizzed about?'

And so the Diana note became a thing of fable. I began to pursue it almost twenty years ago, alerted to its possible existence by a single intriguing paragraph in the book *Panorama: Fifty Years of Pride and Paranoia* – the 2003 history of *Panorama*, written by a former reporter for the programme, Richard Lindley. Referring to the then editor of *Panorama*, Steve Hewlett, Lindley wrote, 'Hewlett said he would provide proof that there was nothing wrong with the interview. Sure enough, says Suter, a hand-written note from Diana soon arrived by courier. It said, in so many words: "This is to confirm that I gave you the interview freely and was not influenced by any documents." There was a general sigh of relief.'

In 2007 I submitted a Freedom of Information request, asking for 'all correspondence between the BBC and the office of Diana, Princess of Wales regarding the *Panorama* interview'. The BBC came back with a reply which I naturally found puzzling: 'The BBC does not hold any correspondence between ourselves and Diana, Princess of Wales regarding her interview on the *Panorama* programme.' But was that true? According to the Dyson report the correspondence was at that time being guarded by someone 'with his life', somewhere, though for reasons we are not allowed to know.

The fact that Lord Dyson should not have interrogated the BBC's bizarre handling of this document seems to me extraordinary, not just for the deep suspicions aroused by the circumstances but for reasons peculiar to the judge himself. Between 2012 and 2016 Dyson was, by virtue of his position as Master of the Rolls, chairman of the Advisory Council on National Records and Archives, advising the government confidentially on which documents the public may see and which must remain secret. The pieces of paper which make up our national story were a principal concern for Lord Dyson; he was in effect the nation's archive-meister. For this reason alone, that it should be treated as unremarkable that a handwritten note from Princess Diana, concerning the most momentous interview the BBC has ever undertaken, should be secreted in someone's study, for unspecified reasons, surely beggars belief. My theory, which seems to me a reasonable one, is that here was a clear attempt at what we can only call a 'cover-up'. Not so much a cover-up of events at the moment they *occurred*, in 1996, but a cover-up designed to last forever and a day.

Although the circumstances for the removal of the Diana note are not explained we do at least know from Dyson's account that it was eventually returned to the BBC by its anonymous keeper. Yet three other critically important documents have disappeared *entirely* from the BBC archives. One of them – a six-page handwritten memo – is by far the most incriminating document in the entire scandal archive. Compiled on 28 March 1996, this memo is the work of Tim Gardam, then the BBC's head of weekly programmes, the man who as described earlier had been closely involved in the handling of the scandal since it first began to erupt in December 1995. Gardam begins soberly, but enticingly:

I am recording my recollection of the allegations surrounding Martin Bashir's obtaining of the interview with the Princess of Wales.

Then, in a spidery script which becomes increasingly untidy, dotted with typos and hasty revisions, he unfolds over 1,800 words the twisting saga of events over the preceding four months, culminating in the dramatic revelation made to him by Bashir on the afternoon of Saturday, 23 March 1996. It was then that Bashir finally admitted that he *had* shown the forged bank statements to Charles Spencer, during his visit to Althorp. Not only that, Bashir had consistently lied about what he had done. Gardam wrote:

> *[Bashir] rung me and told me for the first time that he had shown, despite his specific denials on December 21st, and that morning, the graphicised documents to Earl Spencer. I told Bashir that this over-turned every assurance the BBC had been given and the BBC would have to consider its position.*

Gardam's memo thus becomes the *only* document in the entire dossier in which it is unequivocally stated that Bashir had employed forgeries during his pursuit of Diana, and then lied about doing so. If its contents had become publicly known at the time of compilation, then the entire scandal would have erupted with a force sufficient to consume the BBC's top-most management but also, most poignantly, lay bare the architecture of Bashir's plot to its chief victim, Diana. The memo may smell like the smokiest of smoking guns, yet the fact that it had somehow disappeared from BBC archives was only revealed by accident – and to my utter astonishment – during my own research. Lord Dyson himself does not disclose that this memo, and two other crit-ically important documents, were missing at all.

Dyson's silence on the matter seems to invite the ques-tions which he might have put, but did not. First, and most obvious, why was Gardam's memo *handwritten* rather than drawn up on his office computer? We are not told. What we do know is that the six lined pages of Gardam's script were then photocopied from his A4 notebook, the copy given to Tony Hall, the original retained by Gardam himself. It is lucky for history's sake that Tim Gardam did not fall under the proverbial bus at some point between 1996 and 2021; if he had, it is quite possible that Martin Bashir would still be the BBC editor of religion today. Aged sixty-eight at the time of writing, and now the Chief Executive of the philanthropic Nuffield Foundation, Gardam was astonished to discover, when summoned by Dyson in 2021, that his own yellowed copy of the explosive 1996 memo was the only one still in existence. Because the copy which had been handed to Tony Hall decades earlier has been either destroyed, hidden or lost. And the way that fact was revealed is a story in itself.

Just occasionally in journalism you stumble upon an important story when the direction of travel is headed somewhere entirely different. So it was in this case. I only became aware of the existence of the Gardam memo when it was mentioned, by Lord Dyson, though without any comment on its provenance, in his report published on 20 May 2021. Five days later the BBC Director-General Tim Davie gave his first, much-anticipated interview on the scandal, to the Radio 4 *Today* programme's Justin Webb. When a particular topic was broached, Davie sounded nervy:

JUSTIN WEBB: When did you first know that Martin Bashir had lied about these documents personally?

TIM DAVIE: I, I mean, I think I knew it when I read Dyson. So I'm not being evasive because I'd heard, you

know, obviously I'd heard the claims of Earl Spencer.
I've read reports. But when I knew it was when I got that
Supreme Court judge to go and do the analysis and talk
to . . .

JUSTIN WEBB: A different question then, when did you
suspect it?

TIM DAVIE: Well, when I saw evidence coming. And to
me, that was firm evidence that there was clearly things that
had gone horribly wrong in the investigation. I mean, if
you looked at what happened in late October, documents
were emerging and Earl Spencer has put them into the
public domain. They clearly indicated there were bigger
problems with this investigation than were known about.
And within days, we had announced an investigation.

There is a man thinking on his feet. And as it turns out,
little wonder. I had made the natural assumption that Gardam's 1996 memo, describing Bashir's lies in detail, had been
provided to the Dyson inquiry by the BBC. And, if that
were true, it surely followed that Davie had been caught out
in a lie. Because how could Davie possibly have been *unaware*
that Bashir was a liar until the Dyson report appeared in May
2021? What about this six-page BBC memo of March 1996,
spelling out Bashir's mendacity in stark terms?

Here was what sounded to me like a news story, though as
a documentary filmmaker my opportunities to break stories
are limited. There is a lumbering process of first getting a
film commissioned, and then producing it, something which
usually takes many months. And so here was a case where
it seemed better to let the newspapers take a shot, if they

thought this issue was as significant as I did. I tipped off two reporters who had closely followed the scandal, both of them thorough pros: David Brown of *The Times*, Sam Greenhill of the *Daily Mail*. Both agreed it sounded like a story and set to work, aiming for what should make at least a punchy page lead: **'BBC BOSS. WHAT DID HE KNOW AND WHEN DID HE KNOW IT?'**

Both reporters had stories set to appear on the morning of Saturday, 12 June 2021, the *Daily Mail* ready to run a stinging 1,000-word take-down of Davie. But late on Friday night the BBC news press chief, Charlotte Morgan, killed the story stone-dead. In emails to the *Daily Mail* and *The Times*, in an act which I believe can only have followed much agonized discussion, Morgan announced the startling fact that the Gardam memo had not been presented to the Dyson inquiry at all by the BBC. The BBC, she said, did not have a copy of the memo. And there was therefore no *proof* that Davie had been aware that Bashir was a liar before the Dyson report appeared, making his statement to the *Today* programme just about defensible.

But could this new revelation by the BBC be true? I emailed Dyson's office, receiving this reply on 14 June 2021 from lawyer Martin Smith:

> . . . *Mr Gardam provided his notes dated 28.3.96 to the Investigation direct when responding to Lord Dyson's request for evidence. The notes were not provided to the Investigation by any other source.*

As to the BBC, when asked to explain, I received this emailed reply the following day:

It was not the BBC which gave this memo to Lord Dyson. This is because we did not find this document during the searches which we undertook before passing documents to Lord Dyson.

And so the most critical document of all had, somehow, gone missing from the BBC archives. Purely by accident I had turned up a story much more significant than the one I had been chasing.

But Davie's claim that he was unaware of Bashir's lying, until May 2021, still sounded rickety, for two reasons. In a court statement delivered on 13 February 2024 the BBC's senior-most lawyer, general counsel Sarah Jones, made a remarkable admission. Her statement came during my three-year legal battle with the BBC, described later. But the significance here is what it tells us about what Tim Davie most likely *knew*, and what he did *not* know, in 2021. Jones provided a description of the remarkable eight-page memo written on 22 April 1996 by Anne Sloman, providing a walk-through of the cover-up. In her statement Jones says, 'Its contents gave a detailed account . . . revealing that Mr Bashir had lied.'

And so for Davie's statement on the *Today* programme in May 2021 to be *true*, he would need to say that he was also unaware of the contents of *this* document, which his most senior lawyer certainly *did* know about. Was the man at the top of the BBC really kept in the dark, once again, about this most critical fact of all?

Reason number two is that, quite simply, by May 2021, it is most likely that Tim Davie and Tony Hall had for months been in close consultation over the scandal. Davie took over as BBC director-general in September 2020, a post which had been held for the previous seven years by Hall. But in addition to a long, close working relationship between the two men, we know that the BBC assumed official public relations duties for Hall, the recently departed leader. The BBC press office fielded all questions on his behalf.

And so it is barely imaginable that the two men did not discuss the enfolding crisis, and how they were going to deal with it. Hall, beyond doubt, had long known that Bashir had shown himself to be a serial liar. For Davie to preserve his deniability in 2021, Hall must say that he, the outgoing director-general, did not brief the new holder of the post on Bashir's lying. Why he would *not* do so is far from clear, though that is where the narrative leads. And this creates a remarkable triangle of BBC directors-general, failing to confer on the issue at the very heart of the scandal: is Bashir telling the truth, or is he lying? John Birt is adamant that Hall never passed on this most vital information to him in 1996. Tim Davie's position depends on accepting that Hall once again failed to pass on this crucial information, to him, twenty-five years later.

There is a delicious irony that John Birt made his reputation, as a then thirty-three-year-old producer, helping David Frost pin down former US President Richard Nixon for his iconic interview sessions in 1977. A question which has resounded over the decades was put by a US senator at that time, seeming to neatly capture Nixon's slippery, never-quite-candid response to the Watergate scandal. The senator asked, 'What did the President know, and when did he know it?' To swap out 'President' and insert 'Director-General' might still today be a useful exercise.

And so the Diana note was sent, for reasons unknown, to be 'guarded with his life' by the mystery man. The Gardam memo went missing from BBC archives, again in circumstances unknown. A third document would also go missing, a handwritten note by Bashir, prepared under conditions which sound rather cloak-and-dagger. The memo drawn up by Anne Sloman on 22 April 1996 again provides an invaluable window on events at the height of the panic, days before the *Mail on Sunday* story threatened to expose the scandal. Sloman wrote:

> *Bashir met Suter to write down his version of the events. The master copy – hand written, – was given to Tony Hall. Bashir kept a copy. No other copy was made.*

> **18.   Bashir to Suter, March 28**
>
> Bashir met Suter to write down his version of the events. The master copy - hand written, - was given to Tony Hall. Bashir kept a copy. No other copy was made.

This was Martin Bashir's confession. It seems to me reasonable to assume that the reason for Hall's insistence on its being *handwritten* was to avoid the potential embarrassment of sensitive information being lodged for posterity within the BBC computer system. But, if so, the plan had one weakness. The creation of documents *by hand* means that a physical object has been brought into being. We see from Sloman's memo that actual pieces of paper were handed to Tony Hall, who becomes the last known person to have had custody of them.

And so why did Dyson not simply pursue this when given the opportunity? Why did he not say to Hall, 'You say you do not have the confession now. Yet at one point you clearly did. What did you do with it?' When the copy held by Hall subsequently vanishes from the record, and the BBC cannot say why, we are entitled to ask questions. An investigator acting on the public's behalf, as in Lord Dyson's case, is surely *compelled* to ask them. It is difficult to see why Dyson does not comment on the disappearance of these documents, if only to demonstrate that he has noted their absence, the facts have been weighed and no blame can be attached to the loss of this vital evidence.

And here is where what I see as the malign effect of the Dyson report becomes most evident. I have tried to discover what happened to this missing evidence, both from my standpoint as a journalist and in the context of my three-year legal battle with the BBC, described shortly. In both cases the result was the same. A refusal to engage with the question on a serious level, instead a determination by the BBC to use Dyson as a shield. Hall, retired from the BBC since 2020, the man whom we *know* once held the master copy of Bashir's confession, had only this to say: 'Any questions about the storage and archiving of documents are best asked of the BBC. Please direct your questions to them.' And this, from the BBC press office: 'Had Lord Dyson wanted to make any commentary about the BBC's archiving, he could of course have done so.' It is replies like that which tell you nothing, and everything.

And so, at least for the moment, that is where we stand regarding three pieces of missing evidence. It is item number four which, in my view, is the most troubling of all.

26. Faking It

When I first learned about the disappearance of Diana's handwritten note, the loss of Tim Gardam's deeply incriminating memo, the loss of Martin Bashir's confession, all of it seemed to make sense. Each of them perfectly fits the description of a 'smoking gun'. Of course, I have no *proof* that these three critical documents were treated in a way that is the least bit sinister. But it seems fair to say that the circumstances are, at the very least, suspicious. One could easily imagine a motive for the BBC wanting each of them out of the way.

In the case of the *fourth* item which went missing things seemed to me, at least initially, far more puzzling. This document is a bland-seeming letter, 250 words or so, dated 4 April 1996, addressed to Martin Bashir.

The letter is unsigned but bears the name of executive Tim Suter. At first glance it appears to be a reprimand, for a series of vaguely outlined offences. The letter reads:

Dear Martin,

Thank you for giving me the detailed account of your preparations for the interview with the Princess of Wales.

I have consulted Tony Hall and others within the senior management of News and Current Affairs, and it is clear to us, from the account you have given and from the corroboration we have received, that your dealings with the Princess in securing the interview were absolutely straight and fair. We are completely satisfied that the interview was freely given; that the Princess was placed under no pressure by you or anybody else; and that she was neither shown any documents nor told anything she did not already know.

However, it is also clear to us that the creation and use of some material in the early preparation for the programme was in breach of the BBC's guidelines on straight dealing. This breach was compounded by your failure to inform the then Head of Department of the use made of this material when directly questioned by him.

You should be in no doubt of the seriousness with which we view this, nor of the reprimand that this letter represents. I will be consulting Tony Hall on his return to the office to discuss any next steps.

We believe that no purpose is served by making this a matter of public record. However, we retain the right, if future events require it, to make this letter public and to justify the action we have taken.

Your sincerely
Tim Suter
(Managing Editor, Weekly Programmes, News and Current Affairs)

Martin Bashir esq

4.04.96

Dear Martin,

Thank you for giving me the detailed account of your preparations for the interview with the Princess of Wales.

I have consulted Tony Hall and others within the senior management of News and Current Affairs, and it is clear to us, from the account you have given and from the corroboration we have received, that your dealings with the Princess in securing the interview were absolutely straight and fair. We are completely satisfied that the interview was freely given; that the Princess was placed under no pressure by you or anybody else; and that she was neither shown any documents nor told anything she did not already know.

However, it is also clear to us that the creation and use of some material in the early preparation for the programme was in breach of the BBC's guidelines on straight dealing. This breach was compounded by your failure to inform the then Head of Department of the use made of this material when directly questioned by him.

You should be in no doubt of the seriousness with which we view this, nor of the reprimand that this letter represents. I will be consulting Tony Hall on his return to the office to discuss any next steps.

We believe that no purpose is served by making this a matter of public record. However, we retain the right, if future events require it, to make this letter public and to justify the action we have taken.

Your sincerely

Tim Suter
(Managing Editor, Weekly Programmes, News and Current Affairs)

So what is it about *this* document which meant that its presence in the BBC archives might prove troublesome in some way? Surely, a letter which showed Bashir had actually been reprimanded for his conduct would demonstrate that his bosses were taking the scandal seriously. They were taking firm action to punish his behaviour. But closer examination of this 'reprimand' strongly suggests that it was no such thing and, in effect, a fake.

A very different purpose for the letter is indicated by the 22 April 1996 memo by Anne Sloman. She writes:

> *Suter agreed a letter with Tony Hall which would confirm that the interview was properly arrived at, but that there were questions about the creation and use of the documents. This was a holding letter against possible further press interest. A copy of it was left with Richard Peel to be sent if needed. It was never sent.*

17. **Suter to Tony Hall, Richard Peel, 26 - 28 March**

Suter agreed a letter with Tony Hall which would confirm that the interview was properly arrived at, but that there were questions about the creation and use of the documents. This was a holding letter against possible further press interest. A copy of it was left with Richard Peel to be sent if needed. It was never sent.

Decoding that cryptic account, it appears that the so-called 'reprimand' was not intended for Bashir. It was not written and sent to *him*. Instead it was sent to the man who was then BBC head of communication and information, the corporation's senior-most press officer, Richard Peel. He was to hang on to it, pending what Sloman elliptically calls 'possible further press interest'. And so the 'reprimand', which there is no indication was ever sent to Bashir, was in effect not a reprimand at all, but a press release, falsely suggesting that Bashir *had* been reprimanded, when he had not. The document would be kept secret, only emerging if the scandal got completely out of hand and the press, having first chewed up Bashir, turned their attentions to BBC managers. When reporters put the question, 'So what exactly did you do about the con man?' the BBC executives could at least then wave this piece of paper in front of the press pack and declare, 'See here! We were on it all the time! Kicked his ass good and proper.' The phoney document was held behind glass, marked 'Smash only in emergency'.

For that reason this letter has always seemed to me a contender for the grubbiest fake of them all. It might just be possible for the BBC to argue that what was done was for the ultimate good of the BBC. To protect the corporation's good name, by preventing news of the scandal becoming public. This document is quite different if it was only to be deployed if and when the cover-up had failed, a sham designed to save only themselves. But, as Sloman confirms, the crisis never quite reached that point. Press chief Richard Peel was not ultimately called upon to deploy the letter. Although on 7 April 1996 the *Mail on Sunday* got very close, the BBC's deeply misleading press statement at that time ensured that the crisis was narrowly averted.

If this was the purpose of the 'reprimand', what were the thought processes behind it? In prospect was a situation where in large degree control of the scandal had been lost. But of course, it could not have been known how many details would have entered the public domain when the letter was deployed and so should be included. The letter begins with what sounds rather like a pat on the back for Bashir; his dealings with the princess were 'absolutely straight and fair'. But if Bashir was not to see the 'reprimand' this merely serves as a form of expository exoneration for the authors.

Should it reveal that Bashir had deployed his forgeries, and then lied three times about his conduct? These transgressions would have formed the principal charges set out in the letter if this were a true reprimand based on what was known at the time. But the letter uses woolly phrases; talking about the 'creation and use of some material' and a 'failure to inform'. Phrases like that do not reveal too much. But at the same time they might *just* underpin a defence were this to become a 100 per cent, God almighty disaster.

The most disturbing paragraph comes right at the end. It is as if, nearing completion of the letter, someone raised the question, 'What if the hacks complain that we didn't come clean about Bashir long ago?' The last paragraph has every appearance of an attempt to establish a chronology, something addressed to a future audience but strangely out of place in a genuine letter of reprimand to Martin Bashir.

So what does Dyson make of this 'reprimand'? The answer appears to be absolutely nothing. In a way which is, to say the least, hard to comprehend, he appears to take the document at face value. Dyson writes, 'It seems probable that this letter of reprimand was not sent . . . There is no indication in Mr Bashir's employment records that he was reprimanded.' Yet

Dyson spent many hours not only with Bashir, the supposed recipient of the letter, but Hall and Suter, its creators. How can doubt *possibly* linger on whether it was sent or not? If, unaccountably, the position was still not clear, Dyson might have followed up with Sloman, whom he also interviewed at length, and who describes the creation of the document and its purpose.

All this seems so extraordinary that my concerns must have provisos. Firstly, the letter's creators are adamant that, sent or not, this was an authentic letter of reprimand, genuinely drafted to reprimand Martin Bashir on the basis of what they then knew of his activities securing the interview and preparing the programme. There was no concealment or misrepresentation by them as to the true nature of the letter in their evidence to Lord Dyson. Furthermore, the full array of evidence which was gathered by Dyson remains a secret, immune from disclosure even under the Freedom of Information Act. Although we have the report itself, plus a selection of edited interviews and certain documents which Dyson elected to make public, we are barred from seeing the full picture and therefore it is impossible to know if some of the questions which cry out for an answer were indeed put but not reported. Certain lapses seem so egregious that it is hard to believe that there is not mitigating material in Dyson's private files. Yet it seems also fair to ask why this inquiry, paid for by the public, concerning Britain's public broadcaster, and on a matter of enormous public interest, was ever conceived as a purely private and in large part secret enterprise, reliant upon the binding judgement of a single individual.

The question of whether or not Bashir was in fact reprimanded when his transgressions first came to light, in 1996, is of critical importance in determining the motivation of the BBC executives managing the scandal. Were they really determined to *do* the right thing, or merely *pretend* that they had done it? Summoned before the BBC Board of Governors on 25 April 1996, Hall clearly senses that he should give some indication that Bashir has been disciplined. In the notes (including Hall's own typo) prepared for that meeting he writes:

> *I am writing to him giving him requesting that his action was incautious and unwise, and that he should be a great deal more careful in the future.*

Crucially, Hall does not say that he *has* written to Bashir. He says, carefully, that 'I am writing . . .' But the so-called reprimand bears the date 4 April 1996, exactly three weeks *before* the meeting of the governors. So why does Hall not say that this document has already been sent to Bashir? The answer may be that Hall, appearing before the governors, was happy to play down Bashir's wrongdoing. Nothing to see here. Move along. And so any reference to a formal reprimand might be counterproductive, threatening to rouse the governors from their torpor.

It is intriguing to examine Hall's next move during his critical appearance before the governors that morning. It requires a clear head and a sharp grasp of the detail, even now, to determine what Bashir did, and why. To distinguish between what is a forgery and what is just an innocent mock-up. As the meeting progressed, after dismissing Bashir's conduct regarding the Diana interview as a mere blip, after confirming that Bashir is 'honest and an honourable man', Hall neatly turned the governors' attention to another edition of *Panorama* altogether, the film which had earlier examined the financial dealings of former England football manager Terry Venables.

The tenuous link with the Diana programme is that, in this earlier edition of *Panorama*, a graphic appeared briefly on-screen which was indeed a mock-up, a wholly accurate depiction of a financial statement which the producer had nonetheless decided to portray in graphic form. Before including the graphic in his film, the producer concerned, Mark Killick, had carefully sought permission from both *Panorama*'s in-house lawyers and the BBC department responsible for editorial policy. Both had signed off, something which it is most likely that Hall would have known when addressing the BBC governors on 25 April 1996.

Yet Hall seemed *appalled* at what had happened in this case. And he would let the governors know that *tough* action was being taken. Right away. Regarding producer Mark Killick, Hall told the governors, '. . . the producer concerned will be given a severe reprimand for the use of a "mock-up" background to the graphic.'

I am carrying out the following actions:

- the producer concerned will be given a severe reprimand for the use of a 'mock-up' background to the graphic

In the snug confines of the New Broadcasting House council chamber, if the governors were struggling to follow exactly how one edition of *Panorama* – something to do with football? – related to another – to do with Princess Diana? – and how two forged bank statements were merely innocent mock-ups yet a quite different mock-up was not innocent at

all, it is easy to imagine how Hall's clear and decisive condemnation of Mark Killick might have come as some kind
of blessed relief.

Someone had been *severely* punished. For something or
other. Next item.

The issue of how Bashir was disciplined – if indeed he
was disciplined at all – surfaced once again in 2021. When
veteran BBC reporter John Ware compiled his own *Panorama* programme on the scandal he approached Hall on this
topic. Ware says, 'Lord Hall told *Panorama* Bashir was given
a "severe reprimand" and was placed under "close supervi-
sion".' Yet this statement by Hall in 2021 does not accord
with Lord Dyson's findings. Nor does it accord with Ware's
own research. When he questioned another BBC executive
who was closely involved with events in 1996, Ware says,
'*Panorama*'s then deputy editor Clive Edwards told me he was
"unaware of any supervisory order on Martin. It is difficult
to imagine how any such order could have been in force but
not known to me as deputy editor, since I would have been
the person to supervise such an order."'

The existence of the letter dated 4 April 1996, the 'reprimand', seems to me to be crucial in making a judgement about
the BBC executives managing the scandal thirty years ago.
Their failure to get to the bottom of Bashir's wrongdoing,
their failure to call Earl Spencer, can, at a pinch, perhaps be
explained away because they were 'woefully ineffective'. But
those failings were sins of omission. A sham 'reprimand'
points instead to a game plan for what to do if the full story
of Bashir's deployed forgeries and lies came out.

It seems to me that the creation of a sham reprimand is
not so very different from Bashir's creation of fake bank

statements. Both are designed to mislead. And in terms of ambition the letter could be seen as the clear winner, designed to fool millions, whereas Bashir's fakes were targeted at just one person. What Bashir did has become notorious, the defining event in the biggest crisis ever to engulf the BBC. The letter and its creators have yet to be satisfactorily scrutinized.

But most worrying of all, in my view, is the fact that Lord Dyson did not draw attention to the issues around the letter in his report. The evidence strongly suggests that he simply failed to realize what these were. And, if that is the case, then perhaps his whole assessment of the scandal must be called into question.

27. Not Guilty

Lord Dyson assumed the separate roles of detective, inquisitor, judge and jury. He set himself the task of establishing who did what and, at least implicitly, then determining their guilt or innocence. As we will see Dyson would himself subsequently raise a question mark over the wisdom of such extraordinary multitasking. In any event it is my belief that Lord Dyson founded his general approach to the scandal on a mistaken assumption, one which has not merely led him astray but is hugely unfair to Diana herself. In the very first paragraph of his report he writes:

By early to mid-August 1995 at the latest, she was keen on the idea of a television interview. She would probably have agreed to be interviewed by any experienced and reputable reporter in whom she had confidence even without the intervention of Mr Bashir.

With this sweeping assertion Dyson establishes the context in which he will examine the scandal. But what do his words actually mean? In saying, 'She would probably have agreed to be interviewed . . .' the question arises: interviewed about what? The only important question is whether Princess Diana would have agreed to deliver the same package of bravado and insult which she presented on *Panorama*, not whether she would grant an interview covering, perhaps, an account of her charity work, or something equally anodyne.

The rest of the sentence is less ambiguous. Dyson declares

that Diana would have cooperated with any trusted interviewer, establishing that there was nothing unique about
what he calls the 'intervention' of Martin Bashir. But this
crucial assertion, offered without the least evidence, runs
counter to the evidence which does exist. Despite her anger
at Prince Charles's television confession of June 1994 Diana
was, in 1995, patently *refusing* all invitations to go on TV, despite these invitations having come from 'experienced and
reputable' figures, like the BBC's royal correspondent Jennie
Bond, as well as famous outsiders like Oprah Winfrey and
the then doyenne of A-list interviewers, Barbara Walters,
both entertained for lunch at Kensington Palace but politely
brushed off.

And they clearly came from people, as Dyson puts it, 'in
whom she had confidence'. People like Andrew Morton,
whom Diana had recently trusted with audio tapes of her
innermost feelings for his scarifying 1992 book. In refusing
to dish Diana as the source, in the media storm which followed, Morton had not merely retained Diana's trust but won
her gratitude, creating a conspiratorial bond within which, a
short time before Bashir came on the scene, Morton pitched
Diana the idea of a TV tell-all. He told me, 'I was part of a
consortium, encouraging her to do a documentary for ITV.
We'd even done some filming surreptitiously. But she felt
that it was just too near to the Dimbleby documentary which
went out in June 1994.'

Dyson seems to suggest that Diana would have said what
she said to anyone, that Bashir did little more than find himself in the right place at the right time. In reality it seems to
me impossible to understand the scandal at all unless we turn
Dyson's defining paragraph through 180 degrees. Instead, it
should more accurately read:

*In early to mid-August 1995 Princess Diana **was firmly resisting** the idea of a television interview, even when suggested by experienced and reputable reporters in whom she had confidence. **But this changed with the intervention of Mr Bashir.***

Dyson's analysis is regrettable, and little wonder that it has been so warmly embraced. Martin Bashir's response to the publication of the report in 2021 included this: 'Lord Dyson himself in any event accepts that the Princess would probably have agreed to be interviewed without what he describes as my "intervention".' And to defend himself before the House of Commons committee on 15 June 2021 Hall reached for exactly the same defence: 'an interview, according to Lord Dyson, was very, very likely. In this sense, Martin Bashir got it first.'

Dyson's apparent willingness to believe that Diana was herself half to blame for the interview, that Bashir was simply what he calls the 'charming and empathetic' reporter who caught her at the right time, means that he abandons the inquiry into exactly *how* the interview was achieved on the very day that Diana and Bashir first met. The narrative reaches 19 September 1995, the day of their encounter in the Knightsbridge apartment. And then it ceases. The six weeks following, in which Bashir worked on Diana's fears in order to get her in front of a camera, are not explored in the slightest degree, despite Dyson's clear Terms of Reference:

What steps did the BBC and in particular Martin Bashir take with a view to obtaining the Panorama interview on 20 November 1995 with Diana, Princess of Wales? This will involve a consideration of all the relevant evidence.

Should Dyson not have given at least *some* consideration to what remains the most important piece of evidence we have, important because it is incontrovertible, the fax described in an earlier chapter? The fax signed by Bashir, making startling allegations about Tiggy Legge-Bourke and Prince Charles, and sent to Charles Spencer on 26 September 1995. In it Bashir urges Spencer to '. . . inform your sister asap'. It is surely fair to assume that Bashir would tell Diana what he had been so keen to pass on to her brother, yet Dyson does not put the question.

And what of Lord Mishcon's astonishing record of Diana's most deeply held fears, recorded on 30 October, strongly reminiscent of the lies unfolded by Bashir at his initial meeting with the princess in Knightsbridge on 19 September? Was Dyson not tempted to at least raise with Bashir what seems the obvious conclusion, that it was the BBC reporter who put these terrifying thoughts into Diana's head? Dyson's approach means that we have an account of how Bashir and Diana came to meet. But as to what happened next, the crucial period, as to '. . . what steps did . . . Bashir take with a view to obtaining the *Panorama* interview . . .' we have nothing at all. Dyson seems content to conclude that Bashir is something of a bad apple, though a charming one.

But what is his verdict on the BBC bosses? There seems to me to be a conundrum at the very heart of the report, where Dyson concludes on the one hand that those bosses did, in 1996, intend to *cover up* the scandal, yet he also finds that the inquiry which they conducted at the time was a *genuine* inquiry. Those two concepts cannot sit comfortably side by side. A clear intention to deceive the public is unlikely to be found alongside a genuine attempt to discover the truth. Dyson's position requires the assumption that the BBC were themselves honestly seeking to reveal the facts of the matter, rather than, as the evidence more strongly suggests, being most concerned to build a protective carapace around them. Far from conducting an exercise which was 'woefully ineffective', the BBC managed this so brilliantly that it sustained itself for twenty-five years.

There are two passages in the report which come close to offering a clear answer as to Lord Dyson's verdict on the bosses. Guilty, or not guilty? On page 112 Dyson addresses the question of why, in April 1996, Charles Spencer was never contacted by the BBC to give his side of the story. If he *had* been contacted, he would have learned that he too had been hoaxed by Martin Bashir, just like Diana. The scandal would then have been revealed and all subsequent disasters averted. The two people who might have contacted Spencer at any time, with a simple phone call, were Tony Hall and Anne Sloman. And the verdict? Dyson writes:

I am not willing to make the serious finding that she and Lord Hall consciously decided not to approach Earl Spencer for fear of what he might say . . .

Not guilty.

Upon reading Dyson's verdict in 2021 the BBC couple, one now a member of the House of Lords, the other a high stalwart of Anglican do-goodery, must surely have breathed the most enormous sigh of relief. Yes, they had failed to do the single, simple – one might say *decent* thing – which would have quickly brought the shocking details of the scandal to light. But they would not be *blamed* in any way for that failure. Running directly counter to Prince William's assessment of the situation, that there were '. . . *leaders at the BBC who looked the other way rather than asking the tough questions*', Dyson's verdict leaves one wondering quite why that critical phone call was never made. How the situation was allowed to reach the point where, in Sloman's punchy, and as she identified, 'mafia-like' phrase: 'The Diana story is probably now dead, unless Spencer talks.'

Spencer did not talk. But he most certainly *would* have done, had he been told about Bashir's forgeries. I have discussed this specific point with Charles Spencer and it seems to him an astonishing omission that Dyson did not pursue this crucial line of inquiry. Hall – and director-general Birt too – were both fully aware in April 1996 that a member of the public had been shown forged documents by the BBC, whilst being assured that they were genuine. Had they not at the very least a duty of care to inform that member of the public – Princess Diana's brother or anyone else – that they had been duped? It was not a fear of what Spencer might *say* which made approaching him so ticklish for the BBC, but what Spencer must necessarily have been *told*. That he had been hoaxed, as it would emerge tragically too late, so had his sister.

And what then of the cover-up which Dyson accepts *did* occur, beyond any doubt? On page 121 of his report Dyson writes:

> The documents that I have read and the oral testimony that I have heard do not enable me to make a finding as to who was responsible for deciding that the story should not be covered by the BBC . . . It must have been someone from senior management, but I can't say who it was.

This is a crucial passage. The suppression of the news story, by the BBC itself, is something which Dyson is perfectly prepared to call a cover-up. But *why* is he unable to say who ordered it? During the course of his inquiry Dyson spoke at length with every member of the 1996 senior management team who might conceivably have issued the instruction to cover up: John Birt, Tony Hall, Tim Suter and Anne Sloman. And so, if not one of those four, who *could* it have been? Was there another manager who might have issued the order? And, even if that *were* the case, why was it not immediately countermanded by one of the people whom Dyson interrogated? In the confusion, for the four people named, there is again only one possible verdict.

Not guilty.

A part of the reason for the vast expense of hiring a figure such as Lord Dyson, whose fee in this instance was £260,750, is the aura of respectability which it confers on the inquiry process. It deters criticism or query. But surely, when someone is hired to do a job, whether they are a judge or a plumber, we are entitled to ask whether the job has been done adequately? The fact that a cover-up existed in 1996 is not in doubt, nor was it *ever* in doubt. The important task Dyson had to perform was surely to identify who was responsible, rather than to note that, yes, the cover-up existed: '. . . but I can't say who it was.' It seems to me that the plumber has stared at the leak. Has agreed that it is indeed a prodigious leak. One which really needs fixing. And has then packed up his tools and left.

Judges of Dyson's seniority deserve respect. I understand that a journalist who sets up to challenge a former Supreme Court judge appears not much better than a ruffian lobbing stones at the courthouse window. Yet it seemed fair to put my concerns to Dyson himself, and that he might respond, especially given the passage from his own memoir quoted earlier: 'A judge should respond positively to fair criticism . . .' Despite having set out, in great detail, the concerns I have outlined, the result was disappointing. In early 2025 I received a response from the chief executive of his legal chambers. In a brief reply she said, 'I have spoken to Lord Dyson about your correspondence and he feels that after all this time he is not in a position to engage with any of the details of this.'

But Lord Dyson *has* commented publicly following his inquiry, once, in a remarkable interview which seems to me both admirably frank and at the same time deeply disturbing. In July 2021, two months after the publication of his report, Dyson agreed to conduct a live Zoom interview with the distinguished legal columnist Joshua Rozenberg, for an audience of the British Friends of the Hebrew University legal group. In that comfortable setting Lord Dyson appears to have spoken very openly, conceding that his own process may have been seriously flawed. He told his audience:

I was, for the one and only time in my career, both a detective – I was having to work out how Bashir had got to Princess Diana, because that was an extraordinary story – and I was also counsel.

And so there I was, cross-examining people like Martin Bashir and Lord Birt and Lord Hall and all these other people. There were eighteen of them all together. It took me back thirty years to my days when I was a barrister. You don't forget. There are certain things, it's like riding a bicycle, you don't forget it. And then of course I had to be the judge as well. So this strange combination of functions.

And I think in hindsight I made a mistake in not asking for a counsel to the investigation to take some of the burden off me, to ask some of the questions, which is what happens in, say, public inquiries, as you know. So I had to do it all.

If Lord Dyson's fears are correct, then perhaps we have some sort of explanation for the apparent oversights I have listed. But as to his implicit verdicts of not guilty, regarding the senior BBC staff who presided over the cover-up, what of them? The glimmer of a possible explanation comes when one considers the curious dynamic at work in this inquiry, a collision of lords, real, manufactured and pretend. The injured party was Earl Spencer, an aristocrat through and through and someone Dyson was clearly not disposed to doubt. Two putative wrong 'uns were lords too: Baron Hall of Birkenhead, Baron Birt of Liverpool.

But these were very different, grammar school lads who had come up through their own talents to win the highest honour that the nation can bestow, just as Dyson had so keenly hoped to do. Indeed still *does* hope, writing: 'If I were offered a peerage now, I would accept the offer . . . To sit in the House of Lords would have been a fitting end to my journey from the Jewish community of Leeds.' Is it fanciful to believe that Dyson, consciously or not, sensed the great power he had been granted, the knowledge that with just one or two sharp phrases he could cast Hall and Birt down into the dirt? Unless he were convinced that the two were truly beasts and scoundrels, perhaps it were better that they receive just a gentle wigging, to behave better in the future?

When historians begin to pick over the evidence and make their analysis, if researchers are able to one day discover all that went on behind the closed doors of Dyson's inquiry, I am convinced that a fuller picture will emerge. For now we have an official account which seems to me glaringly incomplete, one which does not apportion blame beyond Bashir, the cringing villain who from the outset had 'GUILTY' inked across his brow.

PART SIX
Looking for Answers

'I don't want a divorce, but . . . I await my husband's decision of which way we are all going to go . . .'

'Would it be your wish to divorce?'

'No, it's not my wish.'

Princess Diana, *Panorama*, 20 November 1995

28. *Panorama* to Paris

Although they are 6,000 miles apart, twelve hours on a plane, there is no time difference at all between France and South Africa. Because it is due south, Cape Town is in lockstep with Paris. And so when Charles Spencer, at his estate known as Tarrystone, received the first phone call on Sunday, 31 August 1997 it was also the small hours of the morning in the French capital. He said to me, 'I was alone in my house with my four children and I had a call in the middle of the night. First it was, "She's had an accident and might have broken her leg or something." Then I got more calls. And it escalated, and escalated.

'Then I was on the telephone to my sister Jane, whose husband Robert was the queen's private secretary. And he was on another line in the same room. I could hear him. And then he went, "Oh no!" I heard him go, "Oh no." And Jane went, "That's it. She's dead."

'And it was just staggering, really. And then I remember watching news coverage. And they didn't know, it hadn't been announced. I stayed up all night, of course.'

As the sun came up he was in that state of shock where you hope against hope you can make it be a nightmare. But each time the bad thing refuses to flee. He had to accept this was real. He said, 'My kids came through for breakfast and I said, you know, "I'm afraid I've got awful news. I'm afraid Diana has been killed." And then one of my little girls, Eliza, just looked at me and she smiled and said, "Not in real life, Daddy?" and I said, "Yeah, I'm afraid it is."'

The rawness of loss, the bewilderment, how life had flipped forever in the time it takes to hear someone say 'oh no', was no different in this instance from any other occasion when a relative receives such devastating news. But it was not going to be possible for Spencer to simply hold the news to himself. To steep himself in shock, in private. Even before it was confirmed that Diana had died, at 4 a.m. Paris time in the Pitié-Salpêtrière Hospital, the media had begun to gather outside his gates.

There was only one story in the world. But as Spencer watched CNN something inside him started to jostle with the grief: 'I saw all these rent-a-quote journalists trying to blame everyone except the paparazzi and the press for this accident and was feeling really very angry about it. And that's why I gave a speech outside my property. I was angry about the role of the press.' He went to his study and put his anger down on paper. When he emerged a short time later holding those notes there was a mass of reporters, more arriving by the minute.

They ceased milling about as Spencer approached. But then the reporters pressed forward with their voice recorders, the cameramen shuffled and elbowed to capture the best shot. Spencer said to them, 'I always believed the press would kill her in the end. But not even I could believe they would take such a direct hand in her death as seems to be the case. Every proprietor and every editor of every publication that has paid for intrusive and exploitative photographs of her, encouraging greedy and ruthless individuals to risk everything in pursuit of Diana's image, has blood on his hands today.'

It was less than a week later, on Saturday, 6 September, when Spencer spoke once again, from a pulpit this time in Westminster Abbey, the audience before him including the queen, Prince Charles, William and Harry, 32 million people watching Diana's funeral service live on television in the UK and perhaps 2.5 billion around the world. What has been remembered from that day is how Spencer captured the sense that Diana had been treated shabbily by the Windsors. His careful reference to William and Harry being part of his own *Spencer* family was intensely awkward, thrilling though, as this rift among the highest born in the land was referenced so boldly: 'On behalf of your mother and sisters, I pledge that we, your blood family, will do all we can to continue the imaginative and loving way in which you were steering these two exceptional young men, so that their souls are not simply immersed by duty and tradition, but can sing openly as you planned.'

But Spencer's other target that day came as less of a surprise. In the days following the Paris crash, the paparazzi whirling on their motorbikes had been fixed as demons, furies pursuing the heroine to her doom. Spencer had summoned a classical metaphor in his eulogy: '. . . of all the ironies about Diana, perhaps the greatest was this – a girl given the name of the ancient goddess of hunting was, in the end, the most hunted person of the modern age.'

The image has been fixed in the twenty-eight years since Spencer's eulogy that, certainly in the final horrific moments of her life, Diana was done to death by the media, the drunken driver of the Mercedes made deadlier still by the pack of manic pursuers. It is not hard to hate the freelance paparazzi who chased Diana for the huge sums of money the right photo would bring.

But in 2021 the picture became more complicated. As

details of Martin Bashir's crimes emerged it became clear that Diana's fate was not solely determined by the paparazzi, the scum. The august British Broadcasting Corporation was involved too. And when this came to light certain people immediately recognized the danger. They knew they must quickly categorize Bashir as having been not really a true BBC guy. He had been one of the scum all along. A low-life trickster who had merely sneaked inside the *Panorama* compound for a short while, disguised as a decent chap.

Bashir was undeniably a pro. His plan was carried out with extraordinary skill, overcoming, as very few reporters were able to do, first Charles Spencer's bristling hostility to the media and then penetrating the very inner sanctum, Diana's sitting room at Kensington Palace. Once there he was able to conjure just the right words and spill them in such a way that Diana, no fool she, was entranced, then terrified, and then done up like a kipper. Those are fearsome skills, as darkly admirable as the paparazzo who can snatch sharp photos single-handed from a racing motorbike or snap the million-dollar picture from a hiding place half a mile away. Bashir's former colleague Jonathan Maitland watched him at work for six years, telling me, 'He was basically broadcasting's fake sheikh, you know? He would do whatever it took – if necessary double-crossing your competitors – and was brilliant at it. I mean, if his target back in 1995 had been a paedophile, or a child trafficker, he'd be a hero, wouldn't he?'

This placing of Bashir among the tabloid demons becomes central to the defence implicitly mounted by the BBC, creating a world of us and them. Saints and sinners. The chief proponent of this argument is John Birt, Lord Birt, Bashir's ultimate boss at the time as BBC director-general. Called before a committee of the House of Commons in June 2021,

Birt said, 'Unless you understand that this was a serial liar on an industrial scale, you simply cannot understand the story.' But Birt understood. He went on to absolve the BBC bosses, and implicitly himself, who had been taken in by the scum: 'Yes, they all believed him, hardened and experienced though they were, and we know they were wrong to believe him, but we also can see some of the reasons why . . . He is a very skilled confidence trickster. He uses emotion. He is very persuasive. He cried in his interview with Tony Hall and Anne Sloman.'

Birt's 'they' are the people who *didn't* catch Bashir. Whose internal inquiry was 'woefully ineffective'. In Birt's analysis they were just as much victims of Bashir's talent for lying as Diana herself. They were all taken for a ride, he said. But although the result was a catastrophe for Diana, for Birt, Hall, Sloman, Suter and Bashir things worked out really pretty well. There were career jumps, knighthoods and peerages, instead of the tsunami of blame, the ignominy, which would have followed Bashir's downfall.

Somehow, though, it seemed that Lord Birt's remarks before the MPs, about how the weeping Bashir was able to fool 'hardened and experienced' inquisitors, were not properly thought through. They didn't really land. But then Birt, as his own former boss at the BBC once pointed out, is not a towering intellect. What makes for a 'hardened' interrogator is precisely that they are *not* taken in by a sob story. Lord Dyson, despite any other reservations about his analysis, had Bashir for breakfast.

Jonathan Maitland put it to me this way: 'People have said Martin can charm the birds from the trees. I think if you're in the business, then you don't fall for that. You can see him coming a mile off. You know that you're being fed a line. But I think if you are a civilian, a normal person, he's very seductive and very charming.' But then Birt was describing a scenario where, quite plainly, if his 'hardened' interrogators had not given their guy a pass, then they would all of them have been sacked within twenty-four hours, Birt too.

In dealing with the fallout from the scandal Birt seems to have pleaded a kind of general befuddlement, saying that he remembered few details of what happened in 1995 and 1996. Although he did very clearly remember that he was never told about Bashir's lying. He could distinctly remember that Tony Hall never told him about that. Absolutely definite. Lord Birt, seventy-six years old at the time, seemed frankly annoyed at the challenges being thrown his way by these whippersnapper MPs, like a grumpy old bear being yapped at by terriers. Was he glad that Bashir had finally been brought to book? That the truth about the *Panorama* interview and the failings of the organization he was running had finally been exposed? Surely he could only answer yes. But the MPs did not ask that particular question. And if there was gladness, perhaps some sadness too: the realization, for Birt, that he will be remembered chiefly for his part in the most tawdry episode in journalism's history.

That will be his legacy. For Diana the impact of the *Panorama* interview was much more immediate. The most chilling aspect of the BBC cover-up which occurred in 1996 is that a line can certainly be drawn from *Panorama* to Paris. A judgement on how thick that line is, how straight, varies from person to person. Diana's alternative therapist, Simone Simmons, seems to have been valued as someone who calls it as she sees it. And on this she does not hold back. She said to me, 'It's unforgivable. To feed her a pack of lies, to make her an emotional wreck, which he deliberately did? Without

Martin Bashir she would never have been in Paris with Dodi Fayed and she would still be alive. Therefore I hold Martin Bashir fully responsible for Diana's death. Not partly responsible. Fully responsible. If it wasn't for him, she would still be alive.'

The link between the hoaxing of his sister and what happened to her in Paris is something which Charles Spencer has considered at length, of course. Sat together in the library at Althorp he explained his thinking to me. I said, 'Let us imagine that the BBC *had* explained the situation to Diana, as soon as they knew that Bashir was both a forger and a liar.' In those circumstances, he said to me, 'I think Diana would have restored her confidence in the right people around her, particularly Patrick Jephson, who by this stage was dying a slow death in office. And was being treated very regrettably, but understandably, given what Diana had been told about him.

'Patrick was really very good with Diana. She could be quite tricky, mercurial, etcetera, because of the pressures on her. But Patrick was the quiet voice of reason. I think she'd have had a much more secure team around her as she progressed into that phase of her life.

'By destroying Diana's trust in the highly trained professionals around her this interview's direct result was to leave her exposed when she needed proper safety. I think it left her totally exposed, with Al Fayed's Mickey Mouse outfit of protection and drivers in place instead. So I think, unfortunately, in terms of consequences, they were lethal.'

I put the same question to Patrick Jephson. Like Spencer, I think he stands above a cheap desire to simply stick it to the BBC. It is just a fact, and a heartbreaking one, that Diana's life was thrown completely off course by the *Panorama* interview.

It was gained through deception, and when the BBC might have revealed that to her, they did not do so. He said to me, 'I think it's easy to see how the line from the *Panorama* interview leads pretty much straight to the night in Paris, where Princess Diana was in the hands of people who were unable properly to look after her. The way Diana met her death was a result of the fact that she was separated from the protection of the royal machine. And a large part of that separation can be traced to the *Panorama* interview.' He acknowledged Spencer's judgement that he, above all, was the one person whose continued presence could have saved Diana. And he added, with a rueful anger simmering for twenty-five years, 'Somebody had got to her with lies about me. And it upsets me more than I can say. Quite possibly the princess died thinking that I had betrayed her.'

There is always a 'what-if?' – what would have happened if Hall's inquiry had *not* been 'woefully ineffective'? Most likely there would have been a small BBC delegation in April 1996 to Kensington Palace. A meeting with Diana to explain that Bashir was a lying fantasist. That he did *not* have a secret source within MI5, that Prince Charles was *not* planning murder. And nor would there be a wedding with the nanny Tiggy Legge-Bourke. It is impossible to know how Diana would have reacted at that moment, although we know how she reacted when it appears she *was* brought up to speed with Bashir's true nature, and cut him off completely. The separation came after she heard snatches of that embarrassing phone call, fielded by butler Paul Burrell. Right there she learned that the BBC man was not so nice as he had appeared. But she was, tragically, still in the dark about the astonishing depth of his duplicity.

It seems to me that had the scandal emerged when it *should* have done, in April 1996, then of course it would have been a temporary media sensation, as newspapers thundered and heads rolled one after another at the BBC. But I think that the only person who truly matters, Diana, would have survived the initial embarrassment of having been duped, and might perhaps have emerged even stronger on the other side. She had been through scrapes before, had she not? The Squidgygate tape of 1992 had caught her chatting with a boyfriend. The tabloids had nailed her for her dalliance with art dealer Oliver Hoare. In the same year, 1994, the nation had learned about her romps with riding instructor James Hewitt. Was it that much worse to have made rather a fool of oneself on the TV? And in circumstances where, so plainly, she had been led up the garden path by the one organization in the country we are all brought up to trust?

The *Panorama* interview, Charles Spencer believes, would have been easy to disavow: 'You have to remember how controversial it was. Sort of 50-50? Some people thought, "Good for her, she's got every right to do it." And others thought, "Wow, that's just terrible." But I think there'd have been sympathy for her. She'd be the victim.' Yes, there would be humble pie, apologies to be tendered. But Patrick Jephson believes Diana would have carried it off with grace and charm: 'I suppose there would have been a bit of an awkward moment over the teacups with Tiggy Legge-Bourke. But maybe — and quite possibly, because she was good at this — Diana would have built a new relationship out of that.'

It is perhaps one speculation too many to wonder whether Diana's divorce might have been halted if the BBC had come clean. The queen's letter ordering that the process must begin arrived on 20 December 1995, one month to the day after the *Panorama* broadcast, yet there is intriguing evidence that Diana remained conflicted on whether her marriage was truly dead. Simone Simmons told me that she was a witness to Diana's doubts, shortly after the letter arrived: 'That really devastated Diana because she didn't want a divorce. She still loved Charles in her own funny way. And she was hoping that maybe this Camilla magic would wear off and Charles would come back to her. And it's very sad. She was crying her eyes out. And I put my arms around her, we had a cup of tea. I calmed her down and said, "Look, this is obviously what was meant to be. Try to get on with your own life, get the boys calmed down, and sort it out. That's your priority."'

An account which I find moving, and has the ring of truth in its halting, second-language delivery, came on the afternoon of Thursday, 17 January 2008. At the Royal Courts of Justice on the Strand, Diana's old friend, Argentinian Roberto Devorik, addressed those who had assembled for the inquest into Diana's death. He said, 'Let me explain to the jury, under oath, it's my belief that the man she loved until she close her eyes was the Prince of Wales. Not because it's the right thing to say. It's because in several occasions we had a conversation about the Prince of Wales.

'Once in my home, during a lunch – who we can provide the names if you need it – somebody make the bad taste to criticize the Prince of Wales. I would not have liked to be that person. She turned. She said, "He is the father of my children and he is going to be the future King of England. And if I have a difference with him, it's my problem with him. But nobody should make mockery about him!"'

29. Cold Case/Cover-Up?

What happened to Princess Diana in 1995 was such a long time ago. It was the year that *Braveheart* and *Waterworld* were Britain's big movies. When the average house in Britain cost roughly £50,000. In the week the *Panorama* interview was broadcast Britpop was a new thing; Oasis were smashing it with 'Wonderwall', their new hit at number 4. And so when I started to look at things again, in 2020, it quickly became clear that this was, in every way, a very cold case. I realize that is something of a cliché but it is, at least for me, a useful way to get my head around what can be a fiendishly complicated tale.

I imagine a police incident room, just as we see in every cop show, coffee cups everywhere, scruffy desks and chairs, garish fluorescent light. Interestingly there are *two* giant whiteboards, side by side. The one on the left is the typical cold-case scene setter, '1995' scrawled across the top in marker pen. There are photographs, Post-it notes, lines of coloured string. In the centre of the board there is a photograph of Princess Diana and next to her, saturnine, a mugshot of Martin Bashir. All around, more pictures of the main players: Spencer, Hall, Jephson, Wiessler.

And on that second whiteboard, the one on the right? Two words scrawled across the top, with a question mark: 'COVER-UP?' This board has fewer Post-its, more question marks. But now something surprising happens. Two of the mugshots are ripped from the first board, the one on the left, and they're stuck bang in the centre of the right-hand board. First Martin Bashir. Then Tony Hall. They are the only two characters who figure in part one of the story and, a quarter of a century later, part two as well. It is impossible to understand the Bashir scandal, how it came to light and how it almost didn't, without noting this generation-long passage of time between the crime, in 1995, and its detection, in 2020. Both men left the BBC, worked elsewhere for many years, and then returned. Hall in 2013, Bashir in 2016.

Hall, having risen to become director of news, then left the BBC in 2001 and was appointed chief executive of the Royal Opera House in Covent Garden, and elevated to the House of Lords in 2010. When he returned to the BBC in 2013 it was in crisis, shaken by revelations over the decades-long sexual abuse carried out by Jimmy Savile. Critics believed that the DJ's crimes had been overlooked and coverage of the issue horribly bungled. The director-general then newly in post, George Entwistle, quit the job after a turbulent fifty-four days, the shortest reign of any BBC leader.

In a curious precursor to the events in this story Entwistle was finally brought down by a tough interview on the BBC Radio 4 *Today* programme. Already on the ropes, he was challenged by interviewer John Humphrys on 10 November 2012, failed to put up a convincing defence and resigned later the same day. But in a statement which seems to mark him down as a decent human being he reflected, 'In the light of the fact that the director general is also the editor-in-chief and ultimately responsible for all content . . . I have decided that the honourable thing to do is to step down from the post of director general.'

Martin Bashir's interim years were far more up and down than those of Tony Hall. After the huge kudos of the Diana interview, he left the BBC in 1999, prospered for five years as a celebrity interviewer on ITV, and then took up a highly paid role as anchorman for the American ABC network in New York. But two scandals blighted his US career. First, a speech at an awards ceremony that was judged to be sexist, and sexually charged. Next, an on-air reference to a female politician that was judged to be crude and insulting. By 2016 his career as an anchorman was finished. He returned to the UK, where things looked equally bleak until, to the surprise of many, he was offered the job of BBC religious affairs correspondent. In 2018 this was elevated to editor of religion.

With this senior position being awarded during the leadership of Lord Hall, someone who *knew* Bashir to be a serial liar, and a forger, questions have been raised about whether it was a wise move. I put the question directly to the BBC in 2020, the press office replying, 'The post was filled after a competitive interview process . . . Tony Hall was not involved in the selection process. Having started his career at the BBC in the mid-1980s, working on programmes such as *Songs of Praise*, it was a role Martin was well qualified to take up.'

And so that was the situation on Monday, 31 August 2020, as Director-General Lord Hall, then aged sixty-nine, pulled shut his office door at New Broadcasting House for the final time. His seven years in office had passed without major crises, the usual small wars and brush fires but nothing existential for either him or the organization he had led. And he was handing over to someone who promised to be an equally safe pair of hands, Tim Davie.

To illustrate the passage of time, in 1995 when Bashir was showing his forgeries to Charles Spencer and hoaxing Princess Diana, Davie was twenty-eight years old, working for

PepsiCo, marketing crisps and soft drinks. Now, a weekend marathon runner, former deputy chairman of the Hammersmith and Fulham Conservative party, Davie was fifty-three years old, a fifteen-year veteran of various BBC roles. But as Davie began to settle in to his spacious new office, in the first week of September 2020, something will have been on his mind, something which would need the most careful handling. In fact Davie's first week in the job must have been one of the trickiest any director-general has faced in the BBC's hundred-year history. He had been informed by his chief of staff that the Bashir scandal was about to blow.

The extraordinary chain of events which unfolded during Davie's first few days was revealed to me in the final stages of a three-year legal battle with the BBC. As described more fully in a later chapter the legal action was not begun to elicit this kind of information, far from it. But in the way that sometimes happens, the court process forced the release of information unlikely to have emerged in any other way. On 13 February 2024 the BBC's senior-most lawyer, General Counsel Sarah Jones, sat down to record a thirty-nine-page sworn legal statement. In it she would describe how, in the summer of 2020, BBC investigators themselves began to look at the Bashir cold case and quickly discovered disturbing evidence.

Jones said that this internal examination began as the twenty-fifth anniversary of the interview, 20 November 2020, grew ever closer. Journalists from outside the BBC had begun to enquire exactly what Bashir had done, all those years ago. Jones said in her statement, 'One of these requests came from Blink Films, with whom Mr Webb was working on behalf of Channel 4, dated 19 August 2020, asking for "any documents related to Princess Diana's *Panorama* interview".'

Jones then described a scenario in which, in her account, the BBC planned to finally come clean about the scandal. Putting a precise date on events she said, 'By 8 September 2020, it was clear that the BBC had information in its archives that had not previously been widely shared about the allegation that the *Panorama* interview had been procured through Mr Bashir's production of fake bank statements.'

The lawyer spelled out how the information which BBC investigators now had might prove damaging for Bashir, the corporation's editor of religion. But also, crucially, for the recently departed director-general, Lord Hall: 'This was clearly a matter that could lead to significant reputational harm to Mr Bashir, including potentially damaging his career and livelihood. Therefore, it was considered important that a process of consultation with Mr Bashir (and also with Lord Tony Hall, who similarly was at risk of reputational harm from the disclosure) should take place.' The critical phrase in that sentence concerns what Jones calls a 'process of consultation'. Jones was saying that the information was *so* damaging it could only be released if it were discussed, beforehand, with the two men in the firing line, Hall and Bashir. And this is where the problem arose.

Once again, dating events to the precise day, Jones said, 'On 9 September 2020, the BBC became aware that Mr Bashir was seriously ill . . . Therefore, the initial plan to disclose the documents following consultation with Mr Bashir was put on hold.' According to Jones's timeline, by 8 September the BBC had assembled its dossier of damaging evidence and had decided to publish. Twenty-four hours later, on 9 September, those plans were abandoned, the deciding factor being Martin Bashir's health. Jones's statement established that there were *two* people likely to suffer what the BBC called 'reputational harm', Bashir and Hall. But the documents relating to Bashir were said to be so closely related to those impacting Hall that *all* of them must remain confidential, for the time being. And so information which might damage Hall would also remain secret, until Bashir was well again.

For journalists like me – though completely unaware at the time of this behind-the-scenes activity – it posed an enormous problem. We did not know what the BBC knew, that there was a dossier of damaging information relating to the scandal. All we were told was that the issue was off the table while Bashir was ill. On 19 October 2020 BBC News head of communications Charlotte Morgan emailed saying:

> With regard to your questions to Martin Bashir, as we told you previously, we are afraid to inform you that he is seriously unwell and we are unable to put your questions to him. In a brief conversation he has asked us to relay that in line with his practice over the past 25 years, he will not be making any public statements about his interview with the late Princess of Wales. The controversy about the mocked-up documents is not new and he has nothing to add.

The BBC say that Martin Bashir remained too ill to be approached about the damaging documents through the remainder of September 2020. They say he remained that way all through October, and also through November. But halfway through November, once the *Daily Mail* had launched its blistering campaign, the scandal had burst wide open in any event. Lord Dyson had been appointed to begin his inquiry on 18 November and so the documents remained under wraps until his report was published, in May 2021.

No official investigator, Lord Dyson or anyone else, has ever been asked to look into the events of autumn 2020, to determine whether or not the BBC pursued a new cover-up, using Bashir's health issues merely as an excuse. The Terms of Reference for Dyson's inquiry, decided by the BBC, restricted inquiries solely to events which happened in 1995 and 1996, excluding the prospect of investigating those in charge of the BBC today. Charles Spencer said to me, 'I was very upset from the beginning with the parameters. It was quite clear to me that they were set so that nobody could look at the current BBC's attitude. For instance, the cover-up that I felt was being perpetuated in 2020, there was no possibility of Dyson looking at that. And I thought that was absolutely germane to the case because it's a conspiracy of twenty-five years. It wasn't just back in the 90s.' This is certainly one of the areas where researchers and historians will continue to dig away as they attempt to paint in every last detail of what happened to Diana. I wish I had the final answer. I do not, but I have been able to pull together enough of the facts to hazard a guess.

The key issue on judging whether the BBC ran a cover-up in 2020 is Martin Bashir's health. Was the reporter *really* too ill to discuss the damaging documents which had been discovered by his bosses, or was he not? In her sworn statement lawyer Sarah Jones said that she heard about Bashir's health issues on 9 September 2020, along with a warning that the reporter was now incommunicado: 'I learned about this having been forwarded an internal email . . . requesting that people do their best "to ensure nobody contacts" him.' But is that how it happened? To discover the answer I once again used the Freedom of Information Act, to see whether discussions did in fact take place between Bashir and his bosses over these crucial weeks.

When the reply came the results were astounding. The evidence shows that Bashir was in regular discussion with his bosses over the scandal, at one point, remarkably, even advising on the wording of a press release saying that the BBC were *unable* to consult him. On the very same day that lawyer Jones says she learned of the ban on contacting Bashir, 9 September, Bashir was simultaneously responding to an approach by the news department's Liz Shaw. Shortly before 9 o'clock on that Wednesday night Bashir wrote to her, his message heavily redacted by the BBC, leaving only tantalizing clues as to the subject under discussion.

> *Dear Liz,*
>
> *I'm quite sure that you'll be sensitive and will explain matters where and when appropriate – so I'll trust your judgment.*
> *There is a certain anniversary coming in November and I'm quite sure that some papers would be keen to splash something gruesome, particularly since they've never recovered from being beaten to the punch.*
> ***[THREE LINES REDACTED]***
> *We can therefore only hope that people inside the Corporation won't decide to talk about my circumstances . . .*
> ***[FOUR LINES REDACTED]***
>
> *All good wishes,*
> *M*

Redactions like that can be made, perfectly legitimately, by whoever has been holding the emails in their archive. The redactions here were made by the BBC to obscure what is loosely called 'personal information', which could possibly have included further details about Bashir's health issues.

> **From:** Martin Bashir [/O=BBC/OU=EXCHANGE ADMINISTRATIVE GROUP (FYDIBOHF23SPDLT)/CN=RECIPIENTS/CN=MARTIN.BASHIR886]
> **Sent:** 09/09/2020 20:48:09
> **To:** Liz Shaw
> **Subject:** FW: Quick update...
>
> Dear Liz,
>
> I'm quite sure that you'll be sensitive and will explain matters where and when appropriate - so I'll trust your judgment.
>
> There is a certain anniversary coming in November and I'm quite sure that some papers would be keen to splash something gruesome, particularly since they've never recovered from being beaten to the punch. We can therefore only hope that people inside the Corporation won't decide to talk about my circumstances...
>
> All good wishes,
>
> M

It is simply impossible to know what lies under those heavy black stripes. It is also necessary to trust that the person at the BBC who made the redactions was scrupulously following the rules, that they did not simply strike out whole sentences because they would prove damaging to the BBC. It seemed to me, having been lied to quite brazenly when I asked for information via Freedom of Information in 2007, and was told that none existed, that I was entitled to be at least a little sceptical.

30. Sick Notes

So what do we know of Martin Bashir's health at this time? BBC lawyer Sarah Jones says in her 2024 statement, '. . . he was about to undergo "major surgery" the following Tuesday (15 September 2020), would be away from work and not deployed.' Martin Bashir entered hospital for elective heart surgery six days after Jones learned of his condition. The procedure, a quadruple heart bypass, typically takes around six hours. The NHS describes the likely outcome like this: 'Generally, you should be able to sit in a chair after one day, walk after three days, and walk up and down stairs after five or six days . . . By six weeks you should be able to do most of your normal activities and by three months you're likely to be fully recovered.'

And so there is no doubt that Bashir underwent a serious, if routine operation. It is fair to conclude that his recovery at least followed the NHS prediction because he was photographed, returning from a takeaway restaurant near his home in London's Maida Vale, on the evening of 6 November 2020, eight weeks after his operation. But the BBC say that Bashir's condition remained so serious, throughout this period and beyond, that they could not raise with him the issue of the damaging information turned up by BBC internal investigators. And, throughout all that time, it seems likely one other person was keeping a very close eye on Bashir's health: the other person with skin in the game, Tony Hall. So long as *Bashir* remained ill, lawyer Jones had said, the damaging information that had emerged involving *Hall* could not be released either.

The evidence I have gathered indicates that Bashir was in fact contacted by managers at the BBC, in emails and phone calls, many times during this period, to discuss the scandal in detail. Trying to pick the bones from the story, to follow the narrative from the massively redacted, mutilated documents which I was sent, is rather like the archaeologist who digs up a handful of pottery shards and, lo and behold, sees a classical vase, the palaeontologist peering at a stripe in the rockface who jumps up shouting, 'T-rex!' But I believe a clear picture does emerge from these fragments. I think it is possible to track the story, to follow each flurry of communication, from 9 September to 13 November, when the trail suddenly goes cold.

The first exchange took place eighteen days after Bashir's operation, on 3 October 2020. Bashir's regular point of contact at the BBC was the then executive news editor, Richard Burgess, and what prompted the burst of activity was the upcoming *Sunday Times* story which, as described earlier, would appear on 4 October. The banner headline would read, **'BBC JOURNALIST MARTIN BASHIR "MISLED DIANA'S BROTHER" TO SECURE BOMBSHELL INTERVIEW'**.

Burgess had been called in to assist with the weekend firefighting. As the *Sunday Times* journalists hurried to complete their story, at 10.22 a.m. on the day before its release, Saturday, 3 October, Burgess wrote to Bashir:

The press office is proposing to say in its statement to the ST [Sunday Times] that you are 'seriously unwell'. This would be for publication.

319

Are you happy with this? I can send you the full statement if
you want to see it?
[LINE REDACTED]
Richard

Four hours later Bashir replies from his iPhone:

Thanks

Thirty minutes later Burgess underlines his previous note:

Just to confirm Martin, we are issuing a statement to the ST
which states you are seriously unwell and unable to address their
questions. The statement then has a BBC response to the story.
  I'm told the ST intend to run the story but it won't be on the
front page.

The next big development in the exposure of the scandal
occurs eighteen days later, with the broadcast of my documentary film, *Diana: The Truth Behind the Interview*, on Channel
4. The film aired on Wednesday, 21 October 2020. Two days
later, on Friday, 23 October, an email which has been very
heavily redacted by the BBC passes from Bashir to Burgess.
Bashir writes:

Dear Richard,

[EIGHT LINES REDACTED]
  I may yet tell the story of my relationship to Royalty and
produce all of the documents that prove there was no
deception. Indeed, I was writing her speeches and cooking
pasta in Kensington Palace for her long before she sat down

to talk about the three people in her marriage. But that's for another day.

[TWELVE LINES REDACTED]

From: Martin Bashir
Sent: 23 October 2020 11:49
To: Richard Burgess
Cc: Jonathan Munro
Subject: ...quick update

Dear Richard,

I may yet tell the story of my relationship to Royalty and produce all of the documents that prove there was no deception. Indeed, I was writing her speeches and cooking pasta in Kensington Palace for her long before she sat down to talk about the three people in her marriage. But that's for another day.

The story is not going away. Burgess has to interrupt his weekend once again when, on Saturday, 31 October, the *Sunday Times* say they are about to publish a follow-up. Among the issues the newspaper will raise is a rumour that Bashir has been spotted in a London night club. At 11.08 on that Saturday morning Burgess emails Bashir. He writes:

Hi Martin

I hope you're ok and I'm genuinely sorry to contact you again about this matter, but The Sunday Times, and a

few other media organisations, are continuing to ask us
questions regarding the Diana interview and how it was obtained.
    I'm very mindful of your health, and not putting any
additional stress on to you, but equally I don't want us
to allow a particular narrative to develop if you have evidence
to the contrary as you mention below. In particular, can
I ask – do you have the handwritten note from Diana
which is mentioned in BBC files and which apparently said the
'faked' documents had no bearing on her decision to do the
interview?
    Also, the Sunday Times are saying that you have been seen in a
club? They have brought this up due to our statement regarding
the seriousness of your health situation.
    If you can help me with either of those two questions – or you
have any further thoughts, let me know.

Thanks,
Richard

The BBC did not release to me any email giving Bashir's reply to the night club question. But it is clear from Burgess's email that now the handwritten Diana note, mysteriously missing from the BBC archives, is starting to become an issue internally. At 11.14 a.m., six minutes after firing off his email to Bashir, Burgess briefs the then top-most journalist in the corporation, BBC director of news and current affairs, Fran Unsworth. Burgess writes:

I've emailed him to inform about the continued media interest, to
ask if he has the Diana note and about whether he has been in a
club recently . . .
    Will see what he says.

But what Bashir says remains a mystery. A little over an hour later, at 12.31 p.m., Bashir replies to Burgess with a detailed email of fifty lines. In the version sent to me all but eleven of the lines have been redacted. The BBC says that the thirty-nine lines of material which have been obscured contain unspecified 'personal information'.

Thanks, Richard.

In reverse order:

[THIRTEEN LINES REDACTED]

2: I do recall the Princess of Wales providing a hand-written statement, on headed notepaper, asserting that she consented to the interview without seeing any 'documents' nor was she coerced in any way. My recollection is that I gave the letter to Steve Hewlett, then Editor of Panorama, and he said that it would be stored in the 'BBC safe', which I assumed was in Television Centre. Unfortunately, I did not keep a copy – foolishly – and so don't have it to hand. I do have other correspondence, one letter in particular, in which she talks about how much she appreciated the interview and how it 'gave her wings'. We also continued to have a warm friendship after the filming – and indeed my wife, our three young children and myself, all went to Kensington Palace in *[REDACTED]* 1996 for dinner. Our daughter *[REDACTED]* remembers it because Prince Harry – who ate with us – took her to the bathroom and there were balloons around the table because *[REDACTED]* was about to celebrate his *[REDACTED]* birthday *[REDACTED]*

[TWENTY-SIX LINES REDACTED]

M

So what exactly lies beneath those unforgiving black stripes? What is the nature of the 'personal information' which the BBC says it is legally entitled to withhold? As

From: Martin Bashir
Sent: 31 October 2020 12:31
To: Richard Burgess
Subject: Re: ...quick update

Thanks, Richard.

In reverse order:

████████████████████████████
████████████████████████████
████████████████████████████
████████████████████████████
████████████████████████████
████████████████████████████
████████████████████████████

2: I do recall the Princess of Wales providing a hand-written statement, on headed notepaper, asserting that she consented to the interview without seeing any 'documents' nor was she coerced in any way. My recollection is that I gave the letter to Steve Hewlett, then Editor of Panorama, and he said that it would be stored in the 'BBC safe', which I assumed was in Television Centre. Unfortunately, I did not keep a copy – foolishly – and so don't have it to hand. I do have other correspondence, one letter in particular, in which she talks about how much she appreciated the interview and how it 'gave her wings'. We also continued to have a warm friendship after the filming – and indeed my wife, our three young children and myself, all went to Kensington Palace in ████ 1996 for dinner. Our daughter ████ remembers it because Prince Harry – who ate with us – took her to the bathroom and there were balloons around the table because ████ was about to celebrate his █ birthday ████

████████████████████████████
████████████████████████████
████████████████████████████
████████████████████████████
████████████████████████████
████████████████████████████
████████████████████████████
████████████████████████████

M

infuriating as it may be, it is impossible to know. In what can seem to resemble some kind of crooked poker game, the only person who knows what the cards say is also the person *dealing* the cards. It is the greatest weakness of the Freedom of Information Act that the organization which may have most to lose from honest disclosure, in this case the BBC, will inevitably be the same organization responsible for either releasing or withholding the information in the first place.

Is it fair to question the BBC's integrity, given its reputation as a truth-teller? At this point in the narrative the BBC's official stance, as reported in press statements to newspapers, radio and TV stations around the world, is that Martin Bashir is unable to discuss matters, at all, because of his health. On Thursday, 5 November, the BBC's Charlotte Morgan fires off a furious email to Richard Kay of the *Daily Mail*. At this point in the timeline his newspaper has begun its exposure of the scandal with a series of devastating front page splashes. Kay receives this rebuke from the angry Morgan:

> *I left you a voicemail. I'm aware that you have sent Martin Bashir several emails.*
>
> *We have repeatedly said that Martin is seriously unwell and that he cannot respond to questions.*
>
> *It's entirely inappropriate you should be mailing Martin at all, let alone with 'urgent' questions which appear to make odd insinuations about him.*
>
> *We have a BBC Press Office. Please stop mailing Martin directly and come through us.*
>
> *Charlotte Morgan – Head of Communications*
> *BBC News*

The following day, Friday, 6 November 2020, there occurs the most bizarre exchange of all, a step into a looking-glass world. BBC news executive Richard Burgess emails Bashir again, to discuss the developing crisis, but also the wording of the BBC's next press statement. And the thrust of that statement will once again be that Bashir is too ill to discuss things. And so Burgess has *contacted* Bashir to discuss the best way of saying that he *cannot* contact Bashir. At 5.50 p.m. Burgess writes:

Hi Martin

The Mail are planning on splashing with the story and running six pages. It is an interview by Richard Kay with Lord Spencer and he has shared his notebook from the September 19th meeting in 1995. These notes say you made a series of shocking claims about the Royal Family.

The Mail are also planning to say: "The BBC has said it is not possible to question Mr Bashir about the events of 1995 because he is 'seriously unwell' with complications from Covid. However sources have told the Mail the 57-year-old journalist is recovering at home following hospital treatment and is 'up and about'."

Our statement is as follows: "As the BBC has already said, we will have a robust investigation. It will have the appropriate independence people expect, and we will set out a process for this in due course. Unfortunately, we are hampered at the moment by the simple fact that we are unable to discuss any of this with Martin Bashir, as he remains seriously unwell."

Let me know if you are ok with this statement or want to know more details of the Mail story.

Richard

Twenty minutes later, the extraordinary discussion continues. Bashir emails Burgess, a little plaintively, from his iPhone. He has been spotted returning from a takeaway restaurant and snapped by photographers as he neared his front door:

[REDACTED] *And as I came home, they took photographs. Two photographers. It's pretty nasty stuff knowing I'm not well.*

Burgess is now called in for what will be his third weekend of crisis management. With the *Mail on Sunday* about to splash further revelations, on Saturday, 7 November Burgess emails Bashir at 12.28 p.m. Referring to material here not divulged to me by the BBC Burgess writes:

Hi Martin

Please see below. We intend to stick to our previous statement regarding these examples below concerning you.
Please come back to me if you have any comments.
Richard

Five minutes later Bashir replies from his iPhone:

*Thanks **[REDACTED]** but my wife says there are several people outside our home. Is there anything we can do to simply tell them that I won't be offering any comment and that they should leave? Its also causing my neighbours distress.*
M

It is at this point, as the scandal rapidly escalates out of control, that the conversations between Burgess and Bashir take on a more formal and legalistic tone. And at the same time we see the first intervention from BBC top-most management. At 12.01 p.m. on this Saturday, 7 November 2020, Phil Harrold, the chief of staff to Director-General Tim Davie, writes an email copied to all members of the BBC board. Briefing them on events so far, Harrold sounds quite cheery as he says:

Good morning all,

It's been a particularly busy week this week, and David and Tim thought that it would be helpful if we put in

*some time next week to update the Board on recent
matters, including the Bashir/Panorama issue, the rollout of
the impartiality guidance, and the latest from the Govt on the
licence fee.*

*I'll ask the team to be in touch regarding your availability for an
hour on Tuesday – and I hope that everyone can join.*

*Specifically on the Panorama issue, it hasn't been
particularly picked up beyond the Mail, but you'll have
seen that they have gone quite big on it over the last week –
no less then [sic] three splashes on something 25 years old.
You'll note that we've agreed to undertake an independent
investigation on this, given new information has arisen.
I've copied below the latest press lines that we are issuing, and
copied John to this email. We will update more on this at the
Board meeting.*

*I hope that the sun is shining where you are, and you can get
out and enjoy a little of it.*

Do be in touch with any queries.

*Best,
Phil*

Cut and pasted to his email is what he refers to as 'the latest press lines'. Despite the by now voluminous discussions with Bashir, Davie's chief of staff confidently assures the BBC watchdogs that Bashir *cannot* be contacted: 'Unfortunately, we are hampered at the moment by the simple fact that we are unable to discuss any of this with Martin Bashir, as he remains seriously unwell.'

Harrold's briefing ensures that the BBC governors are as thoroughly misled as the general public, for whom the press release is intended.

From: Phil Harrold
Sent: 07 November 2020 12:01
To: BBC Board <BBCBoard@bbc.co.uk>
Cc: John Shield - Comms ▮▮▮▮▮▮▮▮▮▮▮▮
Subject: Board Update

Good morning all,

It's been a particularly busy week this week, and David and Tim thought that it would be helpful if we put in some time next week to update the Board on recent matters, including the Bashir/Panorama issue, the rollout of the impartiality guidance, and the latest from the Govt on the licence fee.

I'll ask the team to be in touch regarding your availability for an hour on Tuesday – and I hope that everyone can join.

Specifically on the Panorama issue, it hasn't been particularly picked up beyond the Mail, but you'll have seen that they have gone quite big on it over the last week – no less then three splashes on something 25 years old. You'll note that we've agreed to undertake an independent investigation on this, given new information has arisen. I've copied below the latest press lines that we are issuing, and copied John to this email. We will update more on this at the Board meeting.

I hope that the sun is shining where you are, and you can get out and enjoy a little of it.

Do be in touch with any queries.

Best,

Phil

> "As the BBC has already said, we will have a robust investigation. It will have the appropriate independence people expect, and we will set out a process for this in due course. Unfortunately, we are hampered at the moment by the simple fact that we are unable to discuss any of this with Martin Bashir, as he remains seriously unwell."

> "The focus of the BBC's investigations at the time was on whether the Princess of Wales had been misled. According to our records, the Princess spoke for herself, sending a handwritten note saying she had not seen the documents and they had played no part in her decision to take part in the interview."

Phil Harrold
Company Secretary and
Chief of Staff to the Director-General and Chairman
British Broadcasting Corporation
Broadcasting House, London, W1A 1AA
▮▮▮▮▮▮▮▮▮▮

Five days later, Bashir and Burgess exchange emails once again. The following day, Burgess has a long phone call with Bashir. Burgess reports the result of that call in a formal briefing note, addressed to the BBC head of news and current affairs, Fran Unsworth, as well as Phil Harrold, the chief of staff to the director-general. We get a sense of what Burgess and Bashir have discussed, though two thirds of the content of the briefing note have been redacted, again on the grounds that it contains unspecified 'personal information'. Burgess writes:

Privileged and confidential
Here are the notes from my conversation with Martin Bashir
today:

Record of conversation with Martin Bashir 13.11.20
I informed Martin that the note from Diana to the BBC had been found and that it would be submitted as evidence to the inquiry. I also said we were confirming this to interested parties in the media.

Martin expressed some concern about the decision to tell the media. He feared it would give the story another lease of life, that the media could FOI it and could diminish its contents. I said that as it was being submitted to the inquiry, I did not think it would be released under FOI but that I would try to find that out.

We spoke about how some newspapers were covering the story, that some appeared to have an agenda and were campaigning on it. Martin said he was trying to concentrate on what he could control.

He said he would bring everything he has to the inquiry in terms of correspondence with Diana. He said he had never wanted to publicise these private letters, particularly ones to his wife from Diana, but he felt now he had no choice.
[TWENTY-FOUR LINES REDACTED]

Once again, the black redaction stripes hide far more information than is revealed in clear text. Whether or not those redactions have been fairly made is impossible for an outsider to say. But the broader evidence surely indicates that, during this period in 2020, the BBC consistently and knowingly misled journalists, and through them the public, by claiming Bashir could *not* be contacted, while at the same time having phone conversations, posing questions and receiving lengthy emails on various aspects of the scandal.

And it was not just some junior staff member who had bent the rules, in secret. In the email group here there is the

From: Richard Burgess
Sent: 13 November 2020 16:26
To: Fran Unsworth; Jonathan Munro; Charlotte Morgan
Cc: zzKen MacQuarrie-PRIVATE; Phil Harrold; Elizabeth Grace; John Shield - Comms; Sarah Jones; Sarah Ward-Lilley
Subject: Conversation with Martin Bashir 13.11.20 - privileged and confidential

Privileged and confidential

Here are the notes from my conversation with Martin Bashir today:

Record of conversation with Martin Bashir 13.11.20

I informed Martin that the note from Diana to the BBC had been found and that it would be submitted as evidence to the inquiry. I also said we were confirming this to interested parties in the media.

Martin expressed some concern about the decision to tell the media. He feared it would give the story another lease of life, that the media could FOI it and could diminish its contents. I said that as it was being submitted to the inquiry, I did not think it would be released under FOI but that I would try to find that out.

We spoke about how some newspapers were covering the story, that some appeared to have an agenda and were campaigning on it. Martin said he was trying to concentrate on what he could control.

He said he would bring everything he has to the inquiry in terms of correspondence with Diana. He said he had never wanted to publicise these private letters, particularly ones to his wife from Diana, but he felt now he had no choice.

corporation's senior-most lawyer. The head of the entire news division. The head of communications would write personally to an enquiring journalist, saying, 'We have repeatedly said that Martin is seriously unwell and that he cannot respond to questions,' while the chief of staff to the director-general would assure the BBC watchdog body, '... we are unable to discuss any of this with Martin Bashir.'

So how much does this matter? In his assessment of the BBC's handling of the scandal in 1996 Lord Dyson applies the term 'cover-up' to the way the BBC managed news coverage. He wrote:

Without justification, the BBC fell short of the high standards of integrity and transparency which are its hallmark by (i) covering up in its press logs such facts as it had been able to establish about how Mr Bashir secured the interview and (ii) failing to mention Mr Bashir's activities or the BBC investigations of them on any news programme.

And the evidence strongly suggests the BBC fell short on transparency and integrity again, about its dealings with Bashir at this critical period in the autumn of 2020. So could the Freedom of Information Act be used once again, to find out what had *really* gone on behind the scenes?

31. Freedom of Information

Way back in my introduction to this book I began to outline the three-year legal battle I waged with the BBC over Freedom of Information, culminating in a memorable two days inside a London courtroom. What I was seeking to discover with my Freedom of Information request was, essentially, whether or not the BBC had been fully transparent in the autumn of 2020 as the Bashir scandal threatened to bubble to the surface. Were they telling the whole truth about Bashir's health, and a number of other things too?

I had been suspicious ever since 19 October 2020, when, forty-eight hours before my film went on air, I first received the BBC's bundle of sixty-seven pages of documents, out of the blue. One of those documents contained the false suggestion that Charles Spencer had actually primed Martin Bashir to produce his forged bank statements. But then, in May 2021, the Dyson report was published and also, with it, a further bundle of documents was released. Among these, crucially, was the eight-page memorandum drawn up by Anne Sloman on 22 April 1996, her timeline of the scandal ending in her deathless phrase: 'The Diana story is probably now dead, unless Spencer talks.'

For an investigative journalist, Sloman's memo was critical to understanding how the cover-up developed in 1996. But why had this memo not been released to me earlier? If the bundle of documents had been sent to me on 19 October 2020 in a burst of BBC transparency, why had *this* priceless treasure been left out? Had someone devised a plan to send to me the *false* allegation about Earl Spencer, hoping it would influence my documentary film, yet *hide* the highly prejudicial Sloman memo?

If that were the case it seemed that the plan might be revealed in emails flying between a small circle of senior executives, at their head the BBC director-general, Tim Davie. But could the BBC really have acted in such a devious way? The British Broadcasting Corporation? I decided it was worth trying to find out. And so on 4 June 2021 I put in my request:

> I would like to request all documents that exist relating to email or other correspondence between BBC managers and the BBC Information Office, between September 2020 and November 2020, which has any bearing on the November 1995 Panorama programme with the Princess of Wales.

Despite this simple-sounding request the case would drag on for more than three years, becoming what the BBC would describe as the biggest Freedom of Information case there has ever been. And to keep pace as this monster grew I had to learn how the Freedom of Information Act works. Since it came into force in 2005 the Freedom of Information Act has allowed anyone to ask for what is called 'recorded information', documents like emails, letters, even CCTV, from what are called 'public authorities'. Maybe a government department, a hospital, a school, and certainly the BBC. The body in question has twenty days to provide the information.

But that is where, as I discovered, things become complicated. The holder of the information can *refuse* to release it under certain circumstances. The holder may say, 'Yes, we certainly do have a series of emails from Mr Smith to Mr Jones, but they are protected under section so-and-so of the Act.' There is nothing inherently sinister in these provisions. Section 40, for instance, protects what is called 'personal information', material which it would be wrong to divulge because everyone is entitled to a degree of privacy.

The problem arises because the only person who knows whether the information ought really to be kept secret is the person *holding* it, not the person *asking* for it. When the BBC said they couldn't release certain emails to me because of X, Y or Z, it was necessary to know whether they were telling the truth. And the BBC appeared, at various points over the three years of this legal battle, to be *not* telling the truth. They acted in a way which one of their own lawyers would describe as 'wrong and impermissible' and which the judge hearing my case, Brian Kennedy KC, would describe as 'a cause for serious concern'. Judicial pronouncements are not designed to be pithy. The judge's comment which probably caused most jitters at New Broadcasting House was this one: 'Although the BBC has accepted and apologised for their mistakes, its errors have significantly contributed to the Appellant's scepticism of the BBC's good faith which, in our view, is not without cause.'

The case dragged on for as long as it did because the BBC argued that it had the right to *withhold* the emails I was seeking, because of the kind of loopholes in the Freedom of Information Act referred to above. And to help them do that, the lawyers the BBC were hiring, viewed from my perspective, seemed to be getting scarier the longer the case went on. Throughout 2023 the BBC's barrister in charge of the case was a high-flyer called Jason Pobjoy. Shortly before being matched against me, on behalf of the BBC, he had been hired by Prince Harry in one of his legal disputes. Pobjoy's next paymaster was Boris Johnson, in his attempt to persuade MPs that he had not lied over 'Partygate'.

But as the two days of court hearings in June 2024 grew closer I realized that the BBC had upped their game. Instead of a mere barrister, facing me across the courtroom would be a KC, King's Counsel, a lawyer from the very top of the legal pyramid where fees average around £5,000 per day. The BBC had hired Monica Carss-Frisk KC, described on her own website, rather terrifyingly, as 'the silent assassin of cross-examination'.

The BBC would spend more than £600,000 on these *external* legal costs. Taking internal costs into account as well, a total somewhere around £1 million of licence fee money. To put that in context, to fight this case over the disputed emails the corporation would spend something like 6,000 licence fees, the annual income from a medium-sized town – say, Aldershot, Morecambe or, perhaps ironically, Windsor. The BBC had decided to spend that money not on making TV or radio programmes for those good people, but on stopping me from seeing what one BBC boss had said to another during the autumn of 2020.

The key moment in the case, and certainly the most bizarre moment, came halfway through, a year and a half after I had made my initial request. After a great deal of argument a stalemate had been reached whereby the BBC declared it had discovered eighty emails relevant to my request. All good, except the BBC said that *none* of them could be released. The reason for that is that the Freedom of Information Act allows emails dealing with legal matters, between a lawyer and a member of staff, to be declared exempt, a provision dealt with under the Act's section 42. The BBC said they had done a thorough search and every one of these eighty emails comprised legal discussion which needed to be kept confidential.

I was stuck on what to do next when suddenly the BBC asked for a halt in proceedings. They said that there seemed to have been some kind of mistake. It appeared that there may be *more* emails than they had initially thought, and so they were carrying out a new search. The halt order came in October 2022. I waited for a month, then two, wondering if the BBC had turned up maybe another half-dozen or so emails? Maybe ten? In December 2022 the BBC announced the result of their new search. The correct total was not eighty emails. There were in fact 3,288.

The number of documents had leapt forty-fold, overnight. But how do you *lose* 3,208 emails? Perhaps more importantly, when you go looking for them and just a few turn up, how do you not suspect that thousands were missing in the first place? Those are the kind of questions I put to the BBC. They said that there had been confusion over how the BBC email system worked. One lawyer, they said, had overlooked 2,741 items in his mailbox alone. The number of working days in which those 2,741 emails were generated is roughly fifty, and so they were arriving in this lawyer's mailbox at an *average* rate somewhere in excess of fifty per day. Allowing for the natural ebb and flow typical in a developing crisis it seems reasonable to assume that on certain critical days the number arriving will have been in the *hundreds*. It seems to indicate a period of almost frenzied communication, raising the question: how was the existence of this vast trove of material so quickly forgotten?

So, 3,288 emails after all. It might seem that the more

there were, the better. In fact I feared that it could prove to be a disaster, for reasons which soon became clear. During 2023 I was summoned to three separate hearings, conducted over video, where I was able to put to the judge my case that I should be allowed to see what the emails contained. And in December 2023, a major triumph. The BBC was ordered to hand over everything, all 3,288 emails, including copies and attachments. Together that would comprise 10,336 pages of documents, in twenty lever arch folders. But there was a catch.

Redaction.

In previous chapters the results of redaction, covering up a sentence here, a paragraph there, can plainly be seen. The BBC now argued that the 3,288 emails were riddled with both personal and legal information. They would require six weeks to go through the 10,336 pages of material, striking out words, sentences, in some cases entire pages. And so when the emails finally arrived, two and a half years after they had first been requested, they resembled a horrible harlequin creation, more black than white, 1,824 documents having been redacted for 'personal information', a further 955 redacted for 'legal information', 688 documents having been withheld altogether, completely removed from the original pile.

And so after all that time I had my emails, thousands of them. I just couldn't *read* them. Or, at least, not in any way that made sense to me. It got worse. I could ask the judge to examine the material, page by page, in its original, unredacted form. But was that likely to happen? The tribunal which had been patiently hearing my case had rules under which they had to operate. One rule said that they could only act in a way which was 'proportionate'. In simple terms, they could only do what seemed to make sense, in the time they had. There is a bit of old wisdom: 'Where is the best place to hide a tree? Answer – in a forest.' It was hard for me not to wonder whether the miraculous, overnight forty-fold increase in the number of emails declared by the BBC had something to do with this.

And of course redaction on such a vast scale would make it virtually impossible to judge between a genuine error and a less genuine one. A single extra black stripe, among the thousands already applied? Easily done. I was not expecting there to be pages and pages of smoking guns. I was expecting just a line, maybe a paragraph, which might give a clear indication that the BBC had followed a strategy to release a document they thought *favourable* while supressing one they thought *incriminating*. In the sixty-seven pages of documents released to me on 19 October 2020 it had been just ten words which brought the temple crashing down, when Charles Spencer was falsely accused of assisting Martin Bashir:

He showed him some documents including this man's bank statement.

Just ten words. I needed the judge to look through every page in a vast mass of documentation, equivalent to a book ten times the length of *War and Peace*, and spot those words. It did not seem to me that was likely to happen. As I geared up for the final courtroom showdown an article appeared in the *Spectator* magazine which put it neatly. On 25 May 2024 Charles Moore wrote, 'The BBC has managed to build up, at licence-payers' expense, a haystack so huge that it could hide any possible needles. If the regulator can be swamped in this way, he is proved powerless and therefore useless. Surely Parliament, and perhaps ministers, should challenge such behaviour.'

The only person available to make a challenge in June 2024 was me.

32. Courts and Casinos

I had discovered something about myself as this case dragged on and on, endlessly it seemed, since I had first submitted my simple Freedom of Information request to the BBC on 4 June 2021. Remember, the Freedom of Information Act says you are entitled to an answer within twenty days. We had now reached the 1,000-day mark, and then some. That is an interesting number, given how much public money the BBC had decided to throw at this, more than £1 million. To prevent these emails becoming public they were prepared to spend a thousand pounds a day, every day, for three years, and as far as I could see would go on spending it forever. Of course all this time I still had a living to make, documentary films to direct. But this struggle with the BBC became a point of honour, or more precisely a demonstration that I would not be taken for a fool.

Does anyone *seriously* forget they had 2,741 emails in their inbox, about the spikiest case they have ever had to deal with, in their whole career? Do they? Every absurd twist and turn of the case made me more determined to see it through. In total I had to deal with 402 emails from either the BBC or the court, some of them requiring answers that would run to fifteen pages or more. I actually took a lot of inspiration from Alan Bates, now *Sir* Alan, the campaigner who sat at his desk for years to get justice for the subpostmasters who had been so badly treated by the Post Office, some of them even thrown in jail. A couple of weeks before my case came to court I wrote to him, and received an immediate reply, wishing me well, which I appreciated a lot.

In a case like this there are not a lot of laughs, but one moment did prompt at least a smile. On 13 February 2024 the BBC's senior lawyer, Monica Carss-Frisk KC, wrote to the judge, a forty-nine-page document of just under 20,000 words. Towards the bottom of page 8 she explained how much work the BBC had had to do to provide me with the 10,336 pages of documents I had now been sent, the emails which, remember, I could not read because they were redacted beyond comprehension. All this work that the BBC had done was work I wished they had never done in the first place. The BBC's KC wrote, 'It goes significantly beyond any FOIA disclosure exercise ever conducted by the BBC (or, the BBC anticipates, any other public authority).' The journalist in me immediately thought, 'Wow, that is a big claim. The biggest ever?'

And so I did what any rookie reporter would do before they print a story saying, **'UK's Biggest Ever Freedom of Information Case'**. I checked the facts with the civil servants who administer the Freedom of Information Act. It turns out that, although the BBC had indeed spent a lot of time and effort, at the public expense, on the redaction process, the amount of data they were handing over was not the biggest by a long shot. It was way down the league table. The people who manage the Freedom of Information Act said that the record goes to an environmental group trying to protect the habitat of rare bats in their neighbourhood which were threatened by a new dual carriageway. The government, it emerged, had huge mountains of data on the daily and nightly comings and goings of the furry little mammals, and the bat-lovers were able to extract it, using the Freedom of Information Act, to argue their case.

In June 2024 it was time to go to court. Three times already there had been hearings conducted over video. At one of them, the year before, Charles Spencer had agreed to appear as a witness to help me challenge one of the particular points the BBC were making, with which I strongly disagreed. This time I would be calling no witnesses. It was up to me, in my smart new suit, to convince the judge and his two tribunal colleagues that the public interest would be best served by publication of the information within these BBC emails, rather than keeping it secret beneath more than 3,000 separate redactions. The tribunal had allocated two days of court time, which is unusual in a Freedom of Information case but an indication that they were taking things seriously. At the last minute I decided that, even in my new suit, I would not turn up like Johnny-no-mates to face the team from the BBC. And so I asked my twenty-four-year-old daughter, Effie, to dress up smartly too and be my 'legal assistant'. It was the right move. As well as the hired KC, Monica Carss-Frisk, there was the BBC's general counsel, Sarah Jones, plus their support teams, eight people in all, with huge boxes of lever arch files, hauled in using those wheelie devices which lawyers favour.

I have sat in very many courts over my decades as a journalist. I have watched magicians at work, right back to people like George Carman QC, the man who famously, successfully, defended Jeremy Thorpe, the former Liberal leader who was tried for conspiracy to murder in 1979. I have watched Michael Mansfield KC, now in his eighties, who fought some of the biggest cases in recent history: on behalf of the wrongfully convicted Birmingham pub bombers, and the family of murdered teenager Stephen Lawrence. I have been in enough courts, and watched the very best silks often enough, to know that persuasion works at the near subliminal level, a word here, a glance there. Yes, the tedious recitation of precedent case history. But KCs, the best ones, know how to work a room. And so I knew that my opponent this day would have been chosen by the BBC because they expected a result, they *needed* a result.

I did what anyone would do and googled 'Monica Carss-Frisk KC'. And there, a fascinating clutch of news stories and articles in legal industry publications. It seemed that in 2016 Ms Carss-Frisk had been asked to help defend a billionaire sheikh, a Qatari man, who had been accused of being involved in the torture of a British citizen. Her defence was successful. But it was the comments of the judge in this case which made it a news story. Working alongside a fellow lawyer, Ms Carss-Frisk had put in for a fee not far short of a quarter of a million pounds. Judge Nicholas Blake rejected her claim with the durable remark, '. . . this is a court of justice, not a casino.' I had not the slightest idea whether the billionaire who had hired her was a torturer or not. The evidence indicated no. But silks who operate in that most rarefied realm of the legal stratosphere, who can put in for astronomical amounts of money like that, are simply brilliant at what they do.

I had written a speech, determined to fill the hour and a half I had been allotted, as Effie, my daughter, made sure my glass of water didn't run dry. I made my case for disclosure, discernible from what I have written so far, but outlined more fully in the document appended at the end of this book. Ms Carss-Frisk KC made the BBC's case, to uphold the redactions in their entirety, saying that in every case the pages that had been removed, the words covered over, had been either personal information or legal discussion. Nothing, she assured the tribunal, had been covered over simply because it might prove damaging to the BBC. It bothered me somewhat that roughly half of the proceedings took place in the form of private discussion, between the judge and the BBC's lawyers, without me being present. It was done that way because the matter under discussion was the material I was not allowed to see, and so it made some kind of sense but still seemed a little unsatisfactory.

I had won the first round of the battle, in demanding to be given these 3,288 emails in the first place. But as regards this second round, the important one, being able to *read* them, I lost. The tribunal's judgement, denying me access to *unredacted* copies of the documents, arrived in August 2024 and was for me a huge disappointment. Of course it was. I felt that the public interest had not been served and, in the long term, perhaps more importantly, the BBC had established a modus operandi for any organization in a tight spot regarding Freedom of Information in the future. The more documents you can find, the better your chances of escaping scrutiny may be.

The judge's ruling also puzzled me. Brian Kennedy KC was quite clear: 'The Tribunal's assessment of the BBC's witness evidence is that it was given with candour, credibility and reliability . . . the Tribunal are satisfied this is not a case where the withheld information reveals any form of wrongdoing, malpractice or maladministration or other form of dishonesty.' But at the same time, it was clear that the judgement was made on only a *partial* examination of the 10,336 pages of documents. How could it be any other way? Judge Kennedy wrote, '. . . the closed material (i.e. material in respect of which exemptions were claimed by the BBC) is voluminous and it would have been manifestly disproportionate (and placed an excessive burden on the Tribunal) to review each and every individual document over which exemptions were claimed.' I had argued that it would be impossible to make a final, definitive judgement without examining all of the material. To find those ten potentially damning words. But I also knew it would be impossible to do so, and so it proved.

The truly worrying part of the judgement, for me, came when I saw that the judge had cut and pasted a 1,500-word section of the Dyson report and said, in essence, that everything had been looked at and there was nothing more to see. Judge Kennedy wrote, 'The Tribunal considers that the public interest in transparency and accountability is to a significant extent met by the publication of Lord Dyson's report . . .' But of course that is what one *would* believe, whatever some jumped-up journalist thinks. Martin Bashir has also found it useful to quote Dyson's report in his defence, Tony Hall too. I suspect that the BBC team facing me across the courtroom were equally glad that Dyson could be used in this way, to help them win the day.

Had the judgement gone the other way, had the BBC been ordered to remove their 3,000 or so redactions, to allow the emails to be read, I have not the slightest doubt that they would have immediately appealed. We were, after all, still at the bottom-most rung of the judicial ladder, what is called the First Tier Tribunal, above which lie the High Courts, the Appeal Courts and so on. Of course I considered whether I myself might have grounds on which to appeal. Is there logic in a judgement which essentially says, 'What we have looked at appears to be guilt-free. But then we haven't looked at every-thing.' Perhaps an appeal by me would have been allowed, perhaps not. Either way, I was counselled by friendly legal experts to be extremely careful about such a decision.

For the BBC the expenditure of more than £1 million thus far was no big deal, nor would the rapidly spiralling costs of following the case into the more rarefied legal realms pose any kind of problem. Need another £1 million, £2 million maybe? What is the BBC licence fee for, after all? *Fill your boots*. But from my side of the courtroom things might, just possibly, become vastly more terrifying. What if the deci-sion went against me, again, and a stern-faced judge decided to look at the issue of costs? Could *I* become liable for the several millions of pounds which the BBC would by then have ploughed into the proceedings? I could certainly not afford to hire my own KC, much less pay for those hired by the BBC to keep their emails from the public gaze. And so I concluded that my time playing amateur lawyer must come to an end. One day, I suspect, *someone* will get to see what those emails contain. Just not me.

At the end of the case, because of information which had been extracted from the BBC almost incidentally, I was much better informed than I had been at the outset. As to whether those emails prove the existence of a new cover-up, that is something for future historians to look at. I think I got a fair shake from the tribunal and was glad that Judge Kennedy saw fit to write, 'Succinctly put, the journey on which the BBC has taken the Appellant (and then the Tri-bunal) has been arduously and burdensomely long and hard. It has also come at a disproportionate cost – not only in terms of significant delay to the administration of justice but also in terms of expense to the public purse and to public confidence in the ability of the public service broadcaster to deal with and answer legitimate information requests in a responsible, accountable and adequate way. The Appellant is to be commended for patiently and assiduously persevering in the pursuance of his appeal until this ultimate conclusion.'

All through those three years of struggle, through the endless twists and turns of seemingly intractable court procedure, I knew that it was vital to keep in mind what it was really all about. And so I kept a small photo of Princess Diana Blu-Tacked to the right-hand top corner of my computer screen. It was a reminder that there was a *point* to all this, and a poignant one. It seemed to me that because of what Martin Bashir had done in 1995, and more importantly because it had then been covered up, Diana's life had been sent off on a terribly dangerous course, resulting in her death. Whether this had been the biggest Freedom of Information case in history, or whether it had not, *that* was the underlying horror which had made it worth fighting at all.

PART SEVEN
Open Questions

'If you do not tell the truth about yourself you
cannot tell it about other people.'

Virginia Woolf, 'The Leaning Tower', 1940

33. Paying the Price

What happened to Princess Diana as a result of the *Panorama* interview is horribly, starkly apparent. What happened to the supporting cast – Bashir and the BBC people on the one hand; Patrick Jephson, Matt Wiessler, Charles Spencer on the other – follows two radically different trajectories.

At exactly the same time that Bashir was attending award ceremonies, in the spring of 1996, collecting universal acclaim for his scoop, Tony Hall was back at New Broadcasting House, working out how to deal with, first of all, whistleblower Wiessler. As Hall would announce to the BBC Board of Governors on 25 April 1996, 'We are taking steps to ensure that the graphic designer involved – Matthew Wiessler – will not work for the BBC again.'

Matt was not to know that he had been formally blacklisted by the BBC until the documents I obtained from the corporation told him so, twenty-five years later. Like Charles Spencer, when informed of what the BBC had said about him in 1996, he was first astonished, then outraged. As the work dried up Matt had realized that his dream of graduating from television graphic designer to film director was not going to happen. He became what he calls a drifter, by which he means he did a bit of this, a bit of that, teaching himself new practical skills. To make a living he became a hands-on carpenter, fitting kitchens sometimes, fitting out shops which wanted to change their layout. He quit London and moved to Devon, where he is today, still married to Lucy, whom he met in the *Panorama* office.

Matt is haunted to some degree by what happened and most of all by the effect his own purely innocent actions had on Princess Diana. But he does not play the victim. Life has worked out pretty much OK for him. He told me, 'I did all sorts of interesting work, it was only stressful because it was out of my comfort zone. It never replaced what I'd lost. Creative challenges, working on your wits. All that stuff that I loved about news and current affairs, it never replaced that. And therefore I never stuck with any of it for very long. And that must have had a huge effect on my family and my wife because we struggled financially. And I also feel very bad about the fact that maybe I will only ever be remembered as the graphic designer who worked on the Bashir papers, which led to Diana's death. So there's no positive side to any of that.'

Once it emerged what Hall had done, casting the whistle-blower as a villain, the BBC was forced to accept the blight that had been placed on Matt's life. What could and should have turned into a lucrative career had been cast aside. In recompense, Matt's lawyers got the BBC to pay £750,000, recognizing where his career might have gone instead of where the BBC sent it. The current director-general, Tim Davie, extended his apology, which Matt accepted. But with one reservation. He told me, 'The real apology that I think I deserve should come from the man that was in charge of the BBC at the time, John Birt. When you're the captain of the ship, and something happens, you have to know about it.'

But as described earlier Lord Birt today insists he was kept in the dark. In his appearance before the House of Commons, on 15 June 2021, though pressed by committee chairman Julian Knight MP, Birt would not budge.

CHAIR: Under your watch he was blackballed and did not work for the BBC again. Do you owe Mr Wiessler an apology?

LORD BIRT: Let me explain the circumstances.

CHAIR: No. Do you owe Mr Wiessler an apology?

LORD BIRT: I am going to explain the circumstances. The circumstances, as I have already said, are that . . .

CHAIR: Do you owe him an apology?

LORD BIRT: I am not in a position to. I do not understand enough of what happened.

It was this apology which Matt Wiessler was looking for, not merely a payday. For Patrick Jephson the same is true and, as with Wiessler, the case against the BBC is clear and ugly. Martin Bashir painted Jephson as a money-grubbing informer, a spy, and had forged documents which were said to prove it. Diana was so firmly convinced that she froze Jephson out at the most critical period, just before the *Panorama* interview, and never trusted him again. After eight years constantly at Diana's side Jephson left, in January 1996, never to see or speak to her again before her death eighteen months later.

In his memoir he describes their last meeting, in the equerries' room of Kensington Palace. Diana had received his formal note of resignation, then, after a few moments' consideration: 'She stood up and headed for the door. I stood up also and half made to follow her. Suddenly she turned, colour rushing back into her cheeks. "Well. We can at least shake hands," she said, and so we did. Then she was hurrying back up the stairs. I heard a door slam. I waited for a minute, feeling the sudden silence. So that was it.'

I have seen the document drawn up by Patrick Jephson, refined by his lawyers and submitted to the BBC as the first step in deciding appropriate compensation. As a then thirty-six-year-old ex-naval officer, with unique skills learned during his royal service, he could find a new job without too much difficulty. But what comes through the document is the deep sense of hurt that someone he had so much grown to cherish, in the most platonic sense of that word, to love, had been poisoned against him: 'In summary, Martin Bashir was prepared to, and did, ruin our client's career and life, in order to serve his own ambition and greed. But for the tenacity of a journalist who exposed the truth that had been deliberately and institutionally suppressed since 1995, Commander Jephson would have carried the consequences to the grave.'

After a brief tussle it was agreed that the BBC would pay £110,000. The entire sum was immediately handed over by Patrick to the Tŷ Hafan Children's Hospice in South Wales. Funding the hospice had been the last project he and Diana worked on together in 1995 and the money from the BBC has been used to create what is called the Sanctuary, a retreat for families who have come to visit their children being given terminal care.

The BBC made another payout, on 21 July 2022, when Bashir's lies about the former royal nanny Tiggy Legge-Bourke were finally laid bare. In a hearing at London's High Court, using her married name, the now fifty-seven-year-old Alexandra Pettifer told of the damage caused by Bashir's false allegations of an affair with Prince Charles, the alleged consequent abortion and the so-called letter of proof which Diana said she had been given. As described earlier it was

Bashir's production of this forged letter, almost certainly on the weekend of 28 October 1995, which proved critical in persuading Diana to give the *Panorama* interview. At the last moment she had wavered, but this apparent proof of Prince Charles's treachery is what pushed her over the line.

Mrs Pettifer's lawyer, Louise Prince, said, 'As the allegation of an abortion was totally false, any such letter could only have been fabricated.' She said that the former nanny was questioned as part of an investigation run by the queen's private secretary, Sir Robert Fellowes: 'She felt she had to prove to others that the allegations were completely untrue by revealing highly sensitive matters, including private medical information. Sadly Diana, Princess of Wales could not be convinced, even when incontrovertible evidence was presented.' The BBC paid Mrs Pettifer £200,000.

There were payments of lesser amounts to others who could make a case: Alan Waller, the man named in the forged bank statements; Tom Mangold and Mark Killick, both *Panorama* staffers caught up in the internal witch-hunt which accompanied the cover-up. Hall had confidently told the BBC governors on 25 April 1996, 'Between now and the summer, we will work to deal with leakers and remove persistent troublemakers from the programme.' Yet another victim of the scandal did not realize he had been targeted by Bashir until he found out by watching TV, more than twenty-five years later. As Bashir worked his way down his list of false allegations, at his meeting in Knightsbridge with Diana on the afternoon of 19 September 1995, item number 8 in the notes scribbled down by Charles Spencer read:

Steve Davies (chauffeur) feeds TODAY newspaper; "change your chauffeur"

Davies was sacked, though remarkably it was not until he watched an episode of *The Crown* in 2023, its dramatization of these events, that he realized what had happened, why Diana had suddenly turned on him. In court in May 2024 the BBC agreed to pay compensation. How much is unclear, though Davies' lawyer Persephone Bridgman Baker made it clear that, just as in Patrick Jephson's case, it was not just about money: 'As he now knows, the princess believed that he had betrayed her, and he was unable to correct the position before her tragic death.'

The total paid out in reparations to individuals is around £1.2 million. In 2021 the BBC said it would pay a roughly similar amount to charity, since that was how much money they had earned from selling the Diana interview to foreign broadcasters. The Dyson inquiry, to investigate the scandal, cost a further £1.2 million. The people who have had to pick up the tab for this are you and me – that is, anyone who pays their BBC licence fee. But for the people who brought about this scandal, and then covered it up, what price have they had to pay?

34. No Charge

When I was making my documentary film for Channel 4 in 2020 I consulted a barrister who specializes in fraud and forgery cases, Quentin Hunt from the London chambers 2 Bedford Row. My question was simple: 'Using forged bank statements sounds like it would be against the law. Is it?' His reply was fascinating, a primer on what the law actually deems forgery to be. It turns out it is not a question of someone simply *gaining* something by using a fake document; somebody else also has to have *lost* something as a result.

He explained it this way: 'Let me give you an example. You and I are the last two candidates for a job interview, and you have a degree certificate saying that you have a first-class degree from a top university. In fact, you don't – your certificate is a fake. If you get the job on the basis of the document that you've put forward, you have used a false instrument. And as a result of it, I have been prejudiced because you have got the job instead of me. I have missed out on financial remuneration as a result of you using that false instrument.'

So that is forgery, when what I have done brings not just a benefit for me but causes a loss for someone else. I found out later that it was not just me looking into the legality of this. Charles Spencer was too. He told me, 'I had a junior counsel who had looked at the case and said it was a clear case of forgery in legal terms.' The argument that Spencer's lawyer made was that Bashir's forgeries played a major part in getting the *Panorama* interview, something which turned

357

out to be worth, in terms of foreign sales, around £1 million. And because *Bashir* got the interview it meant that somebody else *didn't* get it. The lawyer I was talking to said much the same, in these terms: 'If a false document is used by Mr A to induce somebody to give an interview, a valuable commodity on the open market, and the person giving the interview decides to favour Mr A over Mr B, then Mr B has obviously lost out. So in those circumstances there would clearly be an argument that a criminal offence has been committed.'

And this is serious stuff. Barrister Quentin Hunt said, 'The law does take it very seriously. Parliament gave a maximum of ten years' imprisonment under the 1981 Forgery and Counterfeiting Act, so you can end up with a long period of imprisonment. And there is no time bar on the launching of prosecutions. The prosecution could be launched at any point if the criminality comes to light.' Lord Dyson established that Bashir had used forged bank statements, not just once but on two occasions, which were instrumental in gaining the *Panorama* interview. And so, has Bashir broken the law or not? I put that question to the BBC shortly before completing my film in October 2020. The BBC News head of communications Charlotte Morgan replied, 'We note that, having spoken to a barrister, you suggest the BBC may have committed criminal activity. This is a serious allegation, but, in these circumstances, a risible one.' Risible. Charles Spencer was not laughing.

In cases like this, especially looking at events which happened many years ago, the police and prosecuting authorities take their steer from the judge who has talked to witnesses and gone through the papers, even if that judge has no formal locus of any kind. If Lord Dyson thought Bashir's use of forged bank statements sounded to him like *criminal* forgery, then he might have discreetly blown a whistle and the police would have at least come running, to see what was up. Charles Spencer had been hoping that was what Dyson would do. He told me, 'I went to the police and I remember them saying we're waiting for Dyson's report.'

Spencer thought that surely Bashir's use of the forged bank statements, to dupe him and win a hugely valuable media interview, must be some kind of crime? Further than that, his lawyer had advised there may be a case against certain BBC bosses for what is called 'Misconduct in Public Office'. This offence is often difficult to establish but is essentially designed to punish officials who have seriously, flagrantly broken the rules when working for a public body, like the BBC. Spencer considered that that is what BBC bosses had done, but then the judgement was not his to make. On 15 September 2021, four months after the Dyson report was published, Spencer received this email from Commander Alex Murray of London's Met Police:

From: Alex Murray
Date: 15 September 2021 at 13:16:42 BST
To: Spencer
Subject: Lord Dyson Report

Dear Earl Spencer
I thought I would follow up our telephone conversation with an email.
Following the publication of the report by Lord Dyson, we again revisited the question of whether a crime may have taken place. The Crown Prosecution Service also gave us the benefit of their detailed advice, particularly around the potential offence of misconduct in a public office (MIPO).
As a result of that careful analysis we are still in a position where we don't believe that there is enough evidence to point to a criminal offence taking place, albeit some of the conduct highlighted was undoubtedly dishonest.
Thank-you again for your sending through the relevant information and I would be more than happy to talk this through with you in more detail if required.
Yours sincerely,
Alex

Commander Alex Murray OBE
Met Police Violence Lead
Metropolitan Police Service

Dear Earl Spencer

Following the publication of the report by Lord Dyson, we again revisited the question of whether a crime may have taken place.

The Crown Prosecution Service also gave us the benefit of their detailed advice, particularly around the potential offence of misconduct in a public office (MIPO).

As a result of that careful analysis we are still in a position where we don't believe that there is enough evidence to point to a criminal offence taking place, albeit some of the conduct highlighted was undoubtedly dishonest . . .

Yours sincerely
Alex

On 28 September 2021, Spencer replied:

Dear Commander Murray,

I'm afraid this is absurd. Clearly forgery is in play here, as is the public office offence. I've read the CPS explanation of both crimes online and there can be no doubt on either point . . . do I have to go to the trouble and expense of mounting private prosecutions?

Yours sincerely,
Charles Spencer

On 30 September 2021, Murray emailed:

Dear Earl Spencer

I understand your frustration here but can reassure you that we examined the law in detail and sought independent legal advice . . .

Yours sincerely
Alex

In an inquiry such as his, not a trial, not even an undertaking with any judicial status, the wording of the report becomes critical for any likely follow up. Although Dyson was clear about Bashir's mendacity, the issue of *criminality* was not raised. As regards the activities of the bosses, the most serious charge laid at the door of Hall and Sloman is that their inquiry proved 'woefully ineffective'. I suspect that is a phrase which Dyson will have decided upon with the utmost care. That which is 'woeful' does not necessarily point blame at those who caused the 'woe'. It is just a shame that the 'woe' was caused at all. Had Dyson chosen a punchier adjective, had he gone for 'recklessly', or even 'criminally', then the result might have been much different. But 'woefully' was Lord Dyson's choice.

Spencer considered whether he should hire lawyers, whether he should spend perhaps hundreds of thousands of pounds to take Bashir and the BBC to court himself. Finally he decided not. And so, case closed.

The fact that BBC employees have entirely escaped legal censure rankles with many journalists in rival media organizations, especially those who saw reporters sent to jail for phone hacking. Richard Kay's newspaper, the *Daily Mail*, was never implicated in that. But he puts the case, calmly and forcefully, that the BBC seems to have escaped real punishment. He told me, 'The idea of cheating and lying undermines the public trust, it has a corrosive effect. You would probably expect me to say this, as someone who works on a popular newspaper, but the tabloid press has had a torrid time in recent years. We all know that the company that owned the *News of the World* is still paying out tens of millions to people whose phones were intercepted and hacked. And the BBC was at the forefront of leading the charge against the excesses of the tabloid press.'

Martin Bashir quietly resigned from his post as BBC editor of religion shortly before the publication of the Dyson report. His colleagues were told in a statement at the time, 'Although he underwent major surgery toward the end of last year, he is facing some ongoing issues and has decided to focus on his health.' Aged sixty-two at the time of writing, Bashir lives in a pleasant town in Hampshire where he is an active member of his local church. But although he has escaped any proceedings, his disgrace is complete. In the Dyson report Bashir was called 'devious and dishonest' and his reputation has been so severely shredded, in media around the world, that he is very unlikely to work as a broadcaster again. His former colleague Jonathan Maitland said to me, 'It must be really, really appalling for him. Emotionally, it must be terribly difficult. But he does have his faith. He's very religious. He's quite strong. And he will be dealing with it by saying, "There's only really one Lord who can judge me, and it's not Lord Dyson. If I have sinned, my Lord will forgive me." And I think he can justifiably say, "Hold on, what I did was bad, but I've admitted it. What the BBC did was worse."'

Lord Hall, aged seventy-four at the time of writing, is a member of one of the committees of the House of Lords. He is also chair of trustees of the Natural History Museum; a trustee of the National Trust; a trustee of the Woodland Trust; a trustee of the Oxford Philharmonic Orchestra; and chairman of the City of Birmingham Symphony Orchestra. Drawing on his experience as BBC director-general, and in the arts, he is listed by an agency which provides well-known figures for conferences in the band between £5,000 and £10,000 per speech.

I asked the BBC whether, in the wake of Dyson's criticisms, and the huge sums of public money spent in reparations, had even a note of censure ever been addressed to Bashir, to Hall or to anyone else, or had their substantial pensions been affected in any way? In every case, no.

35. An Open Wound

Forty-three years old at the time of writing, Prince William is now seven years older than Diana was when she died in August 1997. And as I indicated way back in my prologue, I wrote this book largely as a result of something William said. His speech on television, on 20 May 2021, reacting to the publication of the Dyson report, was to me electrifying. He seemed to have immediately put his finger on what is the real story here, the BBC's failure to mitigate the harm done to his mother when the chance arose. And remarkably, of all the people in the world, he was the one whose view counted most.

William's recorded statement for television, just a little over two minutes long, is a truly remarkable piece of TV. I have never yet seen a victim impact statement of that kind which, even delivered haltingly, from crumpled notes outside a wind-blown courtroom somewhere, does not carry enormous power because of the raw passion behind it. In William's case he was not crowded by shouting reporters. He had had twenty-four years in which to nurse the grief of his mother's death. But here, still, was a devastating analysis of who was to blame, and for me it was compelling. Where Dyson portrays hapless but blameless BBC people failing to nail Bashir, William calls it quite differently. For William there were 'leaders at the BBC who looked the other way'. He makes plain his view that it was not that these BBC men and women messed up. They *chose* to look elsewhere, suggesting a culpability which has gone wholly unpunished.

At the time, in 1996, those responsible for the cover-up could not know just how devastating the consequences of their actions would be for Diana. Now they do, and any refusal to own up or to keep ducking and diving puts the BBC in an extraordinary position regarding, once again, the one person in the world whose concerns it is not just heartless to ignore but foolish too. In the fullness of time it will be *King* William who issues the Royal Charter, the formal statute reissued every ten years under which the BBC operates. In the solemn language used at the time of the first charter in 1927 the monarch's association is intended 'to endow the BBC with a prestige and influence which will be of special value to it'. Yes. But do I trust you?

A couple of times in this book I have cited the journalistic convention of something being off the record, true but unattributable. I do it here again to say that the BBC, at the time of writing in 2025, should be aware that they have an implacable antagonist in William, now taking steps to discover what truly happened inside the BBC, before and after the *Panorama* interview. William has people on the case. And the more the BBC act suspiciously, as they did in 2020 with Bashir's overstated illness, and since then with my battle over emails, the more William becomes convinced that there is something he is not being told. Those at the top of the BBC would do well to consider how powerful the motivation is, for someone whose entire life has been shaped by these events, to discover the truth. The consequence for William has been described to me as 'an open wound which will not heal'.

The clues are all there if the BBC cares to see them. When former royal nanny Tiggy Legge-Bourke, now using her married name of Alexandra Pettifer, brought her case to court in July 2022 it was dealt with by Harbottle & Lewis, the legal firm which William often uses. Following the judgement Mrs Pettifer made a carefully worded statement, one which offered a very clear challenge. She said, 'The distress caused to the royal family is a source of great upset to me. I know first-hand how much they were affected at the time, and how the programme and the false narrative it created have haunted the family in the years since. Especially because, still today, so much about the making of the programme is yet to be adequately explained.' That final sentence. Over a year after the appearance of the Dyson report, which at the very least *should* have provided that adequate explanation of how the programme was made, that is what Mrs Pettifer believes, what William believes and, for what it is worth, what I believe.

What I think the BBC does not appreciate is that this is a story which will not go away. One of the cruellest aspects of what happened to Diana is that, in the way this scandal played out, she was the victim of her own celebrity. Had the *Panorama* interview of 20 November 1995 been with a much lesser person, had it then been revealed that a sly reporter had made things up, as sometimes happens, it would all have been over in less than a week. Reporter sacked, probably the editor too. Newspapers froth and foam. Life moves on.

But in Diana's case the story was too big to fail. Because the biggest scoop of the century had been seen by hundreds of millions of people around the world. Because the chairman of the BBC governors, one-legged Marmaduke Hussey, was already baying for the blood of Director-General John Birt.

That is why the BBC covered up in 1996, and why Diana was allowed to remain in the dark, with such tragic consequences. But, and this is what the BBC leaders today need to understand, the magnitude of these events has not diminished. That *Panorama* interview is still the biggest one the BBC has *ever* broadcast. And so the question raised implicitly by Mrs Pettifer will continue to cry out for an answer.

Dyson performed a useful task, in providing a record of events up to the time when Bashir first met Diana. But his report serves as a menu for historians, not the meal. The fact that we now know – and I have to say, only thanks to my own research, not Dyson nor the BBC – that the most critical documents had been *removed* from the archive, means that it is perfectly reasonable to suspect that other critical documents are yet to be discovered. And it is perfectly reasonable to assume that the BBC will lie about the existence of such documents. That is not a cheap sneer; it is something I am entitled to write ever since the BBC lied to me over the question of whether or not they possessed documents on the scandal way back in 2007. The problem currently at the BBC is that there is now a new cohort of people who, once again, have skin in the game, who clumsily became involved in the events of 2020 and so, still today, have questions to answer. Tim Davie, the director-general. When exactly did he know that Bashir was a liar? Why did he attempt to brush off Charles Spencer instead of going hammer and tongs after the truth when he was offered the chance? Tough questions to answer.

The BBC at the time of writing is also not obviously configured to be jolted into action from above, by the people who are there to act as watchdogs, the BBC board. Its chair is Samir Shah, the man who, when employed by the BBC more than thirty years ago, was perhaps more aligned than most to both John Birt and Tony Hall. I know that Shah has been urged by certain very powerful people to start turning over stones but he may not be the man to do it. It may take the arrival of a future BBC director-general, unburdened by history, to demand some kind of truth and reconciliation process, to throw open the archives just as every incoming US president promises to throw open the archives on JFK. Until that happens, historians, researchers and journalists like me will continue to nibble away from below, and Prince William will continue to try to shine his light down into the cellar from high above. What an extraordinary situation.

I began this book by suggesting that the story of what happened to Princess Diana is so luridly fantastical that it is certain to live on, simply as one of history's most alluring human stories. One of those which playwrights, novelists and filmmakers cannot leave alone, with plot points you would not dare to make up. So it is, and I recognize that that is a journalist talking, making a cold assessment of what happened to a real person, a mother, a sister. But I also hope that this book has served a useful purpose in helping to explain why the image that we have of Diana – inasmuch as that image is the edge-of-crazy BBC *Panorama* black-ringed-eye image – is the wrong one. Again, as Diana's son put it plainly, it 'holds no legitimacy'. Diana was behaving in a way which made perfect sense, in the circumstances, but she was not that person, not for any longer than the poison administered to her by the BBC was allowed to work. The antidote existed, but the BBC would not employ it. The unending tragedy is that Diana would never be allowed to know that was the case.

Appendix

I have put a series of Freedom of Information (FOI) requests to the BBC over the years. The most protracted one followed my question seeking potentially incriminating emails, the request made in June 2021 and finally resolved with the First Tier Tribunal decision announced in August 2024.

By that stage I had first been refused sight of an undeclared number of emails, in July 2021. That refusal was confirmed by a BBC internal review later that year, claiming that all 'responsive' emails were protected from disclosure under sections 42 and 43 of the Freedom of Information Act (FOIA). My request for a further external review, by the Information Commissioner's Office, was granted, and a small number of emails was then released. But these proved to be entirely irrelevant to the case, and so I appealed, arguing that the BBC must surely hold further *relevant* information.

That was the basis for my appeal. In addition to an extraordinary amount of written correspondence, three separate hearings were held, conducted over video, during 2023. The case then culminated in two days of live hearings in June 2024.

The document appended here comprises my summary of my case up to that point, what the court terms a 'skeleton argument', to be submitted in advance of the court appearance. After hearing from the BBC's witness and counsel and after examining a sample of the information withheld by the

BBC, the tribunal would say it found no evidence of wrong-doing, malpractice or dishonesty.

Appeal No. EA/2022/0069

IN THE MATTER OF AN APPEAL
TO THE FIRST-TIER TRIBUNAL
(GENERAL REGULATORY CHAMBER)
INFORMATION RIGHTS
BETWEEN:

ANDREW WEBB
Appellant

– and –

THE INFORMATION COMMISSIONER
First Respondent

– and –

BRITISH BROADCASTING CORPORATION
Second Respondent

Appellant's skeleton argument

June 11 2024

I respectfully ask the Tribunal to consider this document in conjunction with those submitted by me on February 27 this year. To avoid repetition I will not restate public interest arguments which have already been submitted, but beg the Tribunal to give them consideration alongside the separate points raised here.

1 SUMMARY

The Tribunal is being asked to decide whether or not to make public the emails I requested more than three years ago, emails currently hidden by very extensive redaction and withholding. I submit that the BBC has twice attempted to prevent publication, but has been thwarted, and so has engaged a third strategy.

> The **first** attempt centred around the 'blanket response', falsely suggesting that a search had been conducted but had detected only material excluded from disclosure under FOIA sections 42 and 43. This has been described by the BBC as *'wrong and impermissible'*.
>
> The **second** attempt centred around the assertion that the bulk of the material, detected by the BBC's own search terms, had proved to be *'irrelevant'*. This argument, termed *'novel'* by the Tribunal, was decisively rejected.
>
> The **third** and current attempt centres around creating conditions which the BBC has described as resembling *'a large commercial dispute'*. The intention is to ensure that a proper examination of what the BBC has done would exceed the time and resources available to the Tribunal and might be regarded as 'disproportionate' even were such resources to exist.

I humbly submit that in ensuring that this third strategy fails the Tribunal will perform a valuable public service in two regards.

(i) the breach of trust committed by the BBC on October 19 2020 will be laid bare and those responsible called to account.

(ii) an attempt to flout the operation of the FOIA, by one of this country's most powerful institutions, will be shown to have failed.

2 THE EXISTENCE OR NOT OF A 'CONSPIRACY'

The Tribunal has received a witness statement from Ms Sarah Jones, General Counsel of the BBC and it is beyond doubt that the sworn testimony of the corporation's most senior lawyer must be taken very seriously. I welcome the opportunity to question Ms Jones on June 18 but beg the Tribunal to consider the points raised here before proceedings resume.

I ask the Tribunal to give these points special consideration because, I submit, it is crucial to the decision now before you to determine whether certain individuals at the BBC did behave improperly around October 19 2020. I say the evidence shows that on the balance of probabilities they did behave in that way, that the emails I seek will illustrate their behaviour, and that the threat of exposure provides a motive for the current BBC attempt to prevent publication.

In her statement, p20 par 58, Ms Jones argues that what she calls a *'conspiracy'* could not have occurred, in essence, because it would have required the participation of large numbers of people with overriding legal obligations. [For the term *'conspiracy'* I will substitute the phrase I have in fact used, a *'cover up'*.] We know from Lord Dyson's report that a *'cover up'* did indeed exist, as regards the underlying scandal, from its inception in 1996 until the publication of his report in May 2021. This surely presents a difficulty in accepting Ms Jones' argument. I accept without reservation that Ms Jones did *not* know about this cover up, since to have such knowledge would have prompted action of some kind. As Lord Dyson remarks, in covering up the scandal: '... *the BBC fell short of the high standards of integrity and transparency which are its hallmark.*'

The assumption must therefore be that, even though she joined the BBC as a senior lawyer in 1996, and later served as General Counsel for seven years under Director General Lord Hall, Ms Jones remained unaware of a cover up in place during the whole of her BBC career. If Ms Jones was shielded from such knowledge for 25 years, despite her position at the very heart of BBC affairs, then is it not equally possible that she has been kept unaware regarding recent events?

The events of October 2020 seem to me far easier to conceal than the 'cover up' described by Lord Dyson, which must of necessity have involved Lord Hall, Mrs Sloman, Mr Suter, Mr Bashir and a large number of people within the BBC who had been ordered to suppress news of the scandal. None of them, clearly, were restrained by any sense of overriding obligation and managed to escape detection until being subjected to *external* scrutiny. In these circumstances it seems to me perfectly credible that a fresh 'cover up' might well exist; the important issue is whether or not the evidence suggests that it does.

3 THE EVIDENCE REGARDING MR BASHIR

Ms Jones asks the Tribunal to accept that the BBC was forced to conceal documents because of Mr Bashir's health and that decisions were not shaped by a perceived public relations advantage. I submit that the evidence suggests otherwise.

Ms Jones' position is that having assembled the relevant documentation, and in particular the 'Sloman memo', the BBC were, immediately prior to October 19 2020, aware that evidence existed which could be very damaging to Mr Bashir. At p22 par 63 she says: '*This was clearly a matter that could lead to significant reputational harm to Mr Bashir, including potentially damaging his career and livelihood. Therefore, it was considered important that a process of consultation with Mr Bashir (and also with Lord Tony Hall, who similarly was at risk of reputational harm from the disclosure) should take place.*' We are asked to accept that a situation existed where Lord Hall *had* been warned what was coming, but Mr Bashir had not, because he was too ill. In any event, the bad news would certainly be announced and it was simply a matter of time.

Ms Jones is insistent that the 'Sloman memo', describing the worst aspects of the cover up in detail, *would* be published, as soon as Mr Bashir was well enough to be briefed on matters. Yet I invite the Tribunal to consider the BBC Press statement issued to me on October 19. This document gives no hint that damaging material has surfaced which will soon put the BBC in the firing line. It is in fact a robust defence of the BBC position, even including the extraordinary claim, regarding Mr Bashir: '*At the time, he co-operated fully with the internal BBC investigations.*' As the author of this document knew, as indeed Ms Jones tells us that she knew, when it was issued, Mr Bashir had in fact lied again and again during those internal BBC investigations.

It is my submission that the BBC believed the shocking allegation that Earl Spencer had acted as co-conspirator with Mr Bashir would so fundamentally alter the perception of events that trifling details in the 'Sloman memo' would be swept aside by glaring headlines in the tabloid press – *if indeed the 'Sloman memo' was ever released at all.*

It remains a fact that, despite all Ms Jones says, this document *has never yet* been released to me by the BBC nor I suspect was it ever intended to be released. It was purely a result of Lord Dyson's decision to publish the raw document, in an annexe to his report, which brought it to my attention and prompted my FOIA request on June 4 2021. It follows that had Lord Dyson not made that decision we would not be involved in the current proceedings at all.

4 CONCEALMENT AS A S77 OFFENCE

Ms Jones makes reference to my allegation that the BBC's withholding of the 'Sloman memo' in particular amounted to criminal concealment under FOIA s77. It may assist the Tribunal to know that my case has been considered by the ICO Criminal Investigations Team and a decision reached that no further action will be taken.

The circumstances are, I submit, worth noting. Following an investigation which lasted approximately two months, ICO counsel concluded that the complaint must fail, not for want of evidence, but because the complaint fell outside the six-month time limit. Though it was accepted that the BBC had never in fact disclosed the information at all, too much time had elapsed from the moment I say the offence occurred, October 19 2020, to the first *possible* moment when I might even have detected the offence, Lord Dyson's publication on May 21 2021. A period of seven months, when the maximum allowed is six.

I have annexed here the ICO decision in full, but draw attention to this passage: '*Parliament is aware of the difficulty with prosecuting under s77 but chose not to change the time limit. In 2009, a* *proposal to extend the time limit, supported by the ICO, was rejected by the government.'** It seems to me that the s77 aspect of this case is one which may engage the attention of Parliament again.

5 THE BBC'S CONTINUED DEFENCE OF MR BASHIR'S ACTIONS

Ms Jones offers the Tribunal what I submit is a puzzling observation at p34 par 85: '*With the benefit of hindsight, I can see that we should have consulted Earl Spencer.*' I will have the opportunity to put questions on this but I feel it will be useful to share two documents which provide a picture of events, once Earl Spencer had been 'consulted'. As I think the Tribunal will be aware, it fell to me to inform Earl Spencer of the BBC's allegation, soon after I received it.

Earl Spencer almost immediately sent a strongly worded email, annexed here, to BBC Director General Tim Davie. Mr Davie replied in an email jointly authored by Mr Phil Harrold, also annexed here.

The significant paragraph, I say, is this, from Mr Davie/ Mr Harrold: '*You say the BBC's sequence of events is incorrect and that Mr Bashir had shown you the documents before you had introduced him to the Princess of Wales. Unfortunately, the account you give does not accord with the account that Mr Bashir gave the BBC at the time. Our records show that he told us that although he had mocked up the statements before the Princess of Wales agreed to give the interview, you had already introduced them to one another and the relationship was therefore established. With Mr Bashir indisposed, unfortunately the BBC can only rely on what our historic records show.*'

---

* https://www.cfoi.org.uk/2010/01/time-limit-for-prosecution-of-offences-under-section-77-of-the-foi-act/

This readiness to accept Mr Bashir's false version of events, challenging Earl Spencer's true account, seems wholly unwarranted given what Ms Jones has told the Tribunal about the BBC's private understanding of events at exactly this time. Referring to the 'Sloman memo', Ms Jones says at p34 par 86.1: *Its contents gave a detailed account of Mr Bashir's conduct and internal investigations of that conduct at the BBC, <u>including revealing that Mr Bashir had lied to BBC management about not showing Earl Spencer the faked bank statements</u>.'* [emphasis added]

It is plain that when Mr Davie/Mr Harrold composed their reply they knew, beyond doubt, that Mr Bashir had lied repeatedly on this very issue. But they were attempting to ride out the storm, completely unaware that Earl Spencer possessed copious contemporaneous notes [which he would shortly make public, leading to the BBC's hurried decision to appoint Lord Dyson.]

Had the BBC a serious intention to publish the 'Sloman memo' then at the very least, and in the context of this confidential exchange, they might have indicated some doubt about the story which Mr Bashir had been telling; how could it be otherwise, when Mr Bashir would soon be publicly branded a liar? I submit that the picture of events provided by these emails sits uneasily with the account which Ms Jones has offered.

6 THE BBC'S APPROACH TO FOIA SECTIONS 40 AND 42

Ms Jones' statement to the Tribunal is sharply illustrative, in a way which I suspect was not intended, in judging the BBC's policy of redaction and withholding. In my submission of February 27 2024 I drew attention to the BBC's decision to publish, unredacted, Mr Bashir's private and confidential email of July 20 2020, which within three hours became a story on the BBC TV News at Ten and dominated tabloid news coverage the following day.

This email contains highly sensitive personal information, quite apart from twice pleading to be regarded as *'private and confidential.'* The personal information includes Mr Bashir's allegations of racism and class-bias, and betrays tensions in his relationships with colleagues. Ms Jones' statement is the best means of assessing the damage publication would inevitably cause. In her statement at p34 par 86.1 Ms Jones explains why the 'Sloman memo' could not be published in 2020 because: *'It also gave details of <u>tensions in his relationships with colleagues. This constituted Mr Bashir's personal data.</u>'* The BBC's decision to publish Mr Bashir's confidential email is regrettable because it removed attention, as the BBC knew it would, from the serious matters in hand. But having presented this email *en clair*, at least the Tribunal will have a yardstick with which to measure all those redacted and withheld under FOIA s40; it follows that *every single one* of those documents must present a stronger claim for privacy than Mr Bashir's email, twice pleading for confidentiality and, in terms defined by Ms Jones herself, undeniably containing Mr Bashir's personal data.

Given the difficulties which exist in trying to guess at what may be hidden behind redaction, I can do no more than register a general concern at the argument Ms Jones makes in her *Section B – Reliance on s.42 FOIA: legal advice privilege.* Ms Jones creates ten separate categories in which she argues documents might reasonably be withheld; I am no lawyer and therefore respectfully invite the Tribunal to use the legal analytical skills I do not possess. But it seems to me that especially in categories 5 and 9 the door is opened so wide that almost *any* communication might be admitted for LPP. These seem to me a very long way indeed from Ms Jones category 1, a straightforward confidential exchange between lawyer and client, and become a catch-all under which almost any email between BBC staff members and BBC lawyers might be allowed to shelter.

7 THE EXTENT OF THE BBC'S REDACTION AND WITHHOLDING

In order to reach agreement over numbers I asked the BBC to provide figures regarding the extent of redaction and withholding and I am obliged for the following information: **955** documents have been redacted but not withheld in full for FOIA s42; **688** documents have been withheld in full for s42; **1,824** documents have been redacted for FOIA s40. Regarding s40, no documents have been withheld in full though there is an unspecified number of full-page redactions. I ask the Tribunal to consider whether the BBC approach is itself proportionate, or whether by introducing redaction and withholding on such a vast scale it becomes disproportionate even to properly examine what it is that the BBC has done.

In what I submit is a telling phrase, the BBC wrote on February 13 2024 that: *'The task that the BBC has carried out in the present context has been an enormous undertaking, similar to a disclosure exercise is a large commercial dispute. [sic] It goes significantly beyond any FOIA disclosure exercise ever conducted by the BBC (or, the BBC anticipates, any other public authority).'**

*

* Ms Carss-Frisk February 13 2024 p8 par 13

The second part of that statement appears not to be true and one wishes that the BBC had paused before making this assertion that it has been unfairly burdened.* The first part is however true, and in my submission does no credit to the BBC at all. The matter in hand is a FOIA request; it is not a *'large commercial dispute'* where competing giant corporations drawing on vast financial resources spend months before the courts. What is more the tone of this BBC observation has that of an innocent third party, offended at the scale of the task it has been asked to perform and bemused as to the reason for it. The plain fact is that it is the BBC which has decided to employ redaction and withholding to such an inordinate degree that this Appeal from my perspective has become all but unmanageable.

The Tribunal has also been obliged to devote much precious time and resources to a matter which ought to have been settled long ago. The attempt to argue *'irrelevance'* occupied perhaps nine months of these proceedings. In January 2024 the BBC replaced that gambit with one of wholesale redaction and withholding, which has not yet been tested almost six months later. The BBC position may be: *'But we have been* forced *to undertake such measures by Mr Webb's obduracy. We are merely fulfilling our obligations to redact and withhold as the law requires.'* If that is the case I invite the Tribunal to examine Ms Jones' ten separate categories of email allegedly deserving protection for LPP,

---

* I sought clarification on this from the ICO. I was kindly referred to the following site, which deals with a survey of bats. It seems very unlikely that the BBC data bundle, though large, is extraordinary in the way suggested. https://www.mysociety.org/2022/05/26/thats-bats/

and to examine the BBC's inconsistent handling of TPD with reference to Mr Bashir's 'private and confidential' email.

The sheer scale of the BBC's redaction and withholding, and the administrative tasks which ensue, have also ensured that there is no effective check or scrutiny on the work which the BBC has carried out. In the *'large commercial dispute'* envisaged then the opposing party would invest similar resources to check each step of the process. But we are not in that world. For my part it has simply been necessary to acquiesce as each complicated move has followed the other, to take things on trust. The Tribunal will understand my lingering unease given the BBC's history of impermissible behaviour in these matters, their repeated pattern of significant error, and the still unexplained loss of critical material in the closely related Dyson inquiry.

I will say here that the BBC approach, to make matters so long drawn out and complicated, has had an effect which I find almost unsustainable. Since my request was made three years ago I have had to respond to 402 separate items of correspondence and invest many hundreds of hours, all of them unpaid, merely trying to keep pace with what the BBC has indeed caused to resemble a *'large commercial dispute'*. I regret that this experience will surely serve as a deterrent to any other citizen seeking to exercise the FOIA right of inquiry granted by Parliament.

8 THE EXAMINATION OF A SAMPLE OF THE DISCLOSURE

As I understand matters the Tribunal must now decide whether to allow the current degree of redaction and withholding to remain, to remove it, or vary it in some way, and that the

Tribunal's decision will be influenced by an examination of a sample of the material. A study of the ICO explanation of FOIA principles reveals that the content of these emails is irrelevant to the question of whether I should see them. FOIA requests are to be considered purpose-blind; the identity of the requester, and the assumed reason for the request, play no part in the decision as to whether the request will be met. In the present case I am a journalist, firmly convinced that a small number of these emails will betray a breach of trust by the BBC. Yet if I am wrong in that belief, if the emails show no breach at all, that will have no bearing on my right to see them.*

Acknowledging my lack of training in these matters, if the purpose of the examination is not to discover examples of 'bad faith', then is it to determine whether the BBC has always fairly applied redaction and withholding? If that is the purpose, then it seems impossible that it can be fulfilled, since the examination can in the time allowed only be extended to a small sample of the total data. To do more would not just be impractical, it would be 'disproportionate', and therefore beyond the Tribunal's powers. Although one fully understands the constraints, and wholeheartedly welcomes the efforts made by the Tribunal to overcome them, to base a decision in such an important matter on a *partial* examination surely cannot meet the standards which justice requires. By limiting the examination on the grounds of what is proportionate would surely be to reward the BBC policy of employing wholesale disproportionate redaction and withholding in the first place.

---

* https://ico.org.uk/for-organisations/foi/freedom-of-information-and-environmental-information-regulations/consideration-of-the-applicant-s-identity-or-motives/

9 THE BBC EXPERTISE IN MATTERS CONCERNING FOIA

I submit that it is relevant to the decisions before the Tribunal to consider the relationship that the BBC has with FOIA in a broad sense, to understand what seems a bewildering pattern of response over the last three years. In the year following my initial request the BBC appeared to act with astonishing ineptitude. We have heard of mistakes over the dating of emails which sent the process entirely off course; mistakes over a computer search by a senior lawyer which failed to detect more than 3,000 emails; other significant failings have prompted a slew of apologies. Yet in the past six months we have seen a complete change. This vast body of data has been, we are told, rigorously scanned to enact the BBC policy of redaction and withholding. The ensuing data management tasks appear to have been carried out with a brisk efficiency.

I say that we should not be the least surprised by this. The BBC is certainly the most sophisticated practitioner in FOIA matters in this country, and perhaps the world. Uniquely among UK authorities, in FOIA matters the BBC is both consumer and provider, poacher and gamekeeper, with an unequalled understanding of how the system works.

Unlike the NHS, the MoD, the Treasury, all frequent targets for FOIA inquiry, the BBC's day-to-day activities depend on *making* FOIA requests, not merely answering the 2000 or so which it receives each year. Entire *Panorama* programmes may hinge on an FOIA request; the BBC website indicates the vital role that FOIA plays in our national life.*

* https://www.bbc.co.uk/news/magazine-30645383

The BBC has a large FOIA staff, not only within the confines of the Information Rights office but with employees placed directly within programme departments to facilitate a speedy traffic in information.*

It is because of the BBC's pre-eminence in FOIA affairs that I have always greeted with scepticism the notion that in the first weeks after my request was made it was allowed to somehow kick around the lower reaches of the organisation, failing to be addressed through a mix of inattention and simple bad luck. We will see before the Tribunal on June 18 the BBC's General Counsel; we will see one of this country's most lauded KC's, assisted by an experienced team. This is the true measure of the importance the BBC attaches to the threat of publication of these emails, but it is not newly minted. We are asked to accept that the BBC journey began in a rickshaw, and is ending in a Rolls Royce, yet the *destination* has not altered in three years. The BBC has steadfastly focussed on preventing publication, whether through the quasi-mendacious '*blanket response*' or now through massive redaction and withholding. I submit that the BBC's nervousness will have been apparent *from the first moment* my request arrived; the challenge for the BBC, even with its unrivalled expertise with FOIA, has been how to deal with it, given the Tribunal's rigorous examination of the gambits so far employed.

* A valuable description of the way BBC Information Rights works can be seen from the link below. It is ironic to reflect that this letter, in 2021, was in fact a refusal to submit to an audit of BBC FOIA practice requested by the ICO. Yet it was at precisely this date that the BBC was engaged in the 'wrong and impermissible' behaviour subsequently admitted to the Tribunal.
https://committees.parliament.uk/publications/8400/documents/85467/default/

10 THE BBC FAILURE TO DEMONSTRATE ACCOUNTABILITY

In the matters now before the Tribunal it is surely essential to have confidence in the way that evidence has been presented. One of my chief concerns over the last three years is that the BBC has failed to demonstrate best practice in accountability in that regard. The breach of trust which I allege did not occur in some far-flung BBC outpost. It occurred in London, inside the very office charged with mounting the BBC's defence, the Information Rights office. It is likely that certain staff members given responsibility for marshalling arguments to the Tribunal, or indeed managing redaction, are in fact the same people who *wrote* the emails now being redacted. In an authority following best practice one would expect to see an immediate recognition that those even remotely suspected of *'wrong and impermissible'* conduct ought not be allowed to manage the evidence for whether or not that wrongdoing has taken place. There would be a demonstration of independence which would go far to suggest genuine accountability. [In the present case it may be argued that the BBC relies heavily on *external* legal advice, yet it seems to me this is no safeguard, since these external lawyers can only rely on instruction given by the people I have indicated.]

I raise this concern because it seems to me that it must constrain the choices which the Tribunal can now make, if they are to have any meaningful effect. Were a direction to be given, say, to reduce the amount of redaction and withholding by a certain amount, the question must then arise 'but who will decide what is left?' If there seems on the balance of probabilities that a breach of trust has occurred, and we know that those responsible also have effective control of the evidence, what guarantee is there that the evidence will be produced?

11 THE BBC'S LEGAL OBLIGATIONS

In making the decision before you I submit that one should consider the BBC's core legal obligations and the degree to which they have been followed during this Appeal. The BBC operates under a Royal Charter citing principles which are not mere lofty ideals but legal requirements. For present purposes the key considerations, in the Charter's own words, are these:

(i) *The Mission of the BBC is to act in the public interest;*

(ii) *The BBC must observe high standards of openness and seek to maximise transparency and accountability;*

(iii) *The BBC must exercise rigorous stewardship of public money;*

(iv) *The management of all of the BBC's resources must meet high standards of public conduct, robust governance and duly consider the expectations of Parliament.**

The course of this Appeal, dictated not by me but in every event by the BBC itself, has brought us to a point where I believe it is critical to ask whether these principles are being observed.

The public interest

The BBC action on October 19 2020 surely constitutes a breach of the Royal Charter requirement listed here at (i).

The evidence indicates that the BBC's intention on October

---

* https://downloads.bbc.co.uk/bbctrust/assets/files/pdf/about/how_we_govern/2016/charter.pdf

19 was not to *expose* the wrongdoing which they knew had taken place, quite the opposite; the document which would have instantly laid the scandal bare, 'the Sloman memo', was *not* published, instead being concealed behind Mr Bashir's alleged debilitating illness. Though it had been delayed for 25 years, the public interest in the eventual exposure of the scandal is manifest, and dealt with in my submission to the Tribunal of February 27 2024. The BBC therefore acted in a way which went directly counter to the public interest and I believe that a small number of the emails currently hidden by redaction and withholding will make this plain.

Maximising transparency and accountability

The matters before the Tribunal indicate clear breaches of the Royal Charter requirement listed at (ii) At its simplest the BBC has ensured that a member of the public is waiting for an answer to a straightforward FOIA request more than three years after that request was made.

During that time BBC staff with legal professional obligations have engaged in impermissible behaviour, the corporation has attempted to prevent scrutiny citing the novel principle of *'irrelevance'* and has now engaged redaction and withholding to an extraordinary degree. It is surely impossible to judge the BBC's behaviour as meeting even the bare duty of transparency, let alone *maximising* that duty.

Rigorous stewardship of public money

Given the Royal Charter requirement listed here it is appropriate to consider the vast expenditure of public money which the BBC has made during these Tribunal proceedings. An FOIA request demonstrates that as of April 4 2024 the BBC had spent £430,034.71 on external legal assistance alone during this Appeal; by the date of the next hearing that figure must comfortably exceed half a million pounds.

This seems to me wholly indefensible. Were there some point of law which the BBC had steadfastly decided to maintain, then I might still seek to challenge the refusal but would respect the underlying argument. In the present case the only motivation for the spending of these huge sums seems to be a stark terror of exposure. I submit that it now falls to the Tribunal to stop this misuse of public funds which runs directly counter to Charter obligation (iii).

The expectations of Parliament

This Appeal has become the subject of widespread media attention which has in turn alerted Parliament to the issues which concern us. A member of the upper House has recently reflected publicly: '*The BBC has managed to build up, at licence-payers' expense, a haystack so huge that it could hide any possible needles. If the regulator can be swamped in this way, he is proved powerless and therefore useless. Surely Parliament, and perhaps ministers, should challenge such behaviour.*'* I submit that these words should be carefully weighed when considering how far the BBC's actions meet the requirements of Royal Charter requirement (iv).

I feel it has become a matter of the utmost concern, irrespective of the content of the emails in dispute, that the BBC has, against its own long-term interests, built a template which would render the FOIA effectively powerless unless now challenged by the Tribunal.

*

* Lord Moore of Etchingham, under his pen name Charles Moore, Spectator magazine May 25 2024

In summary, the Royal Charter provides surely the best yardstick against which to measure BBC behaviour when considering the matters now before the Tribunal. It is to avoid breaches such as these, and for no other purpose, that I have pursued my case over the last three years.

12 A SUGGESTION FOR RESOLUTION

My main ground of Appeal, that the BBC held further information within the scope of the request, has been conclusively proven. The issue now is that I am barred from seeing that information and have moved hardly further forward than I was on June 4 2021. My preferred outcome is that I am quite simply allowed to examine the emails which were responsive to the search and perhaps the Tribunal will make a decision based upon public interest arguments. If not, and a decision becomes contingent upon examination, then I beg leave to suggest the following.

I have no wish whatsoever to view items *properly* protected for TPD or LPP. But my legitimate doubts about the contents of the data bundle cannot be satisfied without comprehensive examination. Is it then within the Tribunal's powers to appoint an 'examiner', agreeable to all Parties, to study the data and report to the Tribunal on his or her findings? If the conclusion of that report is that there are no instances of impermissible redaction and withholding, and no indication of a breach of trust concerning the October 19 2020 events, then the Tribunal can indicate as much and I will immediately consider my Appeal to have been answered.

If on the other hand the report indicates improper redaction and withholding and perhaps suggests a breach of trust then the Tribunal may order that I be allowed to examine the emails. It seems to me that such an examination could be carried out in the space of two or three days and in no way threaten confidentiality, if it were to emerge that TPD or LPP had indeed been properly protected. If that is not the case then justice will not have been denied, simply because detection is too great a task.

13 CONCLUSION

The issue which has troubled me since these proceedings began has been to consider whether the BBC has *truly* committed a serious breach of trust, since compounded by spending half a million pounds of public money attempting to cover it up. As someone who worked for the BBC for two decades and has still a deep affection for the corporation it saddens me to conclude that that *is* the case. We would like to think that a much-loved institution would not do that sort of thing. We have seen lately in the case of the Post Office that even our most cherished institutions can seek to cover up serious failings by a years-long strategy of deceit.

Were the Tribunal to allow full scrutiny of the emails then I suspect that certain senior members of BBC staff would be called abruptly to account, in exactly the way that Mr Bashir, Lord Hall, Mr Suter and Mrs Sloman were called to account regarding the underlying scandal. That would be a painful process, but a far preferable outcome to allowing those individuals to remain the moral guardians and financial stewards of one of this country's most precious institutions.

As regards the damage done to FOIA, I believe that the Tribunal's denial of the *'irrelevance'* defence was a critical intervention preventing incalculable long-term harm. But the BBC's reckless search for an alternative escape route, burying both me and the Tribunal in near-impenetrable documentation, provides a blueprint for any other authority which finds itself in a tight spot but has limitless financial resources.

This has caught the eye of Parliament, as is right, but I submit that it falls to the Tribunal to make a clear demonstration that the law cannot be swept aside in such a calculated fashion. I call the BBC's actions 'reckless' because they do not only threaten FOIA's general operation; given the corporation's unique reliance on this legislation, if BBC reporters in the future find themselves waiting three years for an answer to a legitimate FOIA request then they will know where the blame lies.

In a way that would have seemed unthinkable when I made my FOIA request more than three years ago, and indeed when these Appeal proceedings began a year later, the decision now before the Tribunal will I submit have profound consequences for our national life. I believe that the correct decision now will:

(i) draw a line under the 'Bashir scandal' once and for all and

(ii) issue a firm warning that FOIA is a body of legislation which must be respected. That FOIA can be invoked, by a citizen, and brought to bear as Parliament intended, despite even the most determined opposition.

I thank the Tribunal for having considered this document and look forward to assisting on June 18 and 21.

Andrew Webb

Acknowledgements

It is a pleasure to offer my brief thanks to the people who have helped me in the writing of this book.

Following the initial default loathing which he understandably feels for most journos, Charles Spencer has, I think, trusted me, and I thank him for that. In a way that is unusual, my key sources have, I think, learned things that were as astonishing to them as they were to me, and that knowledge, though painful, has at least provided some degree of understanding. Matt Wiessler and Patrick Jephson both provided unique insight during many friendly discussions. I am glad that their quarter century of doubt and despair, which could have been ended so much earlier by the BBC, has now at least come to an end.

For my TV colleagues, warmest thanks go to Dan Chambers of Blink Films, who championed the project for years; to Lesley Davies, who brilliantly assisted on the three documentaries we produced for Channel 4; and to Shaminder Nahal, who commissioned them. At Michael Joseph, in guiding a book-writing rookie, Dan Bunyard and Emma Henderson have been delightful, as has my copy editor, DeAndra Lupu.

To the others who offered their time and insight, named in the text but not here, sincere thanks. And to people who cannot be named, particularly people at the BBC who feel a deep sense of shame and regret over what has gone on – is going on – thank you too.

Andy Webb
London, 2025

Bibliography

Birt, John, *The Harder Path* (Little, Brown, 2002)

Born, Georgina, *Uncertain Vision* (Martin Secker & Warburg Ltd, 2004)

Brandreth, Gyles, *Charles and Camilla: Portrait of a Love Affair* (Century, 2005)

Brown, Tina, *The Diana Chronicles* (Doubleday, 2007)

Burrell, Paul, *A Royal Duty* (Michael Joseph, 2001)

Dyson, Lord John, *A Judge's Journey* (Hart Publishing, 2019)

Fromkin, David, *Europe's Last Summer* (Alfred A. Knopf, Inc., 2004)

Harvey, Glenn and Saunders, Mark, *Dicing With Di* (John Blake, 1996)

Hussey, Marmaduke, *Chance Governs All* (Macmillan, 2001)

Jephson, Patrick, *Shadows of a Princess* (William Collins, 2000)

Lindley, Richard, *Panorama: Fifty Years of Pride and Paranoia* (Politico's Publishing, 2002)

Mangold, Tom, *Splashed!* (Biteback Publishing, 2016)

Morton, Andrew, *Diana: Her True Story – In Her Own Words* (Michael O'Mara Books, 1992)

Spencer, Charles, *The Spencer Family* (Viking, 1999)

Stott, Richard, *Dogs and Lampposts* (Metro Publishing, 2007)

Toffolo, Oonagh, *The Voice of Silence* (Rider, 2002)

Credits

Plate section: page 1, images 1&2: Tim Graham / Tim Graham Photo Library via Getty Images, image 3: The Fincher Files / Popperfoto via Getty Images; **page 2**, image 1: by kind permission of Matt Wiessler, image 2: Tim Graham / Corbis Historical via Getty Images; **page 3**, image 1: Buller Louisa Buller / PA Images via Alamy, image 2: / PA Images via Alamy; **page 4**, image 1: Adrian Dennis / Stringer / AFP via Getty Images; image 2: Andy Paradise / Independent via Alamy; **page 5**, image 1: Milica Lamb / PA Images via Alamy, images 2: Richard Gardner / Shutterstock; **page 6**, image 1: Gemma Levine / Premium Archive via Getty Images, image 2: Edward Webb via Alamy; **page 7**, image 1: WPA Pool / Getty Images Entertainment via Getty Images, image 2: Joel Robine / Staff / AFP via Getty Images; **page 8**, image 1: PA Images via Alamy, image 2: © Andy Webb.

Every effort has been made to trace copyright holders and to obtain their permission for the use of copyright material. The publisher apologizes for any errors or omissions and would be grateful to be notified of any corrections that should be incorporated in future editions of this book.

Index